ORIENTAL RUGS

A COMPREHENSIVE GUIDE

ORIENT

A COMPREHENSIVE GUIDE

NEW YORK GRAPHIC SOCIETY

AL RUGS

MURRAY L. EILAND

GREENWICH, CONNECTICUT

International Standard Book Number 0-8212-0506-4

Library of Congress Catalog Card Number 72-89825

Cover and color section designed by Joe Romeo

Printed in Japan

TABLE OF CONTENTS

BLACK AND WHITE ILLUSTRATIONS

ACKNOWLEDGMENTS

During the years of research for this project, considerable information and encouragement has been given to me by collectors and dealers in this country, and bazaar merchants, traders, designers, and dyers in the Middle East. (Strangely enough, almost none of my information has come directly from a weaver.) Without the assistance of these people—who are too numerous to list individually—this book could not have been assembled. I am grateful for their help.

A smaller number of people have been instrumental in producing the book itself. My brother Emmett Eiland, of the Oriental Rug Company of Berkeley, has helped assemble suitable illustrations and provided advice on other matters. Roy Barkas has assisted with the photography, while Peter Saunders has prepared the illustrations of Turkoman guls. David Flattery was particularly helpful in providing background on areas I have not been able to visit.

Pat Forseth's editing greatly improved the original manuscript. She also contributed advice for the layout. I also appreciate Pamela Robbins' generous contribution of time in typing the manuscript.

It was my good fortune to have access to several prominent rug collections, and I used excellent examples belonging to Dr. Gil Dumas and Hillary Black, Dr. S. W. Shear, and Peter Saunders.

Finally, there are those who have maintained their enthusiasm for rugs even in the face of such mind-numbing tasks as merely holding pieces to be photographed. Susanne Curtis and Vivian Curtis have my thanks for this less glamourous but necessary job.

ORIENTAL RUGS

A COMPREHENSIVE GUIDE

GLOSSARY

Warp. Threads running longitudinally through the fabric; these are anchored to the loom at both ends.

Weft. Threads running perpendicular to the warps, thus across the width of the fabric. Also known as woof.

Abrash. Variations in a particular color, usually resulting from the use of different dye lots. Often this effect is intentional.

Gul. Turkoman tribal emblem specific for each tribe, probably derived from floral motifs. Guls are frequently octagonal and often are quartered.

Joval. Bag for bedding and other gear; used by nomads when moving to new area.

Katchli. A type of Turkoman rug with the design elements quartered by a central cross-like structure. These rugs are used as both prayer rugs and tent flaps.

Kobitka. Circular tent of lattice and felt.

Kilim. General term for a pileless rug or cover, woven in one or more flat-stitch techniques.

Mejedieh. Design reflecting encroachment of European styles on Turkish décor.

Mihrab. The arch or niche seen on a prayer rug; this design element derived from a feature of mosque architecture.

Saph. Rug (usually Turkish) showing multiple mihrabs arranged in a series.

Torba. Long, narrow tent bag for small household items.

Yastik. Small mat or pillow cover.

INTRODUCTION

Since the first books on oriental rugs were published in the late 19th century, there have been numerous works approaching the subject in greater or lesser depth. Nevertheless, in attempting to acquire a general orientation in the field, one is struck immediately by the curious contradictions from book to book. For certain types of rugs it is nearly impossible to gather a consistent set of specifications, and overt errors in historical and geographical fact occur in all but a few of these surveys. Data that would facilitate the identification of rugs as to origin or time of manufacture are at best inadequate and at worst misleading. One must approach most works on oriental rugs with a thorough skepticism toward everything from the labels on illustrative plates to the maps, which are frequently so inaccurate as to misplace a city by several hundred miles. Scholarship and art are seldom farther apart than on the subject of carpets.

Among the reasons for this generalized confusion, the most significant is probably the assumption that the dealer in rugs is of necessity the expert, and here we make a mistake that would appear naive in other areas of art. Few of the great literary and scholarly works on painting and sculpture come from dealers, nor do museums depend upon sellers of art as sources of authoritative information. Still we note that well over half the books on rugs are written by people who make their living buying and selling the products they seek to describe in print. Objectivity regarding matters of age, rarity, and value is not of primary interest to the seller. Indeed the dealer often takes it upon himself to give each rug an air of mystery and intrigue, as though the finer specimens had once belonged to royalty and the lesser had been smuggled by camelback across trackless deserts. Often the terms themselves convey a sense of worth, as many perfectly innocent rugs are given such designations as "royal," "princess," and "imperial." Obviously books written from this point of view add little to the world's knowledge and only confuse an already cloudy subject.

The other common source of reference is a group made up of connoisseurs, collectors, and hobbyists. Here the approaches are legion, but generally one finds another type of subtle distortion that inclines steeply toward the subjective. Instead of deliberately disseminating misleading data, these writers are more concerned with their own personal feelings toward rugs. Again we find an aura of mystery surrounding these products of the inscrutable orient, and we are given little information of a concrete nature. In place of the dealer's sales talk, we hear the enthusiasm of the confirmed customer.

There are a small number of books with neither of these prejudices, written from the viewpoint of an art historian and employing more scholarly methods of analysis and evaluation. Most of these present an historical development of the weaving art, with little material about the more recent rugs that one would see in private homes or in dealers' shops. Although these books are admirable so far as they go, few of them provide the sort of information one would require for a broad understanding of oriental rugs.

It is this more general purpose that the present volume seeks to fulfill. The intention has been to include under one cover all the information necessary for the reader to identify and comprehend the background of most rugs he is likely to see or be in a position to purchase. Information has been included about the peoples who make the rugs and the conditions, both geographic and cultural, under which they live. Not only are the rugs described, but also their antecedents and reasons for being.

As in all works dealing with art, the scope must be limited (although some limits must be accepted), and the choice becomes somewhat arbitrary. Rugs of Persia, Turkey, the Caucasus, and the Turkoman peoples are by far the most common in the United States and Europe, and most of the fine carpets, both past and present, originated from one of these areas. We have limited the present volume to carpets of these types, leaving the products of India, China, Pakistan, and Morocco to be considered in a later work. Research is currently in progress for this second volume, which will also include an atlas of color plates, illustrating more thoroughly the rugs described in the current work.

Since there is often a considerable difference between the unusual pieces sought by collectors and the commercial varieties most typically encountered, whenever possible the plates in this book have been selected to aid maximally in the identification of other carpets.

I HISTORY AND DEVELOPMENT

The structural materials of carpets are more perishable than those associated with other design arts, such as painting, sculpture, or architecture. Consequently we have a smaller legacy of specimens from the past, and this has severely limited our ability to trace historical development. The origin of rug making is a subject left for speculation, and its evolution over the centuries is known only in the vaguest outline. As with most indigenous arts, its history has been almost ignored by its native culture. Only in comparatively recent times have efforts been made, mostly by Europeans, to piece together disjointed fragments of the story.

Although most of this material is of little help in identifying the more recent products, we will briefly summarize currently accepted ideas to provide a historical perspective from which to view the great expansion of carpet weaving in the nineteenth century, along with the reawakening of interest in the West.

We may take either of two basic approaches to explain why the pile carpet came into existence. The most popular is that propounded by Erdmann,[1] who suggests that the first products of this type were made by nomadic shepherds (differing from nomadic hunters in that they could not kill their animals for pelts) in an effort to simulate animal skins. The pile would thus be left long and shaggy and only later would design be superimposed over something basically utilitarian. The need for such an innovation would occur only under harsh climatic conditions, which seem to have existed where the first known specimens of pile carpet were found.

Another assumption is that the complex technique of the knotted pile carpet would of necessity have arisen in an established city culture. Some scholars have maintained that carpets were inspired by the artwork of such centers as Babylon and Nineveh, representing something on the order of a portable mosaic. In this form the decorative art could then take its place in a nomadic environment.

Neither position is supported by conclusive evidence, but several factors invite consideration. Greek and Roman sources refer repeatedly to carpets and draperies of the East; obviously this was a decorative medium in ancient times, but we are given little information about the construction of the fabrics. They may have been knotted, felted, or woven in a looped pile technique. The likelihood

that these were pile carpets was supported in 1949 when Soviet archeologists excavated a Scythian burial site at Pazirik near the Outer Mongolian border.[2] A carpet approximately six feet square was uncovered and has been dated with some certainty as fifth century B.C. (Radioactive carbon tests are consistent with this dating.) The design is relatively sophisticated, with five border stripes; the widest depicts horsemen and the secondary band contains naturalistic renditions of deer. The central field has a quatrefoil pattern, and the colors are dark red, light blue, greenish yellow, orange, and other shades. The construction is surprisingly fine with about 225 Turkish knots to the square inch, which is unusual for this type of knot and shows a highly developed technical skill. This discovery leaves us with a question as to what Scythian nomads would be doing with such a sophisticated work of art, although it could have originated either as a product of these people (a nomadic weave is not necessarily coarse) or as a result of trade with civilizations of the Middle East. The existence of similar motifs in Mesopotamian art of that period would suggest strongly that the rug originated there.

Also among the burial mounds at Pazirik were kilim fragments, woven in the slit-tapestry technique still commonly found in the Middle East; these mostly involved simple repeating patterns but were finely executed, and the dyes have been shown to be of the same chemical composition as those used several millenia later. Flat stitch work of a type used later in Gobelins tapestries was also found at the same place. Human figures were depicted in ritual scenes, and another fragment showed lions similar to those occurring on Babylonian bas reliefs.

Subsequent excavations over 100 miles west of Pazirik, at Bash Adar on the River Ursul, uncovered other Scythian burial mounds that were thought to predate the Pazirik finds by one or two centuries. Here was found a pile carpet fragment, used in the manufacture of a saddle, with the very fine weave of over 400 Persian knots to the square inch. This multicolored piece was too tattered for the design to be deciphered, but its weave indicates it to be, like the Pazirik fragment, the product of considerable technical accomplishment. Indeed, these fabrics as a group demonstrate to us just how little we know about the history of weaving, as clearly all skills necessary for the production of

Middle Eastern carpets during the last 700 years (the period for which we have other surviving examples) were already in existence two thousand years before. These pieces are, in fact, so well woven that we could confidently assume that they were in themselves products of a long tradition, probably (judging from features of the design) from the Middle East.

The second oldest carpet finds date probably a thousand years later. These were made during Sir Aurel Stein's early twentieth century explorations of Eastern Turkestan. At Nira and several other locations along the old caravan routes, a number of small carpet fragments were found that have been placed between the fifth and sixth centuries A.D. These fabrics were made with the Turkish knot, but there is little similarity to the Pazirik find, as the weave is coarse, with only 30 to 40 knots to the square inch. Not enough material survives for us to reconstruct the designs. Neither the people who made these carpets nor subsequent developments are known.

No further specimens survive for the succeeding 600 years. Our next evidence comes from Anatolia, where the Seljuks left a number of well-preserved carpets. (There were some older fragments found in old Cairo, but those dating before the Seljuk finds were woven with the cut loop technique rather than the knot.) In 1905, at the Mosque of Ala-ad-Din in Konia, three large carpets and five fragments were discovered which have been dated from the thirteenth century. In 1930 four more fragments of a similar type were found in Beyshehir, just south of Konia. Obviously they are the products of a mature art which may have been brought into Asia Minor by the Seljuks from their homeland in Turkestan. The patterns of these rugs are all geometrical, and the design units—hexagons with latch hooks and other simple figures—are arranged in staggered rows. Marco Polo in 1272 made reference to the Seljuk carpets as the finest and most beautiful in the world.

From the fourteenth and fifteenth centuries we find in European paintings a number of rugs that likely originated in Anatolia; apparently they were brought to Europe in significant numbers and held in high esteem. Still there is a lack of direct information, and the next major grouping, the so-called Holbein or Ottoman carpets, is made on the basis of sixteenth and seventeenth century paintings. (Holbein was particularly fond of including rugs in his portraits, but labeling the rugs with his name is perhaps misleading; many Dutch and Italian masters also depicted rugs in various contexts.)

These carpets are usually divided into three classes, probably because they were made at different times or in different areas, but all share certain characteristics of design and have similar borders. Frequently there are staggered rows of lozenges and octagons separated by vine-like figures, while the borders show a pattern apparently derived from Kufic script and similar to that found in later Caucasian rugs. Clearly there were several centers of production and periods of both development and decline. Ushak was almost certainly an important weaving area, and the Aegean region around Canakkale and Ezine was probably important also. (Obvious likenesses of these rugs are still woven in this latter area.)

Although information about Anatolian carpets is limited, the background of Persian rugs is even more vague. Not a single surviving specimen can be dated prior to the sixteenth century. Nevertheless, we may surmise that there had long been a need for something similar to the pile carpet and that such a fabric was probably produced many centuries before our first examples. Numerous Arab geographers (Yakut, Mukadassi, and Ibn Hawkle[3]) provide references to weaving, and carpets were allegedly made during the ninth century in Fars; there is also evidence that the thirteenth century palace of Ghazan Khan near Tabriz was furnished with rugs from Fars. Persian miniatures from both Herat and Shiraz show carpets extant during the fourteenth century and perhaps before. Still we have no surviving fragments; a partial explanation for this may be that most of the weaving was accomplished at a village level, with the carpets being made for immediate use. Carpets subjected to household wear could hardly have been expected to last into the present era.

Whatever status the art attained, we have one pertinent item suggesting a high degree of development. In 1514 Tabriz fell to the Ottomans and was held by them for several weeks. About this time we find a new group of rugs from Anatolia; these are generally described as of Turkish court manufacture. Several sources indicate that the Ottomans brought with them weavers from Tabriz, and evidence occurs in the use of the Persian knot for these new fabrics. (This rests on the assumption that the Persian knot was used in court factories of Tabriz, although any village art of the area would likely have employed the Turkish knot.) Indeed they have many Persian features of design, with medallions, scrolling vines, and large, lancet-shaped leaves. The question of Persian influence, however, is not so simple, as the Persian knot was used in

Cairo well before the fifteenth century (its origin there is not explained), and when this city fell to the Ottomans in 1517, the carpet industry was already highly developed. These products of the Mamluke Dynasty displayed complex rectilinear designs, but the patterns changed abruptly soon after the arrival of the Ottomans, and we see the familiar palmette blossoms, rosettes, and spiral vines with lancet leaves. Thus during the sixteenth century we have carpets produced in Anatolia and Cairo with similar designs and only slight differences in technique, both possibly influenced by Persian originals. Recent evidence[4] indicates that most of these carpets were from Cairo, although Bursa, not far from Istanbul, was another important center. Rugs of this type continued into the early seventeenth century.

Persian Carpets of the Sefavid Period

The sixteenth century was of great importance to the Persian carpet; here we see a great flowering of local arts under the Sefavids, the first native dynasty since the Arab conquest. The course of these rulers (from 1499 to 1722) includes what is considered to be the classic period of Persian carpet weaving. Before the Sefavids we have no evidence that the art was anything more than a village craft (the first carpets to appear in miniatures were small and covered with repeating rectilinear figures). But under Sefavid patronage design took a revolutionary direction toward curvilinear rather than rectilinear patterns. The new patterns required a highly developed technique, with cartoons drawn before the weaving began. Unfortunately, despite thousands of pages of speculation, surprisingly little is known about these carpets, and there is meager likelihood of our ever acquiring more specific information. Still, we may approach the problem from several directions: attempting to date carpets, to locate their places of origin, and with this information to outline a coherent picture of the development of weaving during the Golden Age.

Our data in the first area are most convincing, although few in number. Among the 2500 to 3000 carpets and fragments that have survived from this period, only a few are dated. Among these is the famous Ardabil Mosque carpet, now in the Victoria and Albert Museum in London; for this we have the date 1539. We also have inventories listing the possessions of various European princes who acquired Persian carpets or commissioned their manufacture, and these provide an approximate date with only slightly less accuracy. The last method of dating is

by inference, drawing conclusions about carpets with design elements similar to those of other arts, such as architecture and miniature painting, both of which are often more datable.

Localization as to place of origin is more difficult and has been done with certainty for very few early carpets. Generally this is accomplished by grouping carpets together according to design and construction, then assigning them to a city where carpets are thought or known to have been made. This has led to great disagreement among art historians. Four major areas are frequently chosen as centers of production: central Persia, Tabriz, Kerman, eastern Persia.

Probably the most important area is central Persia, where we know from good historical data that carpets were woven in Kashan and Isfahan at least since the beginning of the seventeenth century. Kashan has long been associated with carpets of silk pile (a material more commonly used only for the warp and weft in other weaving centers) even to the present, and likely such silk rugs as the so-called Vienna Hunting Carpet were woven there. We also know that in central Persia Shah Abbas established a court factory at Isfahan when he moved his capital there in the late sixteenth century. Many silk and metal brocaded carpets of the period certainly must have been woven there.

Tabriz and the entire northwest of Persia have also long been described as an important weaving center; Pope[5] lists it as by far the most significant. This city was the first Sefavid capital, and a court manufactory could have been located there. But Turks overran the area four times during the sixteenth century, and the seat of government was moved to Kazvin and finally to Isfahan. Rugs may also have been woven in Kazvin, but we have no record of this nor is there any tradition of a court manufactory having been located there; it has not been a weaving center within recent memory.

Evidence of rug production in Kerman is less specific, although there is some probability that weaving continued there after the Afghan invasion. Kerman was little disturbed by this catastrophe, but it was laid in ruins by Mohammed Aga Qajar in 1794. A group of floral carpets, usually referred to as *vase* carpets, is thought to have been woven there.

The last major area, eastern Persia, is also mentioned as a likely source of Sefavid carpets, but many pieces alleged to be from here were probably woven in India. Herat was the major city of the district, and it had been the capital of Shah Rukh in the early fifteenth century. There is a large group of later carpets traditionally known by this name, although weaving in the classical Persian style had apparently ceased by the early nineteenth century.

Early Rugs of the Caucasus

Weaving at a village level has probably been known in the Caucasus for hundreds of years. None of the earlier rugs have survived; the oldest examples attributed to the area are the so-called Dragon carpets, probably beginning in the sixteenth century. Dozens of these pieces still exist, and they have stimulated wide speculation. Their origin is localized anywhere from eastern Anatolia to the eastern Caucasus around Kuba or Baku. Authorities disagree as to whether they were products of a folk art or a larger manufactory system, although the size of some specimens (up to 23 feet) would suggest the latter. The latest of these rugs was likely woven in the mid-eighteenth century.

Nor is there agreement as to the origin of the design. A lattice pattern breaks up the field into lozenges by means of thick, serrated lancet leaves, each of which also contains smaller floral figures. Within the lozenge shaped compartments are a variety of highly stylized animal figures (frequently a dragon and phoenix in combat) or floral forms. From some sources we are assured that these rugs show heavy Persian influences, particularly from the vase designs alleged to have been woven in Kerman. Others trace their development from the Anatolian geometric "Holbeins" (particularly the lattice framework), noting that nowhere is the influence of northern Persia noted (i.e., medallion designs).

Although definite links cannot be proved, one need only study the dragon carpets in chronological succession to notice their evolution toward various well-known nineteenth century patterns, such as the "sunburst" found on a variety of Karabagh rugs.

Weaving During the Eighteenth Century

In reviewing the development of carpet weaving in both Persia and the Anatolia, we note a flowering in the sixteenth and seventeenth centuries, followed by a relative blight in the eighteenth. The only class of rugs to maintain its vitality during this period is the Anatolian village rug, the designs of which developed, in many cases, from the earlier court pieces. Otherwise there was a general decline in industry and inventiveness, even in such peripheral areas as the Caucasus and Egypt.

Among factors contributing to this decline were the almost continual wars in Persia for many years after the Afghan invasion, and the turmoil throughout the Turkish Empire. The economics of carpet production were such that the grand creations of the Golden Age and the court were no longer in demand. The weaving of carpets was again left to the villagers and nomads, who needed such a fabric for household use. One could indeed say that the great flowering of the art had taken its beginning in a folk model, and that it had returned to its origin. In any event, with the dawn of modern interest in oriental rugs, perhaps as early as the beginning of the nineteenth century, there was no such thing as a carpet industry in the Middle East. Its emergence from this lethargy was called forth by demand from Europe. Its gradual increase and the many directions it has taken are the basic subject of this work, which has included these brief historical comments only as an introduction.

A Note on Dating

Occasionally one will find a date woven into an oriental rug, and this is relatively simple to read once one acquires familiarity with the Arabic system of numbering. The figures are arranged from left to right, just as in the European system, although there are times when the symmetry of a rug requires one set of numbers to be written backwards.

0 1 2 3 4 5 6 7 8 9

٠ ١ ٢ ٣ ٤, ٥ ٦ ٧,٢ ٨,٦ ٩

The date ١٢٨٣ is thus read as 1283 A.H. (after the Hegira).

Occasionally on Turkish and Caucasian rugs of the early twentieth century or later one will find dates that correspond to our own system, beginning from the birth of Christ. Most of the time, however, the dating will be in the Mohammedan system, which begins with Mohammed's flight from Mecca to Medina, the Hegira. The conversion of this date to our own system is done by two methods, with the second being a simple matter of addition. The dates on the earlier pieces are calculated on the basis of the lunar year, which is shorter than the solar year. As the Hegira was in July of 622 A.D., this number must be added to the Mohammedan date, while a correction factor must be subtracted to compensate for the shorter lunar year. The lunar system gains one year every 33.7 solar years; so dividing the number of years by this number gives the correct factor.

$$\frac{922}{33.7} \quad \text{equals } 27$$

922 plus 622 minus 27 equals 1517 A.D.

This method is used to determine the date of such historical specimens as the Ardabil carpet, and up to the nineteenth century it can be used without question. With the Russian occupation of the Caucasus in the early 1800s, however, we have some confusion, as this introduced the solar calendar even when Mohammedan dates were retained, although this was by no means uniform. When the solar calendar is used, the conversion factor is no longer necessary, and one converts merely by adding 622 to the Mohammedan date. In the Caucasus both systems existed side by side during the entire nineteenth century, with the cities using the solar calendar, while the lunar calendar was still used in the more isolated, rural areas. Any date on a Caucasian rug may be from either calendar.

In Persia and Turkey the changes occurred during the 1920s, when the solar calendar was imposed by rulers who sought to bring their respective countries more into line with Western institutions. Converting the date on a modern **Persian** rug is thus a simple matter of adding 622. (This is not completely accurate, as the new year does not occur at the same time.)

One must exercise some caution, allowing the possibility that the date has been merely copied from an older rug. At other times it may be fraudulent, particularly on some early twentieth century acquisitions from the Istanbul bazaar, where forgeries were plentiful. At times the clever alteration of one number, perhaps by replacing just a few knots, can change the date by a century. Generally, however, the date is reliable if one uses the proper method of conversion.

NOTES

1. Erdmann, K., *Oriental Carpets, an Essay on Their History,* Universe Books, New York, 1962, p. 15.
2. Rudenko, S. I., *Frozen Tombs of Siberia,* Univ. of Calif. Press, Berkeley, 1970, pp. 204-6, 298-304.
3. Serjeant, R., "Materials for a History of Islamic Textiles Up to the Islamic Conquest," *Ars Islamica,* 1943, p. 99.
4. Kuhnel, E., and Bellinger, L., *Cairene Rugs and Others Technically Related,* National Publishing Co., Washington, D.C., 1957.
5. Pope, A. U., *A Survey of Persian Art,* London, 1938-39. Vol. III, Chap. 55A.

II THE ELEMENTS OF DESIGN

Oriental rug designs are so numerous and richly varied that we cannot even begin to describe all the possible approaches and combinations of motifs. Yet we may make a few basic observations to clarify their classification and identification, so that any given rug may be placed into one of several broad categories on the basis of its design. Considering the myriad ways in which a surface can be decorated, we are immediately struck by the essential similarities that cross class lines and occur in virtually all oriental rugs from the beginning of weaving. The development has been extensive and imaginative within a framework that has clearly limited itself in materials and outline, while many other alternatives have been virtually ignored. We observe, for example, that carpet design, with few exceptions, has traditionally been two-dimensional, and that the addition of depth through different thicknesses of pile has been only superficially explored. Also notable is the uniformity of material composing the pile, which might well be more varied or enriched by the addition of other ornamental objects. Numerous materials could easily be incorporated into the design of carpets, either for use on the floor or as wall hangings, but such innovations have been used only rarely. The modern carpet has been both flat and uniformly of one material, with infrequent attempts even to provide surface effects by means other than color. Indeed, of all the many ways of creating design, color has been used virtually to the exclusion of all else.

Even the shape of the oriental carpet has shown little innovation, as we find almost invariably some form of rectangle, with such minor deviations as the square uncommon. Carpets in round or hexagonal shape are seldom found, although they present no special technical problems in weaving. One is led to speculate why such possibilities have been generally ignored in favor of a rectangular layout. Clearly the art has been more circumscribed by tradition than need have been the case.

Accepting these limitations, we are left with the problem of covering a flat, rectangular surface. Again we see development along narrow lines, with nearly all designs involving a division into border and field, while several other alternatives are possible. Design could have developed without borders, leaving the rug to be placed in a proper setting much as the painter allows a work to be framed without his considering the frame as an integral part of the composition. There could also have been a greater use of the striped patterns that were so highly developed in meso-American weaving, particularly in the fabrics of Peru and the Guatemalan highlands. Enormous variety is achieved through complex stripes of varying widths, while there is no arbitrary orientation as to specific dimensions of the fabric. Oriental rugs have indeed been woven with such designs, but this has been relatively rare and almost entirely limited to flat-stitch pieces.

1. Medallion
design in a Tabriz rug

TYPES OF DESIGN

Field design may be approached from two distinct directions. One basic design may serve the entire field, or the surface may be covered by a repeating pattern that recurs throughout the rug.

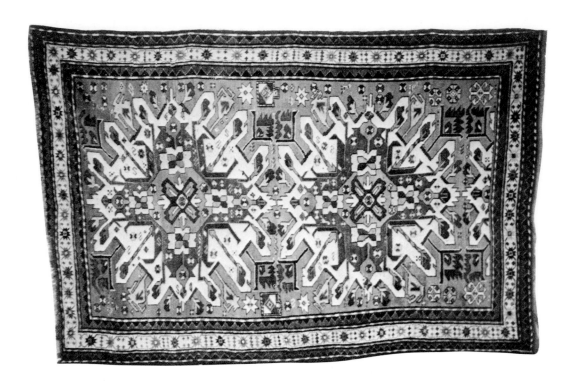

2. Multiple
medallion design in
Caucasian "Sunburst"

The single-design type has several variations; the most common is a medallion pattern with one basically symmetrical figure occupying the center, and the corners usually drawn from similar elements. There may be one medallion (as in many Kerman, Tabriz, and Kashan rugs) or several in a series, arranged at intervals across the field. Medallion forms are found both in curvilinear city rugs and rectilinear village products. The form probably originated during the Sefavid period in the great court carpets, as adaptations of figures found in illuminated manuscripts.

Intermediate between the medallion and repeating designs are various compartment or panel arrangements in which the field is broken up into rectangular, square, or lozenge-shaped areas containing similar or diverse design motifs. These circumscribed areas may be arranged diagonally or parallel, and they are sufficiently varied in size so that the field may be covered by several or dozens of compartments.

3. Yuntdag rug from Bergama area, with
design elements arranged in compartments

Blending almost imperceptibly with the latter approach are designs that repeat a single figure. These occur in characteristic forms in all rug weaving areas. Most simple in layout are the repeating forms in Turkoman rugs, although the figure itself may be complex and may show some internal variation. Even more common is the repeating "Boteh," which in Persian literally means a cluster of leaves. Explanations as to what it represents are legion; it is called in various books a pear, cypress tree, pine cone, and leaf. It has been likened to the sacred flame of Zoroaster, the bend of the River Jumna as it leaves the vale of Kashmir, and the shape of a clenched fist making a seal in blood. Its origin is, however, less important than its multitude of forms, as it appears in curvilinear guise in the city rugs of Qum, Kashan, Arak, Kerman, and many others; at the same time rectilinear forms are frequent in the Caucasus, the nomadic rugs of Fars, and the Kurdish village rugs of Northern Persia. Kerman designers probably made the most varied use of the device, with adaptations from the shawls that were made there in the mid-nineteenth century. Saraband rugs are woven almost exclusively in the Boteh pattern, as are many Hamadans. In some rugs the figures all face the same way, while in others alternate rows vary in direction.

Examples of Boteh figures in rugs from different areas are shown below and on the next page.

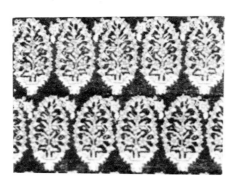

a) Tabriz adaptation
of Saraband

b) Caucasian Gendje

c) Nineteenth century
Kerman

d) Caucasian rug from
the vicinity of Baku

e) Caucasian Shirvan

f) Qashgai rug from Fars

4. Boteh figures: seven examples from rugs of varying provenance.

Other repeating designs may be more complex; several of the most common apparently evolved over a period of many decades from the scrolling vinework patterns of sixteenth- and seventeenth-century Persian carpets. The so-called "Herati" pattern is certainly the most widely used, and forms of it appear in city, village, and nomad rugs even so far afield as eastern Turkestan. It was woven in Anatolia and India during the 1920s, and machine-made versions have been produced in the West. (The name derives from the former Persian city in Afghanistan, although we have no evidence that the pattern originated there.) Basically the design consists of a lozenge, around which are arranged four "fish" or lancet-shaped leaves, and this is repeated in the same scale throughout the carpet. The form employed in Khurassan often does not contain the lozenge, but otherwise the pattern is similar over a wide area; it is found around Hamadan, Arak, Tabriz, and the Kurdish villages. The classic Feraghan carpet was usually woven in the Herati design.

There are two other common Persian repeating patterns besides the Herati, the Gol Hennae (literally, henna flower), and the Mina Khani (a name of uncertain origin). These occur mainly in Kurdish, Hamadan, and Arak weaves, although they also have a more limited use elsewhere.

5. Crudely drawn Herati pattern on a Bidjar rug

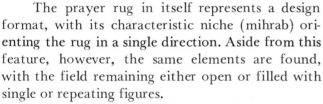

6. Mina Khani design
on a Hamadan rug

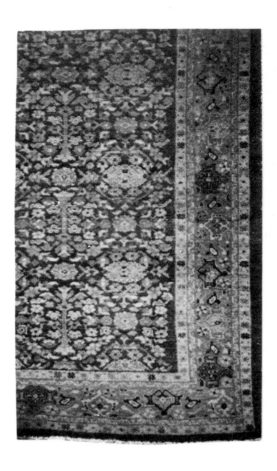

7. Gol Hennae pattern on a
Mahal rug. The border is the
so-called turtle.

The prayer rug in itself represents a design format, with its characteristic niche (mihrab) orienting the rug in a single direction. Aside from this feature, however, the same elements are found, with the field remaining either open or filled with single or repeating figures.

This applies also to a class of rug (usually Turkish) known as *saphs*, with multiple mihrabs arranged in a series. In Turkey these may be found in mosques, but they are often used in houses simply as rugs; their alleged function as "family prayer rugs" is rather dubious.

THE BORDER

The border presents less of a problem, and there is more similarity between the major classes of rugs in this area than in field design. Although the number of border stripes on a given rug may vary from one to well over ten, the usual practice is to provide one wider stripe as a major border and for this to be surrounded by smaller stripes of approximately equal width. The dividing lines themselves may be so ornate (with alternating colors or reciprocal serrations) as to form separate stripes, or they may be merely simple lines. The main border usually involves the repetition of a relatively

complex floral or geometric device, while the subsidiary stripes may be meandering vine figures or simple elements like the reciprocal trefoil. Again, as with field patterns, there has been little exploration of other possibilities outside the conventional realm; yet many other directions could have been developed. One radical departure is the concept of broken borders, or rather those not bounded rigidly by straight lines. The most common use of this innovation has been in some recent Kermans (and their copies), where the inner border is encroached upon by the field design. This was adapted from French models, and although it may often seem inappropriate with the Persian medallion pattern, it promises possibilities that could be developed more within the native tradition.

THE ORIGIN AND "AUTHENTICITY" OF RUG DESIGNS

In discussing the history of rug weaving, we have considered the lack of information surrounding its origin and development, and the same doubts apply to design. One may easily speculate on the relationships between various design elements in modern rugs and the figures decorating ancient art and architecture, but again we cannot say what was derivative and what original. There is, however, some reason for believing that the first rugs were geometrical, as the technique for reproducing curvilinear design is more complex and requires either scale drawings or detailed sketches. Likely the earliest designs were based on floral or animal forms, which gradually became more stylized. Even the earliest known rug, from the Pazirik find, shows the separation of border and field.

Most of the present literature on rugs leads one to the view that design development during the last fifty years is little more than the encroachment of foreign tastes upon a well-established art form with a many-century tradition. Interaction of the native art with the corrupting influences from Europe and America is thus seen as a struggle between the pure and the impure, bringing about an eventual debasement of original models through the exigencies of commerce. Such alarming conclusions are, however, not necessarily supported by our observations, as the issues tend to blur on closer examination. Questions arise in at least two distinct areas: 1) How do we distinguish between the "authentic" expression of native Middle Eastern culture and the products of this culture which are primarily meant for export to another area? 2) How do we derive origins for design motifs which appear in rugs from such diverse peoples as the Turkomans along the Oxus to the Kurdish nomads of Anatolia? Is there such an entity as a pure Persian design or a pure Turkish design? Does one find rug designs that can be described, with confidence, as representing local or tribal forms with no trace of outside influence? The answers are by no means obvious or comforting to the traditionalists, who assure us that we are now witnessing the death gasp of a great art.

Our first speculations could center on the question of which rugs are strictly commercial products of a folk art that could just as readily be intended for local use. This is not merely an academic matter, but a frequent criterion by which a design is adjudged to be either authentic or corrupted. Obvious examples of commercial rugs are the products of Arak during the 1920s, when Sarouk rugs were made in sizes to fit American houses, designs supplied by Western merchants to appeal to American housewives, and colors to match the schemes of typical American interiors. We might go so far as to say that there was nothing Persian about these rugs except the technique of pile knotting, and the same judgments could be made upon thousands of Turkish weaves of the early twentieth century. Surely these are not collector's rugs, and are at best merely a form of floor covering desired by people who place greater emphasis on other features of decoration. They bear little resemblance to the great Persian court pieces of the sixteenth and seventeenth centuries, nor do they relate to any present Middle Eastern culture. To a lesser degree we can confidently assign a great bulk of all twentieth-century rugs to various commercial categories, and few would argue the point. The controversy would arise, however, when one tried to find rugs that are not commercial, as virtually nowhere do we find examples that are woven in designs most pleasing to the weavers for use within their own homes. The more we penetrate into the village life of Persia and Anatolia, the more we find that even in the most remote areas, the rug output is seen almost exclusively as a means of earning capital from the outside, or rather of converting a relatively abundant material—wool—into either cash or items that cannot be produced locally. If, for example, we were to take rugs from the various nomadic tribes of the Fars Province of Iran, we would be tempted to assume that they certainly represent a traditional native craft. But would our judgment be influenced if we were to consider that virtually all these rugs are made for consumption outside the country, that their sizes, thick pile, and largely synthetic colors are ultimately determined by what is salable in Western Europe, and that even their designs in many cases can be traced to widely diverse origins in other countries? Would we not then be tempted to call these commercial rugs, or would we develop other criteria for adjudging them as honest, native products? We might actually entertain the notion that such a distinction is highly artificial at best and likely to be misleading.

We could also expand this analysis to include the past, speculating that even the best Turkoman and Caucasian rugs of earlier generations were woven with some commercial incentive, either local or remote. At the same time, we can bring forth no ready evidence that this is necessarily to be deplored or that it adversely affects the aesthetic appeal of any given rug. There are fine commercial products and coarse, brazen commercial products. Such has always been the case and no doubt always will be.

The next question is related and requires a similar abandonment of prejudice. Are the designs of a given type of rug the fruits of a long, local tradition, or are they also the results of an intricate and commercially influenced transaction? Again we may adduce little evidence that the designs are strictly local in origin or any reason why they should be. Artistic motifs flow freely from one culture to the next, and this process is much more readily recognized in other forms of expression than carpets. Taking as an example the same tribal products of Fars, which we could not clearly label as commercial or traditional native art, we may find a wide variety of patterns whose origins would take us far afield. One of the most common is the Boteh, which covers many of these rugs and which forms a minor part in the pattern of many others. Although it has been widely assumed to be of Persian origin, we have no direct evidence for this, and, indeed, its first widespread use and development occurs in the Kashmir shawls, which reveal an evolution from rather crude, graceless forms of the late eighteenth century. Surely none of the classic period carpets display this design, nor is it found on earlier Persian textiles. Our conclusion that it is a foreign-derived element is surprising when we consider that this figure is so pervasive from one end of the country to the other, and virtually all weaving areas have produced their variation of it. This leaves us all the more confused when it comes to classifying designs as to their "authenticity"—that is, whether they are part of the native art or a later commercial infusion. Further exploration shows that other elements as well are the result of complex interactions between Iranian art and that of surrounding cultures. Chinese motifs may well be found on the same rug as design features that would appear to be Indian, Arabic, or Turkish. As has always been the case, the art of each culture has been influenced by that of neighboring cultures and has achieved its identity and individuality by its success at making the combination aesthetically pleasing and internally consistent. The process is still going on, and additions from the West are no more unique than earlier material absorbed from the East. Carpet weaving regions will undoubtedly continue this process of adaptation just as in the past. Commerce and the arts are as ineradicably linked as the forms of artistic expression from one culture to another.

SYMBOLISM IN DESIGNS

Much was written in the older rug books about various design elements relating to beliefs and superstitions, and many rug dealers are adept at fabricating exotic stories from these vague shreds of symbolism. We are given tales of bloody battles, hidden treasures, evil spirits, and the inevitable luckless weaver who was killed during his work and whose duties were taken up by another hand. As most oriental rugs today are commercial products—and this has been the case with the majority of rugs for the last hundred years—these pieces of supplementary information appear most improbable. One has only to talk with some of the weavers to quickly dispel the notion that each figure is laden with mysterious significance. Indeed, we may well consider the design elements as merely part of an arrangement of form and color that produce a pleasing effect.

III   THE PROBLEM OF DYES

The art of the dyer may well be considered of equal importance to that of the designer, as the manner in which a rug ages is to a large extent dependent upon the types of colors imparted into the wool. We have ample evidence that various forms of fabric dyeing have been practiced since Egyptian times, if not before, and references to colored garments in classical literature are legion. We know, for example, of the Tyrian purple extracted from shellfish in a large industry around Sidon and Tyre from at least 1000 B.C., and this later became the Imperial purple, so expensive that it could be worn only by Roman nobility. Indigo was known to the ancient Greeks, and the name is probably derived from India, its country of origin. Marco Polo reports its use by the Chinese, and there is evidence of a similar plant among the Incas and Indians of Central America.

For centuries natural substances were the only source of color, and many of these were not only expensive but demanded long and complex techniques for their proper application. It was only natural that the resources of modern chemistry should be set to the task of finding substitutes. Early in the nineteenth century much work was done with derivatives of the benzene nucleus, but it was not until 1856 that W. H. Perkin, a British chemist, discovered the first aniline dye, a mauve, with a structure based on the benzene ring. A revolution in color occurred during the next several decades. In 1858 a magenta was discovered by R. W. Hoffman, and a year later fuchsine, another magenta dye, was discovered by Vergium. In 1862 aniline black was developed, and two years later the first azo dyes were synthesized. In 1868 there was a major breakthrough in the reds, with Graebe and Liebermann discovering the alizirine colors, which are of the same chemical composition as the natural madder dyes. Previously the latter had been the most important source of red in many types of textiles, but it was expensive and difficult to use properly. With the synthesis of an artificial indigo in 1880 by Baeyer, the two major colors were brought securely within the realm of the chemist. Succeeding years have only added to the profusion of shades, as now a great wealth of color is available that could never be obtained with the old natural dyes. Many of the new colors are chemically the same as their prototypes, so identical colors may be obtained, and in theory this could have marked a great step forward in the carpet industry.

On the contrary, as the use of these dyes increased there was some question of their having wrought a great injury to the oriental carpet. Rug collectors and connoisseurs throughout the world raised a cry against the new dyes, and, although nearly all the modern products of the orient are well dyed by synthetic means, considerable prejudice remains. Most of the older rug books were published during the height of the controversy, and we may read a number of absurd statements. Norton, for example, asserts: "Vegetable dyes are the *sine qua non* in a rug; all other dyes will disappear or change into ugly colors with the test of wear and washing."[1] She adds: "The unfailing test as to the kind of dye used in a rug is to rub the surface with a cloth moistened with saliva. If the colors are made from any but vegetable dyes, they will rub off on the cloth." The older books are full of such admonitions, but almost all such statements show a basic lack of understanding of just what the process of dyeing sets out to accomplish and how these ends may be approached by varying methods. To dispel the old prejudices we should first examine the properties of dyes.

Dyes may be described in terms of their source, physical structure, chemical composition, color quality, fastness, dependance upon external agents such as mordants, and methods of application. Most dyes consist of complex organic molecules which, when dissolved in a solution or applied to a fabric, have the quality of absorbing light in such a way as to reflect other wave lengths which the eye perceives as a particular color. Although we are not here concerned with the physiology of vision or the physics of light waves, we do need to know certain basic data on those chemical properties of a dye that determine its effect upon wool. (Dyes affect other fabrics differently; cotton, and particularly silk, are more resistant to color.) Of primary interest is the degree of color fastness, as a dye would be of little use if the colors bled with washing, or if they faded or changed markedly upon exposure to light. Many dyes not only become lighter, but actually assume a different color on aging, and this is potentially disastrous in a fabric that depends on a harmony of colors for its effect.

The same might also be said for the bright, harsh quality that limits their integration with other colors. For any dye used in a rug, we want to know how it will stand up under daily use and how it will respond to washing.

Another area of interest is the damage that the dyeing process inflicts upon the material. This has been particularly important with wool dyed black. Any process involving the boiling of wool or its immersion into liquids of either an acidic or basic character will have some effect upon its strength. Some natural oils will be removed, and the fibers will consequently become more brittle. Tensile strength may also be diminished by the caustic action of mordants and dyes. In numerous older rugs one may examine the texture of the pile and note how each color seems to have worn at a different rate. Often there will be an effect of relief, with some colors nearly obliterated and others intact.

The method of applying dyes has aroused much discussion. This is a crucial topic, particularly in the areas where rugs are made, as some observers insist that the newer dyes are defective in rugs not because of their intrinsic inferiority, but because they have been improperly used. In weaving areas of Persia the dyer has always been classed as an artisan, and he enjoys a certain prestige in the villages. Around his art a mystery has grown, undoubtedly fostered by these craftsmen, as to the exact formulas and methods employed in obtaining various colors. Secret processes have been handed down from generation to generation, and many of the older rug books speak as though there is something mysteriously but inevitably superior about the results of such traditions. Actually there is little that is secret about what goes into Persian vegetable dyes, and the same techniques are used throughout the Middle East. Any competent Western dyer would likely have a better understanding of the processes and chemical reactions involved than the best informed Persian dyer.

Basically the problem is approached quite simply. Among the many stages at which material may be colored (from the raw, unspun fibers to the finished, woven fabric), the Middle Eastern dyer has traditionally applied his colors at the yarn stage, when large bundles of material can be immersed in vats and then left in the sun to dry. In most cases a mordant is applied first, then the yarn is immersed in vats of dye and allowed to remain for varying times, depending upon the shade desired. When the wool is dried, it is given to the weaver. The controversy arises over both the types of dyes and the mordant.

Three major categories classify the dyes used in rugs: the natural vegetable or animal dyes, the so-called anilines (acid or basic dyes), and those dyes known as chromes. For any understanding of the controversy we must consider each in detail.

DYESTUFFS OF THE MIDDLE EAST
Natural Dyes

Traditionally the most important natural dyestuffs have been the sources of red and blue, the madder root and the indigo plant. Madder has been used throughout recorded history, and the plant grows wild in many parts of Persia and Anatolia; in other areas it is cultivated as a crop. It is a perennial growing several feet high, and from its thick, pulpy root a substance can be extracted that oxidizes into a red dyestuff. The root does not develop this property until its third year, and after the ninth year the plant is again of little use. The roots are pulled up in the fall and, after drying, are ground into a coarse powder. Dyers generally prefer to grind the roots themselves, as the powder is expensive and can be easily adulterated.

The most commonly used dyeing process is to first boil the wool in an alum mordant. Figures for the alum concentration vary, but it is usually given at about ¼ pound for each pound of wool. This mordanting process is usually repeated before the yarn is added to a vat of madder which has previously been prepared by dissolving a weight of the powder nearly equivalent to that of the wool. The amount of time in the dye depends upon the desired shade, usually several hours, then the yarn is rinsed thoroughly, preferably in a running stream. Variations in technique may produce hues of widely differing character, as, for example, in the process formerly favored in the Sultanabad area. The characteristic rose color was produced by leaving the wool for two days in a bath of madder and whey, followed by scouring in running water for 24 to 48 hours.

Indigo presents a slightly different problem, as it is not widely grown in the Middle East, and most of it must be imported from abroad. The synthetic has almost completely replaced the natural substance; its use is a simple process involving sodium hydrosulfite. The older process is quite complex: indigo is fermented with clay, slaked lime, sugar, and potash. The basic mixture takes several days to prepare, but the efforts are justified by the enormous range of blues that may be obtained. There are some who maintain that the same results are possible using the synthetic indigo with the old fermentation method. The added difficulty, however, makes this unlikely.

Cochineal is another important dye substance. Although known by one name, it actually comes from several chemically related substances. The first to be used widely is derived from a scale insect cultivated extensively in northern India. The insects puncture the bark of certain trees and suck the sap, producing a resinous exudate which imprisons them to the tree. From twigs encrusted with these insects a red dye is extracted. It is also called "lac" and has been exported from India for centuries. It was widely used in Kerman and Khurassan, probably because of their geographical proximity to India.

The other cochineal, by far the most extensively used now, comes from an insect growing on several species of cactus in Mexico and the Canary Islands. The dried bodies of these creatures are used to produce a dye that is almost identical to the Indian lac; when export began from Mexico, it largely supplanted the Indian product. Use of this color never penetrated into northern Persia (and not widely into Anatolia), probably because madder was much more plentiful there. The dyeing process resembles that used for madder, and sometimes this latter dye is added to vary the shade.

Among other natural dyestuffs there is a great deal of regional variation, as the desired colors may be obtained from several substances. Numerous plants produce a yellow dye, and many greens result from first dyeing with indigo and then yellow. Probably the brightest yellow is from saffron, but this is seldom used now and was always costly. More common is the yellow from weld, a delicate vine of the reseda family, which grows wild in many parts of the Middle East. Flowers, stems, and leaves are all used, and the amount added to the vat varies between five and forty percent of the weight of the wool, depending upon the shade desired. The leaves of Sumac and other vines are also used, but the color is not so vivid as weld. Pomegranate rind, which is cheap and plentiful, produces an acceptable yellow or yellow-brown.

Walnut husks are used for any number of brown shades, most commonly the beige which many dealers describe as natural camel hair. Oak bark and gall nuts also produce rich browns, and if madder is applied in heavy concentrations and heated for several days, the result can be a reddish brown.

Shades of orange are frequently dyed with henna leaves, but there is much variation; vine leaves and madder will also produce a good orange. Black has presented probably the greatest problem to the dyer, as one would judge by the number of carpets with this color worn off. The easiest solution is to use naturally dark wool, although this is not always available. (Some sources indicate that dark wool does not wear so well as white, but this seems unlikely.) In some areas dark wools may be dyed with indigo, producing a particularly deep, rich shade. Most other blacks are unsatisfactory for a number of reasons. The black from oak bark contains a high concentration of iron salts, which weaken the wool and make it brittle. Among the earliest aniline dyes was a black so acidic that it severely damaged the fibers.

Throughout the Middle East there are doubtlessly dozens of other botanical sources of dyes used in different villages. Those we have described, however, are certainly the most important.

Aniline Dyes

The term *aniline* is not chemically accurate so much as it is descriptive of the first class of synthetic dyes that began to be manufactured in Europe during the 1860s and which, within a decade, penetrated to almost all corners of the earth where fabrics were woven. At once it was clear that the new dyes were both cheaper and easier to use than the natural dyestuffs, and the colors could be standardized within much lower limits of variability. It was also not long until many of their defects became apparent, as carpets made from aniline-dyed wool showed a tendency to lose color by bleaching and running. Great quantities of poorly dyed carpets were exported, and a public awareness of this inferiority began to be felt upon the market. By the late 1890s the first of a long succession of measures were taken to counteract the use of these synthetics, and various regulations continue up to the present. At first there were laws calling for the confiscation of aniline dyestuffs, then edicts authorized the seizure of carpets produced in this manner. Law enforcement, however, is somewhat less rigid in Persia than in Europe, and nothing was effective in preventing a gradual replacement of the natural dyes. Finally laws were passed that added an extra 3% export tax to carpets made with anilines, and the proceeds of the tax were to go toward dye research. The tax was subsequently raised several times and began to constitute a source of revenue more than research money. There has probably never been a time during the last seventy years in Persia when synthetic dyestuffs were not available to those who wanted to use them. The possible exception is during both world wars, when the chemical plants of Germany turned their resources toward other areas.

In sifting out all the complaints leveled at aniline dyes, there is obviously much that is unfounded and of a prejudicial nature. The traditionalists, as in all the arts, have shown their customary rigidity toward any innovation, and had the anilines been superior substances, undoubtedly they would still have met with resistance. Still, there seems to be much ground for complaint, particularly as to the dye's effects on the wearing qualities of wool. As most of these dyes are strongly acid, the reaction on the wool leaves it considerably weakened. (A strong enough solution of acid would, of course, dissolve the wool.) At least as objectionable, however, is the manner in which anilines age. This often involves a greater change than mere fading, as the tonality of a color can shift enough to upset the rug's color composition.

Chrome Dyes

This term has been loosely applied to a new class of synthetic dyes mordanted with potassium bichromate. Developed and nearly perfected during the last thirty years, they are clearly becoming dominant in all areas where rugs are made, particularly India and Pakistan. Most rugs exported from Persia today are made with chrome dyes, and they can hardly be held inferior for the same reasons as the anilines. They are fast to water, alkalis, and sunlight, and they seem to cause minimal impairment to the wearing qualities of wool. They are easier to apply than natural dyes and provide a greater variety of shades. Indeed, the chromes would seem to be an ideal solution to the problem of dyes in oriental rugs. To some connoisseurs and dealers they are quite acceptable, but this approval is by no means unanimous. Oddly, objections arise from the very qualities that could be considered virtues.

The colors produced from chrome dyes may actually be too fast and unyielding to the effects of time and wear, although even vegetable dyes had a period of newness in which the colors seemed too bright. The newest rugs may hardly be judged on the basis of a somewhat stiff appearance, but there is considerable question as to whether the chrome dyes will ever mellow or age gracefully. The richness that the years gave to the old Persian carpet does not develop; the colors maintain their same intensity year after year. Many observers remark on the hard, metallic look in carpets dyed with chromes. This look could result from the almost total lack of abrash, as the dye is absorbed into the fiber more evenly, and concentrations of dye can be rigidly controlled. One gram of a chrome dye will always maintain a standard ability to produce a given color.

Other opponents of the new dyes are even more vehement. One can often hear statements to the effect that all carpets not dyed with natural substances are inferior. In essence, however, the primary issue seems to be an emotional one, the traditionalists desperately clinging to the old. In this case we observe the anomaly of the most conservative elements occurring in our progressive Western society, while the tradition-bound Persians eagerly accept innovation. This leads us toward two important conclusions: synthetics will replace the natural dyes, and likely they will eventually be of a better quality. Conceivably modern chemistry will produce dyes that are better for any purpose than naturally occurring substances. An analogy may be found in the field of pharmacology, where even the most effective natural remedies have been supplanted by chemically similar but often superior drugs. Whatever has been produced from natural dyes will be produced from synthetics, and likely the results will be better. The traditionalists talk as though all the old carpets were well dyed; yet we may find countless inferior specimens made with the most respected of natural dyes.

A NOTE ON CHEMICAL TREATMENT

While considering the subject of color, we should turn some attention upon the practice, primarily an American one, of artificially changing the colors of a rug after it has been imported. Treatment with strong bleaching agents was common by the early years of the century (as described by a 1906 article in *Country Life in America* by George Leland Hunter). By the 1920s most large rugs were "chemically washed."

American demand for oriental rugs reached crescendo proportions, and the material available did not always coincide with what the American housewife had in mind. The colors of the new rugs exported from Persia were too bright and garish for American tastes, attracting more attention than the floor would seem to deserve. Oriental products of a less oriental nature were demanded. In Persia designs were woven to please the American taste, and dealers purchased only the few patterns deemed acceptable. But the problem of color remained; some process was required to tone down the brightness of the rugs. To supply this need the chemical wash was developed in various forms in New York, London, and Europe. In all cases the rugs were treated with a bleaching agent to remove the excess color. Chlorine water and a great number of other substances were used at times. Bleaching was probably practiced most vigorously in New York. Many rugs were considerably lightened in the process, and of course the wool was affected. The thinnest carpets were damaged to the point of greatly diminishing their lifespan, and even the thicker carpets survived with more brittle, lifeless wool. Also, some of the colors were more fugitive than others, leaving rugs with the design somewhat obscured by the loss of contrast.

To guard against seriously weakening the fabric, dealers ordered rugs made with a thicker pile and generally heavier construction. Of course this excluded the finer, more intricately delineated designs. For the fugitive colors a new technique was developed. The painting process was born, particularly for rugs from the Sultanabad area. The rose field of these Sarouks and Mahals lightened considerably with bleaching, while Americans seemed responsive to rugs with a rich, maroon field. This discrepancy was remedied with a paintbrush, as labor was then cheap enough to allow many workmen to be employed painting in the fields with dark, artificial colors. (Labor costs now prohibit the practice in this country.) The American Sarouk thus became like no other rug in the world, with rich maroon fields and subdued subsidiary colors. The dull, listless texture of the wool after all this chemical treatment was remedied by another process, usually involving glycerine or mineral oil. Thus treated, the rug could also have a sheen, at times appearing richer than an unbleached rug. Of course this quality would not last, but it seemed to sell rugs.

Many old books tell us that we may distinguish an aniline-dyed rug by looking at the back and front and noting that an inferior dye will be much brighter on the back, while on the surface light will have caused fading. With painted rugs the opposite is true. The back will be a lighter red, as the bleach penetrates the entire rug, but only the front will be darkened from the painting. Rugs treated in this manner are easily distinguished if one examines both sides.

Many rugs other than Sarouks were bleached, but repainting was less common. Few Kermans were sold in the United States without a moderate bleach; this practice is responsible for the drab, colorless appearance of many medallion rugs imported during the 1920s. Generally the blues remained firm, but the greens, light browns, and mauves virtually disappeared, and reds diminished in brightness. Many Turkoman rugs were considerably lightened. There is a variety of Caucasian rug that was drastically changed by the chemical wash;

virtually all red (usually a synthetic) was removed by the bleach, leaving a gold-like color in its place. With the unchanged blues and whites, this often created a pleasing effect, but one quite different from the original intention.

The practice has diminished in the United States, but unfortunately, there is still some rug painting in Persia, although generally not on a large scale. At times only one color, thought by a dealer to be objectionable, will be darkened or otherwise altered by the application of a dye. I have observed this in the Tehran bazaar, done by young men using small, pencil-shaped pieces of wood, dipping the instrument in a pan of dye and quickly transferring it to the rug. Such efforts are expended mainly on the finer rugs, often in a manner that would leave the prospective buyer with virtually no suspicion that the colors are not original.

A NOTE ON COLOR VARIATION

Frequently one may note that the colors in a rug vary from one portion to the next. The field color, for example, may be bright red in one segment, switching to a horizontal band of more subdued red, then undergo further changes. This variation in shades of the same color is called *abrash*, and it results from the practice of dyeing yarn in small batches. In larger rugs a given color may be the result of numerous dyeings, giving subtle differences in color intensity. American buyers have ordinarily not been fond of abrash, considering it a defect, while many rug collectors insist that it increases the appeal of a rug. Abrash is seldom found now in city rugs, while in nomadic and village rugs it is more common.

THE USE OF DYES IN DATING RUGS

Some enterprising researcher may one day study the records of European dye manufacturers and determine exactly which dyes were exported to the Middle East in what years. In the absence of such data, however, we may still make a number of observations regarding the use of synthetics, allowing the dating of a rug with reasonable accuracy. If we begin by looking for colors not produced by natural dyes, we immediately recognize shades that are obviously a legacy of the chemical laboratory. When these occur in dated rugs, we are on safe ground in assuming that other rugs with the same colors may well have originated from the same period.

The two most obvious synthetics, found frequently in Anatolian, Caucasian, and some Persian rugs, are a bright orange and a mauve-magenta, which likely originated from several different synthetic dyes. In some rugs the mauve has faded to a dull gray on the surface, while the underside remains a vibrant violet; in others it becomes a dull brown. The amount of change resulting from bleaching is unclear, but the orange was apparently impervious to these chemical agents, and in many Caucasian rugs it glistens brightly from a field on which the reds have been removed. Both of these dyes seem to have appeared in the 1880s, as there are corroborating dated specimens, the mauve appearing less frequently after 1900.

A slightly later generation of synthetics is clearly recognizable from the 1890s in a number of Anatolian rugs. These are characterized by a rather fugitive green and a deep carmine similar in appearance to cochineal. The green often fades to a dull gray on the front of the rug, while the deep red is noted for its instability in water. Many rugs with this dye show a great deal of running; they assume a general "muddied" appearance except for the unchanging bright orange. The dyes apparently remained in use throughout the early twentieth century.

Recognition of other synthetic dyes is more difficult and requires an experienced eye. Many times one cannot be certain of blues, particularly dark blue, which may be natural or synthetic indigo. While some shades of red, particularly a common type of light rose, are easily recognizable as synthetic, other hues are not distinguishable on visual evidence. Even when the synthetic color does not provide a precise date, its recognition at least allows one to be certain that the rug was made after the mid-nineteenth century. The first aniline-dyed rugs could hardly have appeared before the late 1860s.

NOTE

1.   Norton, E. D., *Rugs in Their Native Land,* Dodd, Mead, and Co., New York, 1910, p. 25.

IV THE CONSTRUCTION OF CARPETS

Before we can describe the various types of carpets, we must devote some discussion to their manner of construction. Among the many methods of weaving and decorating fabrics, the knotting technique of oriental carpets is relatively simple and involves only minor variations within the entire Middle East.

The process begins with cotton or woolen cords stretched longitudinally between two beams which constitute the ends of a loom. Subsidiary beams are then inserted, allowing alternate strands or warps to be raised and depressed so that the cross strands (the wefts), also of wool or cotton, may be inserted perpendicularly to the warps. If these were the only steps, the result would be a thin, pileless fabric, but the oriental rug acquires depth when tufts of colored wool are knotted over two (and sometimes four) warp strands. The fabric begins with a narrow band of plain weave, then rows of knots are inserted, followed by a number of weft strands, which may vary from one, as in most rugs from the Hamadan area, to four or more in the coarse Kazaks. Design is produced by alternating the color in these tufts of wool.

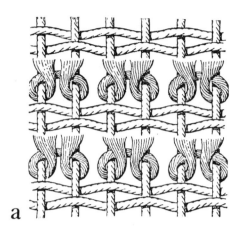

KNOTTING TECHNIQUES

The major variable is the manner in which the wool is twisted or knotted around the warp strands, and here we have one of the identifying features of a rug. There are two types of knot, usually called the Turkish or Ghiordes, and the Persian or Senneh knots. For our purposes we will use only the country names, which in themselves are misleading (as many Persian rugs are made with Turkish knots), but we will abandon the names of the towns with which they have been associated. Ghiordes has no particular claim to the Turkish knot, as weaving was likely practiced by the Turks long before they entered Anatolia, and the Persian city of Senneh has even less claim to the Persian knot, as the rugs made there (contrary to what one finds in the older rug books) are Turkish knotted. Basically the difference is as illustrated:

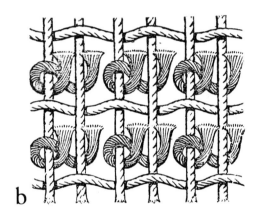

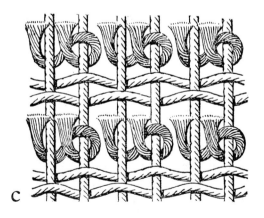

8. Types of knots. a) Turkish knot. b)Persian knot, left-handed, with 1 weft strand between each row of knots. c) Persian knot, right-handed, with 2 weft strands between each row of knots.

The Turkish knot is symmetrical, but the Persian knot differs from side to side and can therefore be tied in two different ways, with the loop on the left or the right and the pile emerging from the opposite side. (These are called left- and right-handed Persian knots.) The right-handed variety is much more common, and passing the fingers lightly across the surface of a carpet will usually show the direction in which the pile is inclined.

Often the warp threads do not all lie on the same plane, with alternate strands depressed toward the back of the carpet. This alteration may be very slight, causing a mild ridging effect, or may be so pronounced as to make only half the warps visible from either surface. With the Turkish knot this ridging is rarely extreme, but the knot may incline either to the left or right. With the Persian knot, however, the encircled warp thread is almost always the one lying toward the front of the carpet. (Some commercial Chinese carpets are an exception, as are a few modern Turkish rugs that are Persian knotted.) Most Persian-knotted rugs have alternate warps that are at least partially depressed, and the city rugs of central Persia (Kashan, Qum, Isfahan, and Kerman) show two distinct levels of warp. Often they are described as double-warped.

A variation of the above knots is one in which the pile is looped around four strands, thus diminishing the knot count by a half. This makes the fabric weaker and more susceptible to wear, but it speeds production and keeps labor costs lower. This knot is known by the term *jufti*, or double knot, and during the last several decades it has swept the Persian carpet industry like an epidemic disease. In Khurassan the jufti has long been used as standard practice, and it has been used in other weaving centers for the cheaper grades. It is now widely used in Kerman, although some areas try to prevent its use. But with the inevitable increase in labor costs in the Middle East, the jufti would seem certain to become more common.

a

b

c

10. Types of jufti knot: a) Turkish jufti knot, b) Persian jufti knot, Kerman type, c) Persian jufti knot, Khurassan type.

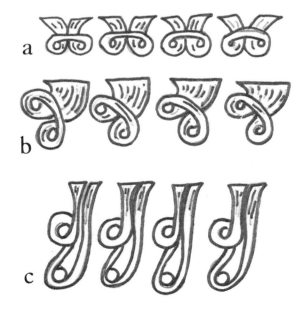

a

b

c

9. a) Turkish knots with warps on the same level. b) Turkish knots with markedly depressed warps. c) Persian knots with warps on two levels.

There is one other type of knot, but it need not concern us here as its incidence outside of Spain is limited to parts of North Africa and Cairo—if indeed specimens found in Egypt were not of Spanish manufacture. It is tied around one warp, but it is placed in such a way as to leave gaps between knots to be filled by those of the next row.

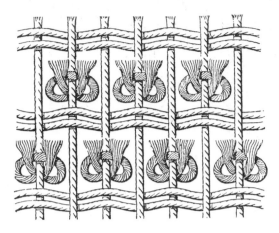

11. Spanish knot with two weft strands between each row of knots.

LOOMS

The looms on which carpets are woven are not of great complexity, and the designs have changed little through centuries of weaving. The basic loom, which is most certainly the earliest and most primitive, is the horizontal type used in the smaller Persian villages and by the nomads. The principle is simple and involves little preparation. Two strong beams are selected (usually poplar, which is common in rug-weaving areas and has relatively straight branches) and are placed in a simple frame created by driving four stakes into the ground. Between these beams are strung the warp threads, with tension maintained by stakes which push the beams farther apart. With the warps thus stretched taut, the weaver is able to begin her work in a kneeling-sitting position, which apparently can be maintained all day without discomfort.

Insertion of weft threads is made easier by two subsidiary beams that also have their counterparts on vertical looms. One beam is thrust through the warps just as a weft thread, dividing alternate warps into two sets of leaves, but for the reverse passage of the weft a reverse shed must be made. This is usually accomplished by attaching all the warp threads of the back leaf (every other warp) to another beam by means of short cords. If this beam is drawn forward the warps attached to it will be drawn in front of the other set, forming a reverse shed and allowing the weft to be passed again. While the one shed is permanently set on the loom, the reverse is formed by drawing forward the other beam. Passing the weft may also be facilitated by wrapping it around a shuttle, a long stick that can easily be passed from one side of the loom to the other.

Advantages of the horizontal loom are its simplicity, economy, and the ease with which it may be taken from the ground and moved to other locations. This is necessary for the nomadic way of life, as more complex equipment would be too heavy and cumbersome. The disadvantage of this system is the great amount of space occupied by the loom, particularly in climates where weaving must be done indoors. In this case the size of the rug will be limited by the size of the dwelling, and larger rugs are cumbersome when made by this technique. It is best suited to the weaving of narrow rugs and runners. Rugs of superb weave and quality have been made on such crude looms, and the simple design provided a prototype from which the more complex versions derive.

Three types of vertical looms are now in use, and these may be described by a number of terms. Edwards,[1] discussing **Persian** rug weaving, labeled them as village type, Tabriz type, and roller beam type. Beattie,[2] surveying Turkish techniques, describes essentially the same mechanisms by a different set of terms, referring to the Tabriz loom as the Bunyan type, while the roller beam loom is labeled as the Isbarta type.

The basic principles are the same, but there are definite advantages to the latter two. The village type loom is, indeed, little more than an upright adaptation of the old horizontal loom. Instead of stakes driven into the ground, the two beams supporting the warps fit into slots along strong vertical beams. The lower ends of the warp are usually tied to a rope which is laced to the beam, and tension is maintained by driving wedges into the slots, forcing the beams farther apart. As weaving progresses, the weavers must work at ever higher levels. The plank on which they are seated may be raised slowly to higher rungs of ladders on each side of the loom. If the carpet is to be larger, the tension is slackened, and the rug is moved downward. The woven part is sewn along the rope laced to the lower beam, and the upper warp ends are retied to the upper beam. Weaving then proceeds as before until the rug is finished or the woven portion is to be lowered again. The added steps of this method are time consuming and inconvenient; clearly there is room for improvement.

The Tabriz loom is only slightly more complex. The warps are looped around the upper and lower beams so that, as work progresses, the tension can be loosened and the finished portion turned up behind the lower beam. A rug can thus be woven that is twice as long as the height of the loom, and the lowering operation is accomplished so easily

12. Young weavers in Isfahan. The scaffolding on which they sit can easily be adjusted upwards so that the rug need not be moved often.

that the weavers never need change the level at which they sit.

The roller beam looms, used most commonly in more advanced centers such as Kerman, carry the innovation of the Tabriz loom one step farther. Here both the upper and lower supports of the warp turn in sockets, and tension can be obtained merely by tightening the levers. As weaving proceeds, the finished part of the rug is wound around the lower beam, and the warp is unwound from the upper beam. This allows carpets of virtually any length to be made, and the even tension that can be maintained on the warps produces probably the straightest carpets woven. There is one disadvantage, however, in that the completed portions of carpet cannot be inspected as in the Tabriz loom. But this is not of great necessity when the designs are being woven with scale paper diagrams by experienced artisans. The roller beam loom is also most popular throughout western Turkey.

14. Instruments used in weaving: scissors, type of hook used in Hamadan, metal weft beater, and type of hook (with blade) used in Tabriz.

INSTRUMENTS

Few instruments are required for weaving oriental carpets; basically these include only devices for cutting the yarn and for combing each row of knots tightly against the last row. Usually the cutting is done with both a knife, for clipping the yarn after the knot is tied, and shears for trimming the pile after each row is tied. In some weaving centers this clipping is done as the work progresses, in other areas after the carpet is finished. In any event there is usually a finishing process in which the pile length is made uniform throughout the rug. The weavers of Tabriz and those areas where weaving was introduced from Tabriz use a hook for tying the Turkish knot, and one edge of this instrument is often sharpened to function as a knife. (A hook may also be used in the tying of Persian knots.)

There are several varieties of comb for beating down the wefts. Usually this instrument has teeth about the width of the distance between the warps, and it is pushed vigorously (often hammered) to pack the knots as tightly as possible. In the Bidjar area this is supplemented by further beating with a nail-like instrument that is inserted above each row of knots and then hammered with considerable force. (This explains the heavy, inflexible quality of Bidjars.) In some areas another tool, a steel brushlike device, is used for combing each tuft of pile and tightening the knot. In any event, equipment for the most modern production plant is much the same as that of the primitive nomadic weaver.

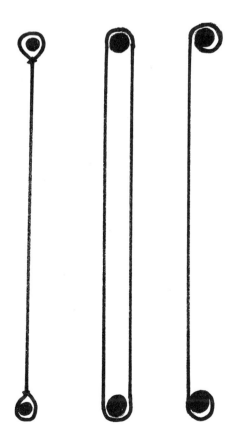

13. Diagram of three types of vertical loom: a) village type with warps tied to upper and lower beams; b) Tabriz type, with warps forming continuous loop around upper and lower beams; c) roller beam type, with both beams rotating in a socket.

MATERIALS USED IN RUGS

The materials used in weaving vary widely throughout the Middle East, and some attention must be devoted to the ingredients of any rug to be examined. Wool and cotton are by far the most important, of course, but there is occasional use of other materials. Silk has been found in carpets at least since early Sefavid times, when it was used as pile material or for the warp strands, as it has greater tensile strength than either wool or cotton. Recently its use has been limited to a few centers, with Kashan being the most important in Persia. During the late nineteenth and early twentieth centuries the weavers of Tabriz and the Anatolian cities of Kayseri and Hereke also produced some silk carpets, usually copies of earlier masterpieces. Silk also is an occasional component of some Turkoman rugs, usually only in small patches. In the rugs of eastern Turkestan and China silk is occasionally found in the pile, although here it is not necessarily accompanied by fineness of weave. In Persia silk rugs often attain the highest knot count per square inch.

The wools available to the weaver vary so greatly from one region to the next that detailed consideration will be deferred to the discussion of each individual rug type; yet there are some basic factors influencing the type of wool that one might expect from a given area. The major variables are the breed of sheep and climate, as both influence the texture, color, and wearing qualities of the wool.

Another matter of concern is the method by which the wool is removed from the sheep. Several processes have developed other than the usual shearing; the wool produced by them—which has the name "skin wool"—is taken from dead animal skins after immersion in a caustic solution that weakens its adhesion to the skin. The fiber is thus easily scraped off, or its base is dissolved so that it floats off in solution. This wool is cheaper than shorn wool and is readily available in many areas. In two important aspects it is inferior. One is that the caustic solutions remove the natural oils, leaving the wool brittle and prone to rapid wear. The other disadvantage is the difficulty in dyeing skin wool, as the hair remains intact, with a hard surface not only along the shaft, but also at both ends. When wool is cut, there is a break in this surface, and dye penetrates more easily than it does through an intact membrane. Rugs made of skin wool may be difficult to distinguish and often may be undetected, but the texture is generally noted to be flat, dull, and lusterless.

Other qualities of wool depend upon such factors as altitude and pasturage. For example, areas of northwestern Persia inhabited by Kurds are mountainous, and even the towns have elevations of five and six thousand feet. In this climate the wool becomes thicker and heavier in texture than that found in warmer, more arid climates. There is no inflexible rule, however, as variation exists in the breed of sheep. In many regions there is a considerable difference between the spring and fall shearing, but again this depends upon altitude, climate, and pasturage.

Cotton is becoming increasingly important as a carpet material, particularly as rug production turns from Persia toward India where cotton is more readily available. Although cotton has been used occasionally in the pile, usually for white, it has been limited almost entirely to the warp and weft. There is some reason for considering it superior to wool for this function: the knots of the pile are thought to tie more firmly to a cotton foundation, and the finished fabric lies more evenly on the floor.

Cotton is grown in many parts of the Middle East, particularly around Isfahan, Kazvin, Kashan, and many parts of Anatolia. The quality, however, is poor, as the fiber is short and does not produce the strongest yarns. There is also a problem of distribution, especially to nomads and small villages. The nomads produce their own wool, but they must purchase cotton from outside sources, an added expense that is sometimes prohibitive. However, even in rural areas the use of cotton is becoming more common.

When treated under tension with strong alkaline solutions, cotton thread takes on textural qualities that give it some resemblance to silk. The "polished" cotton of modern fabrics has been treated· in a similar manner, and mercerized cotton (named after John Mercer, the man who developed the process) has been used in oriental rugs as a silk substitute since the late nineteenth century. Mercerized cotton has a greater affinity for dye than ordinary cotton; initially it has a greater tensile strength, but it tends to decompose after a number of years. A mercerized cotton rug fifty years old would likely show a relatively brittle pile that would wear very poorly. Initially its luster makes mercerized cotton difficult to distinguish from silk, but wetting the two fabrics is a fairly reliable test; mercerized cotton then feels more like ordinary cotton. Many Kayseri rugs were woven of this material and sold as silk to the unsuspecting.

Camel hair may also be found in carpets, although the beige-colored wool in many Hamadans and Kurdish village rugs described as camel hair is almost always ordinary sheep wool dyed with walnut husks. Actually the camel has two distinct types of hair: an outer coarse layer that is basically stiff and straight, and an under layer more like wool in softness. When the latter is used (as seems to be the case in some earlier Turkoman rugs), it can be distinguished from wool only with a microscope.

A few other materials have had minor use. Goat hair is sometimes used as pile material and in the selvage of some Baluchi, Afghan, and Ersari Turkoman rugs; it may also occur in the weft of some Anatolian nomad rugs. This is usually dark brown or nearly black, and makes a yarn of little strength. Other substances found occasionally are jute (mixed with wool or cotton in some wefts), and linen, which has been used in rare instances as a foundation material.

The manner of spinning wool and cotton into thread has some effect on the finished product, as there are variations in thickness, compressibility, and tensile strength. For ages the yarn was spun by hand methods that varied little from the cities to the villages, but recently machine-spun thread has become available from India (with exports beginning in bulk just after World War II) and from domestic industrial development within Iran and Turkey. This has both advantages and disadvantages. Whereas the machine-spun thread makes strong warps that would probably have uniform shrinkage characteristics throughout the rug, the wefts are less compressible and thus less easily incorporated into some of the heavier types of rugs. Wool for the pile is still hand spun in most areas.

FLAT WEAVES

Several types of rugs are woven without pile, and these are intended to serve as inexpensive floor coverings, draperies, or various utilitarian or decorative functions. Flat weaves are more quickly produced than pile carpets and use a number of brocading and embroidery techniques. Likely flat-stitch rugs were made before pile carpets, and, without evidence of known specimens, we may assume that various types have been woven for many centuries.

The most common form of flat weave is the slit tapestry kilim (also gilim or kileem), which is found throughout the Middle East. The technique resembles that used in European tapestries; both sides of the fabric are left essentially the same. The warp is arranged on the loom just as for a pile carpet, but the design is formed entirely by the weft which completely hides the warp from view. The pattern is formed by using different-colored wefts. The simplest flat weaves are only stripes of alternating colors; much more commonly, however, a

design is produced by introducing discontinuous wefts in different colors. Each thread is taken only so far and then is passed back again, eventually forming a patch of solid color. Where the demarcation between two colors is a vertical line, there is a discontinuity in the fabric, resulting in a slit.

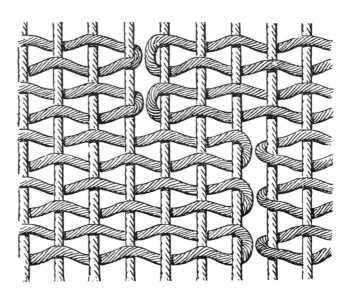

15. Slit tapestry kilim technique.

Less common in the Middle East (although it is standard in American Indian flat weave rugs) is the technique of "warp sharing." In this case the slit is eliminated by allowing the wefts from two adjacent color areas to share the same warp, thus strengthening the fabric. One seldom finds older kilims with this technique, but it seems to be spreading. Most recent kilims from Kurdistan are woven in this fashion, and among the piles of kilims I recently examined in Shiraz, about ten percent showed this feature. Hazara kilims from central Afghanistan apparently all have shared warps.

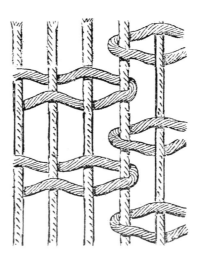

16. Warp-sharing technique.

The fineness of a kilim is a function of the number of warp threads for a given measurement (usually ranging between 6 and 20 per inch), and ordinarily there are four to six times as many weft threads for the same area. Usually the same density of wefts is found from one portion of the rug to the next, and they are all at right angles to the warp. Some Senneh kilims, however, achieve a curvilinear effect by slightly slanting the weft in some areas and by allowing the density in some patches to exceed that in others.

The Turkish kilim has several distinctive features that make identification easier, and the two sides are often distinguishable by loose threads at the back connecting patches of the same color; the design also may be outlined in brocade. Larger pieces are often woven in two strips that are then sewn together. Frequently there is a slight size difference between the two halves; so the design does not completely match up.

Kilims are found in all sizes from very small to over 20 feet in length. Those of Fars and the southern Caucasus tend to be long in relation to their width, with design elements arranged in broad stripes across the breadth of the field. Kurdish kilims, particularly the Senneh type, may be smaller; most kilims woven as runners, often with repeating figures in the field, are Kurdish.

The other common type of flat weave is the so-called *Soumak*, allegedly named after the Caucasian city of Shemakka, and often erroneously assumed to be primarily Caucasian. The technique, however, which is a type of brocading, is found in all weaving areas. Basically the design is produced by a method of weft wrapping in which the weft is passed forward over four and then behind two warp threads (the ratio may be two to one in exceptionally fine pieces). The loop at the front of the carpet thus does not lie at right angles to the warp, but slants uniformly in one direction. Alternate rows usually reverse the slant, creating a herringbone effect, and the loose ends left after a patch of color is woven are left hanging at the back of the rug. This has caused the Soumak to be classified at times with the Kashmir shawl, which has the same peculiarity, but the two are unrelated.

Most Soumaks have a supplementary ground weave of thin wefts passing the width of the rug which do not contribute to the design; rare pieces have no ground weave. The Soumak technique is found classically in a variety of Caucasian fabrics, but there are many small Soumak pieces, particularly bag faces, from both Kurdistan and Fars. There are fewer Turkish examples of this type, but a common species of Yomud Turkoman bag is woven with the Soumak stitch.

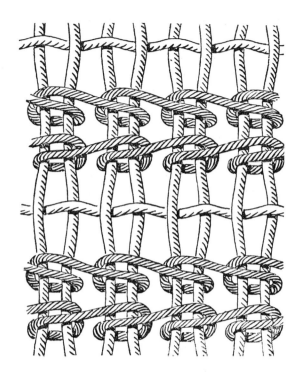

17. Soumak weave.

Among less common flat-weave techniques, the most important is probably weft-float brocading. This involves the introduction of design elements through supplementary wefts on a ground weave. Often it occurs on a plain weave or Soumak ground, and it may be used to decorate the woven bands at the ends of many rugs. A group of large Turkoman rugs is done exclusively in weft-float brocading, as is the so-called *Verneh*. This latter type has been described as Caucasian by most rug books, but most examples show evidence of an origin among the nomadic population of eastern Anatolia. (Recently flat woven rugs have been well described in print by a Textile Museum publication, *From the Bosphorus to Samarkand, Flat Woven Rugs*.[3])

EXAMINING A RUG

We have outlined the manner in which oriental rugs are woven, and further details will be given in later sections of the book. At this point, however, it is important to determine a method by which carpets can be methodically examined. The carpets illustrated in this volume have been subjected to such analysis, with data provided about the warp, weft, pile, sides, ends (both upper and lower), and colors. Different authors have employed a variety of abbreviations; ours are adapted from those of the Textile Museum, Washington, D.C.

The Warp: The material of the warp is stated first, and it may be discerned by examining the ends. Wool and cotton are readily distinguishable, and if a small amount is burned there can be no doubt—the odor of burning animal hair is unmistakable. Silk is even more obvious, and when burned it leaves a small hard ball of resinous substance.

The manner of twisting the material into thread is also significant. In all areas where carpets have been woven except Egypt, the wool, cotton, or silk has ordinarily been "Z" spun, or rather the fibers have been twisted counterclockwise (to the left) to run at the same angle as the stem of the Z. The individual strands are then plied into cords, always in the opposite direction, in this case clockwise (to the right) like the cross of the S. Most fibers we will have occasion to examine are Z-spun and S-plied; the only exceptions within the area we will survey are probably random. (Several of the spinning mills in central Persia produce cotton thread spun to the right.) The warp is usually made of three strands in Turkey and the Caucasus, and four to six strands in most Persian city rugs. We will abbreviate this as follows:

EXAMPLE   *Warp:* C, /4\ .

(The C stands for cotton, while the / refers to a Z spin; the figure 4 indicates the number of strands, and the \ means that these are S-plied.)

Spin and ply of threads ordinarily are not crucial to the identification of recent Middle Eastern rugs; yet this data has been useful in answering some questions on historical issues. Many carpets that were formerly described as Turkish court manufacture are now thought to have been made in Cairo after the Ottoman conquest in 1517. The major reason for this conclusion is that the threads are S-spun and Z-plied, which was the practice only in Egypt.[4]

The Weft: Aside from the characteristics noted for the warp—the material, spin, and ply—we are concerned with several other features of the weft. While the warp is seldom dyed (except in a few Oushak and Bergama rugs), the weft is very often dyed red or blue. The number of times it crosses between each row of knots is also of diagnostic importance and can usually be determined easily. In rugs with one weft between each row, alternate warps are exposed at the back of the rugs, as the weft covers only every other strand. This grainy effect may often be noted at a glance.

When there are two wefts, the warps usually cannot be seen at the back. With three or more wefts there may be some difficulty in determining

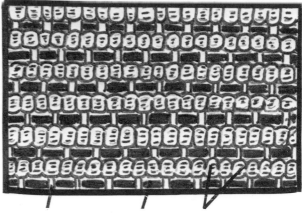

Exposed portion   W eft.   Knots — loops seen
of the warp.   from the back.

18. Appearance of single-wefted rug (from the back).

the number of strands, as in the triple-wefted Kerman, with one of the strands very thin and buried. Also the material is more difficult to determine, particularly in a tightly woven intact rug.

Other features that should be noted about the weft relate to how tightly it is pulled across the rug. In cases where a thick weft is drawn taut, the warps are placed at different levels, one on each side of the weft. If the next weft is loose, alternate warps will remain depressed. We can thus describe the weft as follows:

EXAMPLE
Weft: W, /2\, dyed red, 3 or 4 shoots between each row of knots, all loose. (Wool, 2 strands Z-spun and S-plied.)

The Pile: The spin and ply of the pile are relatively unimportant as diagnostic features; often the yarn is twisted lightly or not at all. The type of knot, however, may be of great importance.

Persian and Turkish knots are distinguishable by several methods, but the easiest is accomplished by folding the rug perpendicularly to the warp so as to expose the base of the knots. Here one may see the loop of pile yarn encircling either one warp or two (if the weave is fine, it is difficult to tell which) and also one sees the tuft of pile. The relationship of this tuft to the loop is the important element. In the Turkish knot it is seen to originate within the loop, while in the Persian knot it emerges from one side or the other. After examining a few rugs, one may use this method with ease.

Another technique is to fold the rug parallel to the warp. In the Turkish knotted rug, each parallel row shows part of a loop of pile, while in the Persian knotted rug, alternate rows reveal only the warp and weft.

The Turkish knot can be tied in only one way, but the Persian knot may open either to the right or the left (right-handed or left-handed). Throughout the area where this knot is used, the right-handed version is found much more frequently (with the weaver holding the knife in his right hand). There seems to be no significant regional variation.

The Turkish knot, however, can incline either to the right or left, depending upon which warp strand is depressed. (In the Senneh rug, alternate rows of knots incline in different directions, as each warp is first depressed and then raised by the single, tightly drawn weft.) We can thus describe the pile as follows:

EXAMPLES
Pile: W. /1, Knot: T-R, 25° h.6, v. 12, 72/sq. inch. (The pile is wool, of one strand Z-spun, Turkish knotted, with the right warp depressed 25 degrees; knot count 6 horizontally and 12 vertically.)

Pile: W. /2\, *Knot:* P-L, 75°h. 12, v. 12, 144 knots/sq. inch. (The pile is wool, of 2 Z-spun strands, S-plied, Persian knotted with the left warp depressed 75 degrees; knot count 12 horizontally and 12 vertically, 144 per square inch.)

The Sides: The finish applied to the sides is exposed to great wear. Since it often needs reinforcement, one must be cautious in determining whether the material examined is original or was added at a later date. There are basically four ways in which the sides of a carpet may be finished, and somewhat arbitrarily we may give these the following labels: 1) weft overcasting, 2) double overcasting (with extra yarn to reinforce the weft overcast), 3) weft selvage, and 4) double selvage (also with added yarn). The simple weft overcast is not common; it is formed merely by turning the thread back toward the other side after wrapping it around the terminal warp, which may be thickened or composed of several threads. A selvage is formed when the weft is woven in figure-of-eight fashion around a series of three or four terminal warps, which also are usually thickened. When additional yarn is added in the double overcast and double selvage, this may be the same or a different color than in the rest of the carpet, and it may vary along the length of the edge. At times in a double selvage, the weft only loops around the nearest of the terminal warps, thus attaching to the carpet a selvage that includes several additional warps. We may describe the sides as follows:

EXAMPLE
Sides: Double selvage, 4 warps, black goat hair.

The Ends: Like the sides, these are often subject to damage and repair, and one must interpret observations with caution. Also one must inspect

19. Types of side finish. a) Weft overcast. b) Double overcast, with extra yarn added. c) Weft selvage (over three terminal warps). d) Double selvage. This is the same as a weft selvage, except that extra yarn is added in a figure-of-eight fashion.

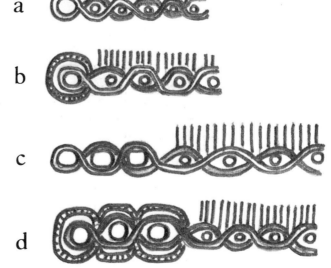

both ends, as there are often differences between top and bottom.

The simplest finish consists of a few rows of weft after the last knots, leaving a loose fringe at both ends. This band can also be lengthened to well over a foot of plain weave, and decorations can be added by various techniques. In Turkoman rugs there are stripes of different colors, while in many Baluchi rugs there are stripes of weft float brocade. Often one of the ends will show cut warps, and the other end will show intact loops where the thread encircled the lower beam of the loom or the rope holding the threads in place.

There are also a number of ways in which warp ends can be tied or braided together. In many Caucasian rugs (particularly from the northern Caucasus) one finds the warp ends tied in a series of small knots. Yürük and Bergama rugs of Turkey often have ends braided together into thick strands. In some Persian rugs the warps at one or both ends are woven together into a thick selvage. At times one finds a fringe left in addition to the selvage. The ends may be described as follows:

EXAMPLE

Ends: Upper; red weft plain weave, 1", selvage band, ½", and loose warp ends. Lower: 4 rows of red weft, loose warp ends.

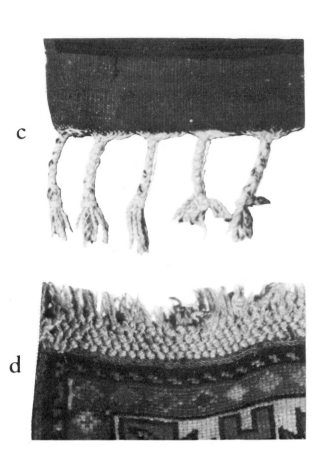

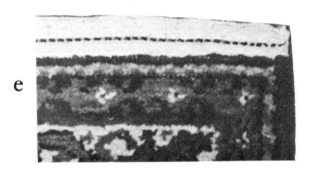

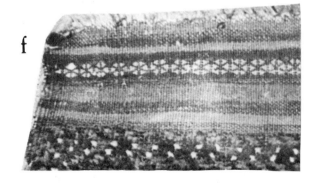

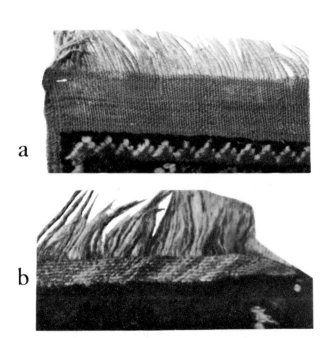

20. Types of end finish. a) Melas rug with plain weave band. b) Yuruk rug with selvage and loose warp ends. c) Bergama rug with warp ends braided together. d) Kuba rug with warp ends knotted together. e) Hamadan rug with plain weave band doubled under. f) Baluchi rug with ornamentation in weft float brocade.

21. Young weavers at a shop in Hamadan.

Other Features: A number of other observations can be made about any given rug. Often it is valuable to count and list the number of distinct colors, and the feel or texture may also furnish some clue toward identification.

Some rugs, particularly in larger sizes, show vague diagonal lines at the back ("zigzag" lines), which result from a particular method of weaving. When one weaver is working at a loom that is too wide to permit tying a complete row of knots without moving, often to save time one portion of the rug will be completed several inches above the rest, and the next section subsequently added on. As the wefts are discontinuous (doubling back at the junction of these two areas), faint diagonal lines are left. This does not significantly weaken the carpet and shows only that some portions were woven before others.

With a little practice one may learn to accurately describe a rug, a skill that may help considerably with identification. The following sections will often place considerable emphasis upon structure, as it is usually a more helpful distinguishing feature than design. In areas where designs have changed to fit the fashions of the day, the weavers have been more reluctant to alter their basic techniques. More often than not, an analysis of these details will provide the decisive information that allows a certain identification.

NOTES

1. Edwards, A. C., *The Persian Carpet*, Duckworth, London, 1953, pp. 22-24.

2. Beattie, May H., "Background to the Turkish Rug," *Oriental Art*, Vol. IX, No. 3, pp. 3-10.

3. Landreau, A. N., and Pickering, W. R., *From the Bosphorus to Samarkand, Flat Woven Rugs,* The Textile Museum, Washington, D.C., 1969.

4. Kuhnel, E., and Bellinger, L., *Cairene Rugs and Others Technically Related,* National Publishing Co., Washington, D.C., 1957.

Supplementary Bibliography

1. Emery, Irene, *The Primary Structure of Fabrics,* The Textile Museum, Washington D.C., 1966.

V THE RUGS OF PERSIA

The name of Persia (modern Iran) is intimately associated with oriental rugs, as a large number of the world's great carpets have been woven there. The tradition still flourishes today, both as an art and as a commercial enterprise, but changes have been numerous within the last several decades, and there will doubtless be many more before the end of the century. We hear from some sources that the Persian carpet is dying, that social reform will make the craft economically unsound within the next generation. At the same time we see in the better modern fabrics a dynamic fusion of modern and past designs, with craftsmanship rivaling even the best court pieces of earlier periods. That such should be the case is only one of many contradictions within a country that has not resolved its identity as a modern nation. A land that was only decades ago a medieval Islamic backwater is ardently applying itself to the task of Westernizing its institutions, and the carpet seems to belong more to the past than the future.

THE LAND AND PEOPLE

Geographically Persia consists of a central plateau tilting in a southeasterly direction, surrounded by rugged mountain ranges. The climate is generally extreme, with harsh winters and dry summers, modified by altitude in many of the cities (Hamadan, Isfahan, and Kerman are nearly 6,000 feet, while Tabriz is 4,500). Rainfall is sparse, except in the relatively humid areas bordering the Persian Gulf and on the western slopes of the Zagros Mountains, which run from Azerbaijan to the South of Shiraz and in places reach heights of 14,000 feet. The eastern central portion of the country contains the barren and virtually unoccupied Great Desert, a drainageless basin into which the small, inland rivers empty. The outer slopes of the mountains drain toward the Gulf or several salt lakes, such as Lake Urmia in Azerbaijan. Lack of water has prevented Persia from becoming a great agricultural land, although there is enough moisture to support grazing over wide areas. Sheep are raised in virtually every part of the country, except, of course, the Great Desert, and this has provided readily available wool for carpets.

The population of Persia (approaching 30 million) is composed of a basic Aryan racial stock with several large minorities. Sometime during the second millenium B.C. the area was invaded by Indo-European groups generally described as Medes and Persians. These pastoral nomads succeeded in establishing themselves in Mesopotamia and what is now Persia, where they absorbed whatever peoples had preceded them. In the course of the following centuries they were invaded by Greeks and Romans, whose influence was transitory; but the Arab conquest of the seventh century brought considerable change, and Arab remnants are still extant in Fars and areas bordering the Gulf. The next conquerors also profoundly affected the populace, as the Seljuks settled large areas of Azerbaijan and Hamadan, where Turkish is still the predominant language. The Mongol invasion produced no such enclaves, but it left a liberal supply of Mongoloid racial features.

Other minority groups probably entered the area with the Persians, as they are related in language and customs. The Kurds are by far the largest group, numbering perhaps two million in Persia and another four million in Iraq and Turkey. Living in small villages or as seminomads along the western mountains, they are closely related to the Lurs (about 100,000) who live to the south in Khuzistan, and the Bahktiaris (400,000), a tribe whose influence has outweighed its numbers. The Baluchis in Khurassan and Baluchistan are more distant relatives, while the other nomads, Qashqais and Afshars, speak a Turkic dialect and are later offshoots of the Seljuk migrations. The Khamseh Federation of Fars is a combination of Persian, Turkic, and Arab nomads. Only a scattering of Jews, Assyrians, and Afghans are found in the cities, while about fifty thousand Armenians live in isolated clusters of villages. Generally these groups are well integrated into the social fabric, although there are some forms of intolerance.

All Persians, with the exception of the few Jews, Assyrians (Nestorians), Zoroastrians, and Armenians, are Mohammedans, and the Shi'ah sect constitutes the state religion. This includes the great bulk of the population, the exceptions being isolated groups of Sunni Mohammedans throughout the country. Most of these are Kurds but there are also Sunnis among the Baluchis and Turkoman tribes in the east. All together they probably number more than 2,000,000. A much smaller group,

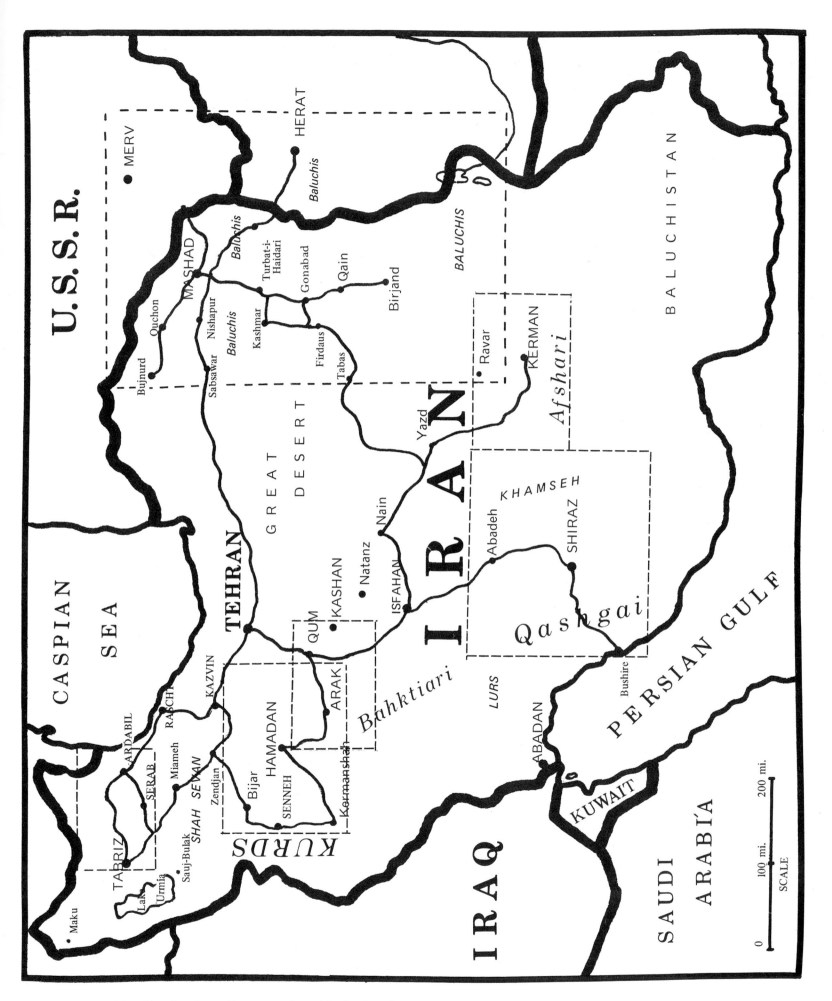

Map No. 1.   Iran. (Areas enclosed by broken lines are covered by more detailed maps.)

the remnants of a religion that once was dominant in Persia, are the Zoroastrians, who number about 20,000 and are found mainly in the vicinity of Yezd and Kerman. At the time of the Arab conquest many of them are alleged to have migrated to India.

RUG WEAVING IN PERSIA

The origin of rug weaving in Persia is not known, although many theories have been put forward. Our first literary references clearly applying to knotted, pile fabrics (as distinct from those described by Greek and Roman writers, which could have been produced by any number of methods) occur in the tenth century, but the Pazirik and Bash Adar finds certainly suggest that the art in the Middle East was several thousand years older. We can no longer give much credence to theories that either the Seljuks or the Mongols brought carpet weaving to the area. As our information is so incomplete, historical discussion must begin with the Sefavid era, from which many examples still survive. This dynasty was established in 1501 and was not overthrown until the Afghan invasions of 1722-23; under these enlightened rulers Persia experienced its most glorious artistic flowering in recent history.

The first years of Sefavid rule were occupied by wars and the establishment of national sovereignty; but the second ruler, Shah Tahmasp (1524-1587), could devote much of his attention to the fine arts. It was under his reign that court factories were established to weave the great carpets we now list among the finest examples of textile art. The weaving was carried on even more avidly by his successor, Shah Abbas the Great, who moved the capital to Isfahan and ruled until 1629. For the next century the empire declined, and finally the Afghans invaded the country and forced the last of the royal line to capitulate in 1723. At this time all city weaving throughout Persia seems to have diminished greatly or ceased, as the country remained in great turmoil for decades. Nadir Shah came to power from 1736 to 1747 and carried on successful wars with Persia's neighbors. The Qajar dynasty ascended in 1796 and ruled with neither inspiration nor vigor until Shah Reza Mohammed Pahlavi took the throne in 1925.

Little is known of carpet weaving in the 150 years after the Afghan invasion. Its development from the late 1800s will be detailed in subsequent portions of this work.

TYPES OF PERSIAN RUGS

In discussing the rugs of Persia, we have made a division between city rugs and those from various nomadic tribes. Curiously enough, the list of cities does not include several of the nation's great population centers, most notably Tehran, a metropolis of nearly three million; Rasht, Abadan, and Kermanshah also exceed 100,000, but they have never been known as weaving centers. In Tehran there was at one time a weaving industry, but it died out as a result of the higher wages necessary to live in this Westernized city. The other cities have also had a small output of carpets, but other industries have remained more important. Thus the areas described in this work are not the only places where rugs were produced, but those whose names are most closely associated with the art.

Tabriz, with its surrounding areas of Heriz, Karadja, and Serab, will be described first, as it was here that the commercial spark stimulating the large-scale export of rugs was cultivated by the merchants. We next consider the various Kurdish weaves and rugs of the Hamadan villages. The Arak area, including Saraband, follows, along with Qum, Kashan, Isfahan, Joshogan, and Nain. The rugs of Yezd are grouped with those of Kerman, while all the city and village rugs of Khurassan are included along with those of Meshed.

Nomad rugs are described by location and tribe. This includes the rugs of Fars (both Qashgai and Khamseh), the Baluchi rugs of Khurassan, Afshar weaves, and those of the Bahktiari.

TABRIZ AND THE DEVELOPMENT OF THE CARPET INDUSTRY

Tabriz is the capital of Azerbaijan, Iran's most populous province that borders on both Turkey and the Soviet Union. As in the Caucasus, with which the ranges of Azerbaijan merge, a profuse variety of ethnic, religious, and linguistic factions lives within the province. It has been settled by successive migrations from the north and east. It contains ruins of the cultural or political centers of at least two pre-Aryan peoples, the first national center of the Persians (before they moved southward to Fars), and the first capital in the Middle East of both the Seljuks and Mongols. Moreover, it has been central in the histories of the Armenians, the Kurds, and of the Nestorian or Assyrian Christians. Today the language of the province is Azeri, a dialect of Turkish, which contains almost as much connection with Persian as it does with the national language of Turkey. The name of Azerbaijan (or

"Land of Fire") is in reference to the fire temples of the Zoroastrian priests, who, until the Islamic conquest, made the area their center.

Tabriz has not produced quantities of carpets to compare with the output of Hamadan, Arak, or even Kerman, but the city perhaps has played a greater historical role than the others in the development of the carpet industry throughout Persia.[1] Indeed the Tabrizi merchants probably were the most significant force in establishing the international reputation of the Persian carpet, beginning in the 1860s, when there was virtually no weaving for export. At that time most of the rugs sent to Europe were Anatolian, shipped from the great markets of Istanbul and Smyrna.

Business increased from a rather modest beginning to enormous proportions within a few decades. At almost all levels of European and American society, a great upsurge of interest in the Orient coincided with an increased cultural and political contact with the Middle East. This was stimulated by the decline in Ottoman influence and the resultant power vacuum that seemed to beckon outside intervention. First Napoleon made his venture into Egypt, opening up untold archeological treasures to French researchers. Next came involvement by the British that continued through the entire nineteenth century and which, during such efforts as the Crimean wars, included the deployment of large numbers of Europeans in what had, since the Crusades, been territory almost unknown to the West. By the middle of the century Russia had also extended her power southward, taking the Caucasus from Persia and exerting pressure on the Ottoman Empire. Clearly Europe had established an interest in the Middle East.

During this period, Eastern influences were also surfacing in the West, both in music and painting. Clearly there was an enormous enthusiasm toward products of this mysterious and unknown vastness, and, as carpets were conveniently marketable items, produced in a relatively accessible region, the stage was set for a great tide of commerce.

Merchants of Tabriz were at the forefront in Persia, as this city had long been one of cosmopolitan traders, and it was well situated for shipment via Trebizond and the Black Sea to Istanbul. Many Tabrizi firms opened up offices in that city, and during the 1870s and 1880s they began the export of Persian carpets on a large scale. Up to that time weaving had been carried on at a modest level to meet local needs and also, in the realm of fine carpets, to provide investments for the affluent. Banking in Persia was in a rudimentary stage, and no Middle Eastern currency was noted for its stability. Used carpets, or rather those that had mellowed with age, were found to bring a better price than new ones, and merchants gathered carpets from homes and bazaars throughout the country.

At one point, however, the supply seemed to be diminishing, as certainly this process would be limited. The merchants were forced to become manufacturers, or at least to stimulate greater output. By 1880, in a number of centers, carpets began to be made for distant markets. Tabriz was a collecting center, although the many diverse activities of the city prevented it from devoting its entire attention to the carpet trade. In other areas, where the traditional textile industries were experiencing a decline brought on by competition with Western machine-made articles, carpet weaving took proportionately more of the resources. Kerman and Kashan soon came to depend almost exclusively on the industry, and Sultanabad (Arak) experienced a similar development.

Since its beginning there have been many drastic changes in the carpet business, as it passed into the hands of foreign businessmen after World War I and then to local Persian interests after World War II. Now, with the enormous markets of Europe and the somewhat diminished market in the United States, the industry is flourishing as never before, although competition is developing from other countries where the labor is even cheaper. Tabriz has little part in the commerce; yet the tradition of weaving fine rugs continues, and some of the better new rugs are still woven there.

THE RUGS OF TABRIZ

The Tabriz carpet traditionally has been a double wefted fabric on a cotton foundation, with Turkish knots and a rather harsh wool from the Maku district of the extreme northwestern part of Persia. Manufacture takes place in factories of ten to one hundred looms, rather than in the homes, with a number of apprentices working for a master weaver. The quality of Tabriz rugs varies more than is usual within a single city, as the weave is from about 6 x 6 to occasional fine pieces with over 20 x 20 knots to the square inch. The pile is short, and the carpet is not known to be particularly durable. The Tabrizis appear to use less wool per square yard than other weaving areas, and this may be easily demonstrated by weighing a Tabriz rug and comparing it, for example, with a Hamadan of equal size and pile length. Tying of the knots is accomplished with a hook, which prevents use of the jufti knot. Synthetic dyes are almost universal,

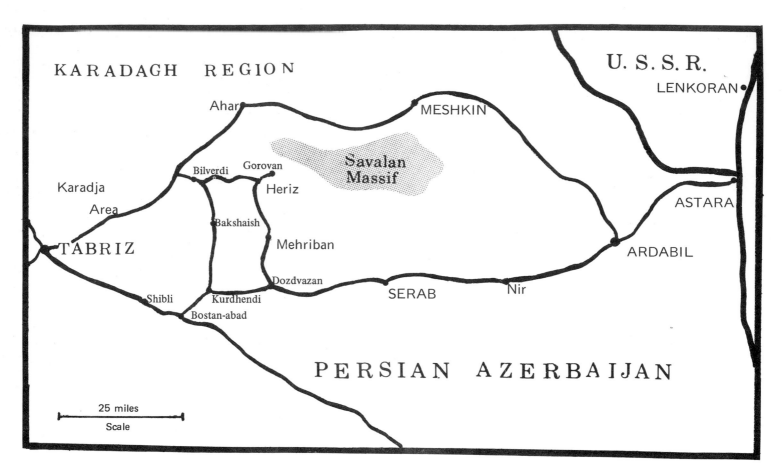

Map No. 2. Tabriz and the Heriz Weaving Area

and these vary enormously in quality. Since the late nineteenth century the best synthetics have been used with great skill in Tabriz, but the poorest grade Tabriz carpet is likely to be made of skin wool colored with harsh, aniline dyes and woven with yarn too thin to provide good wearing qualities.

The Tabriz carpet may appear in virtually any shape or pattern. Medallion designs may well have been used first in Tabriz carpets of Sefavid times, and they are still found in many forms, both in curvilinear and rectilinear patterns. There is no traditional color scheme, as in Kerman or Kashan, and the weavers make what the market demands at any particular time. A great number of diverse elements have found their way into Tabriz rugs. They are precisely drawn and executed with care, and perhaps this has led to the charge that these rugs often have the stiff appearance of machine-made fabrics. Perhaps this is also related to the early commercialization of the Tabriz carpet by foreign firms, who, by the turn of the century, virtually controlled production in the city. While the British and Ameri-

cans dominated the Arak area, German organizations were more important in Tabriz. The firm of Petag was particularly notable, and it marketed several grades of carpet designed to European tastes. Although the industry is now controlled by Iranian businessmen, most Tabriz rugs still go to Europe.

A novelty among the new rugs is the appearance of a number of pictorial designs, with human and animal forms against a landscape of trees and mountains. Although they have not been woven in quantity since before World War I, old Tabriz silk rugs may still be encountered in the trade, and they have recently been bringing enormous sums of money. These rugs are thin, pliable, and may occasionally be woven with the Persian knot. (Some show the novel feature of dyed warps, often in stripes visible at the back of the rug.) A panel design of small squares enclosing floral motifs is common, and often this is modified to consist of numerous miniature prayer niches. Adaptations of Anatolian prayer rugs (often the Ghiordes type) are frequently found, and these are distinguished by a more naturalistic

23. TABRIZ PRAYER RUG, late 19th century, 4'1'' x 6'2''. Warp: C. /4\, white. Weft: C. /3\, white, 2 shoots. Pile: W. /2\. Knot: T-L, 75°, v. 9, h. 10, 90/sq inch. Sides: double selvage of rust red wool over 3 warps. Ends: .... Colors (8): rust red field, yellow, apricot, dark and light brown, light blue, mauve, ivory. Tabriz prayer rugs, of both wool and silk, may be found in curvilinear adaptations of Turkish designs or elaborately floral tree-of-life patterns. This example, with its columns and hanging lamp, appears to be influenced by earlier Ghiordes types.

22. TABRIZ MEDALLION RUG, 19th century, 4'9'' x 6'. Warp: C. /6\, undyed, light. Weft: C. /2\, undyed, 2 shoots. Pile: W. /2\untwisted. Knot: T-L, 45°, v. 14, h. 14, 196/sq inch. Sides: double overcast of rust red wool over 4 warps. Ends: white cotton plain weave and loose warp ends. Colors (7): rust red field, light blue, dark brown, tan, dark brown, yellow, ivory. Superficially Tabriz medallion rugs are often suggestive of Kashan or even Kerman designs, but they are easily distinguished by their use of the Turkish knot.

24. HERIZ MEDALLION RUG, late 19th
century, 4'3" x 5'7". Warp: C. /6\, dull gray
(unbleached). Weft: C. /4\, 2 shoots, undyed.
Pile: W. /2\. Knot: T-L, 25°, v. 8, h. 6, 48/
sq. inch. Sides: double overcast of brown
wool over 6 warps. Ends: .... Colors (7):
brick red, red-brown, dark blue, dark brown,
ivory, light blue, yellow. Heriz medallion designs have changed little during the last 90
years, although figures in the field have tended to become more concentrated. Likely the
original inspiration for these rugs was provided by the curvilinear designs of Tabriz.

drawing than the originals. The prayer design, with a flowering tree of life and scrolling vines, may often be found expanded into a large format, perhaps 9 x 12 feet, and some of these rugs exceed 20 feet in length. With a knot count at times greater than 400 to the inch, these were some of the most expensive products of their time, and even before 1910 they were exceedingly expensive. Today, however, their artistic merit does not seem to justify such attention; they were never an organic part of the heritage of Persian weaving so much as a very successful commercial enterprise, with designs probably oriented to accommodate Western tastes.

THE HERIZ AREA

About forty miles east of Tabriz, south and west of the Savalan Massif, lies a group of about thirty villages, the largest and most important of which is Heriz. Carpets have probably been woven in this vicinity at least since the beginning of the nineteenth century, although the industry received its greatest stimulus from later efforts by the Tabrizi merchants. Recently in the American market virtually all these rugs have been labeled as Heriz and Gorevan. Both villages weave the same basic patterns, and the names were used to label quality rather than origin. In the early twentieth century Gorevan was the best grade rug, but more recently this name has been used to designate the lowest quality. Today the most tightly woven rugs are labeled as either *Mehriban* or *Ahar,* after two of the larger villages that produce the finest rugs. (*Ahar* is also used to designate rugs with some curvilinear aspect in the medallion.) This should not be taken as an actual description of origin, but merely as a commentary upon quality; any village could produce fine or coarse rugs, and only the carpets of Bilverdi, which are single-wefted, can be distinguished on structural grounds.

Almost all products of the Heriz area are in larger sizes, with scatter rugs relatively rare. For years these tended to be more squarish than other Persian weaves (with many 10 x 12 foot sizes), but now they conform more to Western specifications.

Formerly the wool was purchased from tribesmen of the surrounding seminomadic Shahsevan tribes, but more recently this has come from the markets in Tabriz and Ardabil. Quality has deteriorated with an increasing use of skin wool from slaughtered animals. The dyes too have fluctuated in quality, with synthetics having captured the market during the last several decades. Older Heriz rugs had madder grounds and medallions mostly of indigo; the red could be either a deep brick or a light, brilliant shade. When synthetics were introduced, the colors became muddied and often fugitive to light. Much of the dyeing is still done in Tabriz.

The typical Heriz carpet has a strictly rectilinear medallion design that has changed little over many decades; repeating patterns are less common. Knotting can be as coarse as thirty to the square inch, while the finer specimens seldom exceed eighty. The pile is heavy, and the edges have a thick double overcast. The very oldest extant Heriz rugs are on a wool foundation, but for the last eighty years cotton has been used, with two wefts, often dyed blue and of equal size. The cotton of the warp may have a grayish, unbleached appearance.

Heriz fabrics are available in great quantities, and they are among the least expensive Persian carpets. Their designs are particularly appreciated in Europe, where the bulk of the market is absorbed. During the last decade there has been an increase in the output of this area. As a historical note, we may mention the name of Bakshaish (Bakshish), a village now producing the region's characteristic carpet, but which in the late nineteenth century had a tradition of weaving carpets similar in design to those of Arak. The typical Bakshaish was similar to the so-called Feraghan of the time, with an overall Herati pattern, usually with a more squarish shape than the narrow Feraghans. They are double wefted and Turkish knotted, differing from the Arak pieces.

One still finds occasional silk rugs that are described as having originated in the Heriz district, and in many respects they resemble the turn-of-the-century silk rugs of Tabriz. The colors are often quite bright, and they are more pliable than Tabriz silks. Curvilinear medallion designs are the most common. Whether these rugs actually originated around Heriz cannot be determined with certainty, and they bear little resemblance to wool rugs of a similar vintage. Possibly they are a variety of Tabriz silk from other workshops.

25. KARADJA RUNNER (portion), early 20th century, 3'2" x 14'. Warp: C. /3\, undyed, white. Weft: C. /2\, unbleached, gray, 1 shoot. Pile: W. /2\. Knot: T, v. 9, h. 7, 63/sq inch. Sides: double overcast. Ends: narrow plain weave band and loose warp ends. Colors (7): brick red, beige, dark brown, light and dark blue, deep yellow, ivory. The modern Karadja almost always includes medallion figures similar to those on this rug. Many examples show a strong Caucasian influence.
(There is a variety of runner with similar medallions and particularly lustrous wool that probably dates from the 19th century and even earlier. These rugs usually show a dark blue field, a striking use of white, and excellent, clear colors. They are all wool and usually double wefted, which suggests that they were made by different people than the weavers of modern Karadjas. They are usually called "Karadagh" rugs, although some have definite Karabagh features. Quite possibly they were made by nomadic groups of the area, and the modern Karadja represents merely a village adaptation of traditional tribal designs.)

KARADJA

The village of Karadja is situated on the Tabriz-Ahar Road about thirty-five miles northeast of Tabriz. Along with several smaller villages, it has become identified with a particular type of rug. In the earliest pieces, the foundation was of wool but is now exclusively of cotton. The construction, however, is distinguished by the use of a single weft strand, giving the fabric an appearance similar to Hamadan village rugs. Although lighter in weight, these Karadja rugs are Turkish knotted and of about the same density as Hamadans. The colors are usually more subdued than those of Heriz rugs. Design remains the most important diagnostic feature, as nearly all Karadjas show the same basic types of medallions arranged along the vertical axis of the rug. There is much talk about Caucasian influence in the pattern, but this is not at all clear. More likely they were influenced by neighboring Shah Sevan nomads. Large Karadjas are uncommon; most are to be found in runners and the smallest scatter sizes.

Karadja rugs are not to be confused with those labeled as "Karadje" or "Karadj," although with some justification they may be called "Karadagh," a term referring to the region just south of the Araxes, opposite the Soviet Karabagh. Although common in the rug trade, these terms do not refer to well-defined classes. "Karadje" is often used to label various Kurdish village weaves, while Karadj is a village near Tehran where rather coarse kilims are made. Still, many rugs are woven by villagers and Shah Sevan nomads living in northern Persian Azerbaijan, and these seem stylistically to combine Persian and Caucasian features. For these rugs we might appropriately use a Karadagh label.

SERAB

The town of Serab is located about seventy miles east of Tabriz on the highway to Ardabil. It provides a market for rugs from some twenty surrounding villages. The fabrics from this area are quite distinct from the Heriz type made about thirty miles to the north. The Serab is almost invariably a runner, and Edwards[2] notes that looms of the town are not appropriate for the production of any other sizes. The rugs are compactly made, with a medium to heavy pile. They are usually a few inches over three feet in width, with the length variable up to twenty feet or more. Typically they show a pale madder and indigo medallion on a camel-colored ground. Some sources indicate that Serabs are all made of camel hair. The origin of this misconception is difficult to trace, as the rugs

26. SERAB RUNNER (portion), 19th century, 4'2" x 13'7". Warp: W. /3\, undyed. Weft: W. /2\, undyed, 2 shoots. Pile: W. /2\. Knot: T-L, 40°, v. 8, h. 7, 56/sq inch. Sides: double selvage of camel color wool over 3 warps. Ends: .... Colors (9): camel colored field, brick red, pale rust red, light blue, dark blue, dark brown, yellow, pale orange, ivory. Most Serabs are found in only two patterns, almost always on a camel ground.
(Older Serabs are likely to have a wool foundation, although the newer pieces are woven on cotton. They tend to be more "double warped" than other village rugs of Azerbaijan. Many old pieces have alternate warps depressed up to 90° and resemble a Bidjar in thickness. Recent Serabs are among the only camel ground runners still made, although this type was common during the 19th century. The origins of many of these pieces are obscure, but Serab borders seem to be fairly consistent and aid in identification. The other common Serab design involves similar, but generally smaller, medallions on a field in which dark camel lines form a simple gridwork on a light camel background.)

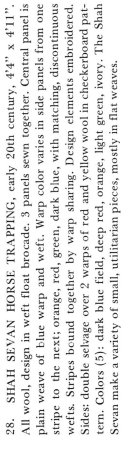

28. SHAH SEVAN HORSE TRAPPING, early 20th century, 4'4" x 4'11". All wool, design in weft float brocade. 3 panels sewn together. Central panel is plain weave of blue warp and weft. Warp color varies in side panels from one stripe to the next; orange, red, green, dark blue, with matching, discontinuous wefts. Stripes bound together by warp sharing. Design elements embroidered. Sides: double selvage over 2 warps of red and yellow wool in checkerboard pattern. Colors (5): dark blue field, deep red, orange, light green, ivory. The Shah Sevan make a variety of small, utilitarian pieces, mostly in flat weaves.

27. MESHKIN RUG, Ca. 1970, 3'2" x 4'5". Warp: C. /6\, white. Weft: C. /2\, undyed, 2 shoots. Pile: W. /2\. Knot: T, v. 5, h. 6, 30/sq inch. Sides: double overcast of pale red wool. Ends: loose warp ends. Colors (6): ivory, pale red, medium and light blue, medium green, dark brown. These adaptations of older Caucasian rugs are usually bland in color; there are only a few designs in common use. Courtesy of the Oriental Rug Co., Berkeley.

clearly are made from sheeps' wool dyed beige with walnut husks or some other substance.

A generation ago the name "Serapi" was often applied to various carpets of the Heriz area, particularly those with a camel ground. This name derived from Serab, although most of the rugs likely did not originate there. A dealer may call any unusual Heriz carpet a Serapi.

MESHKIN and ARDABIL

Rugs from the vicinity of Meshkin (a town fifty miles northwest of Ardabil on the road to Ahar) have achieved a wide popularity during the last decade. Prior to World War II the villages of this area wove an undistinguished fabric of a vaguely Caucasian character. More recently, however, Caucasian prototypes have been more carefully copied, particularly the old Kazak designs, and dyers have been at least moderately successful in approximating old colors. Meshkin rugs are double wefted on a cotton foundation and, as they are woven by a population of Turkish derivation, employ the Turkish knot. While they are not to be mistaken for older Caucasian rugs, they succeed on their own terms in capturing a similar vigor and harmony.

The town of Ardabil, site of an important Shi'ite religious shrine, has also turned, during the last several decades, to weaving rugs in Caucasian patterns. These are somewhat more finely woven and thinner than the typical Meshkin rug, with designs more often adapted from the Shirvan area. Cream fields are common, with bright red, blue, and green figures. These rugs are also woven on a cotton foundation with the Turkish knot.

OTHER WEAVES OF AZERBAIJAN

There are many other woven products from Persian Azerbaijan that are seldom exported in great numbers and have not established a clear identity in the West. Probably most of these are made by Shahsevan nomads, particularly the Soumak stitch bags that have recently become so sought after by collectors. Usually these are sold as Caucasian products, although they are woven in Iran. They are also produced in great numbers by many villages south of Astara and around Ardabil. Saddlebags and larger storage bags (often described by dealers as cradles) are woven, and slit-tapestry kilims are made for local use. In some of these pieces the white is in cotton, while the foundation may be either cotton or wool.

KURDISH RUGS

If we were to designate a fifth major category of oriental rug, there would be convincing arguments to suggest that Kurdish weaves are an entity in themselves, although the Kurds are split between three countries (Turkey, Iraq, and Iran), and their products have no national identity as do the rugs from such peripheral areas as India and China. Nevertheless, judging by the variety of patterns and techniques, by their large output for probably many centuries, and by the quality of their best pieces, the Kurds should certainly rank among the most imaginative and prolific of weavers. Their rugs occupy a spectrum from the most crudely designed and woven nomad rugs to the minutely drawn and impeccably executed Senneh pieces of the nineteenth century. In texture Kurdish rugs vary from the thinnest, most flexible pieces (the pile of the Senneh possibly being the shortest found in all rugs) to the heaviest pieces from Bidjar, which are often so tightly packed and thick as to make folding difficult. Some Kurds inhabit tiny villages or live a seminomadic life, while others occupy fairly progressive urban centers like Senneh (modern Sanandaj). They number about as many people as inhabit the Caucasus, and they greatly exceed the Turkomans in population. Indeed, if more were known of their individual tribal and village weaves, they would likely be classed separately from other areas, but Kurdistan has generally been even less accessible to visits from the outside than either the Caucasus or the Transcaspian area. Our information on the Kurds is fragmentary.

The first historical references to peoples we assume to be Kurdish date from the writings of Mesopotamian civilizations three thousand years ago. From that time Indo-Aryan elements, presumed to be Kurdish, inhabited the same area of the Zagros and eastern Taurus mountain systems as today. They were mentioned by Greeks, Romans, Sassanians, Arabs, and later by the Turks, even then assuming the role of raiders and occasional invaders of the more civilized lowlands. The most famous Kurd was Saladin, who led the Saracens against Richard I of England during the Third Crusade. Under the Ottoman Empire, the Kurds became prominent in many wars with the Sefavids of Persia. At times they more or less achieved autonomy, although most of them remained allied to the Sultan in Istanbul. This is probably accounted for by their religious differences from the Shi'ah Persians, whom the Sunni Turks and Kurds regard as heretical.

Ethnic origins of the Kurds are uncertain, although they are obviously related to the Persians and probably arrived in the Middle East at about the same point in history. There are many Kurdish dialects, but they all fall into two major categories, both showing great similarity to Persian. Obviously the two languages derived from a common source. Current population figures indicate that there are about seven million Kurds, with less than one million in Iraq (where most agitation around the creation of a Kurdish state has been concentrated), nearly three million in Turkey, and over two million in Persia. Other concentrations of Kurds are found in the southern Caucasus and in Syria and Jordan. Aside from the few who reside in larger Persian towns, most Kurds live in great isolation from the rest of the world, and efforts of outside powers (notably the Soviet Union) to exploit the Kurdish political situation have done little to change this. Whatever their national boundaries, the Kurds enjoy a certain autonomy in managing their own affairs.

The area roughly described as Kurdistan covers over 200,000 square miles, although the Persian province of that name, where most of our interest is centered, is half that large. The western part includes portions of the Zagros range, with ridges of 6,000 to 8,000 feet elevation running in a northwest-southeast direction. The eastern part is a plateau, 4,500 to 5,500 feet high. The climate is extreme in nearly all parts of this area, with winters leaving snow on the ground for five months. Summers are hot and dry, although the differences in elevation allow both winter and summer pastures for the grazing animals. Much of the area is cultivated, with crops ranging from rice and corn to cotton. Industry has been slow to develop here, and until recently rugs have constituted a significant portion of the exports.

Kurdish rugs considered in this section are predominantly of Persian origin. The large Kurdish population of Anatolia once also included many weavers, but their products have not always been readily distinguished from those of surrounding peoples, and doubtless there are many rugs described merely as "Yürük" that were made by Kurds. One could even suggest that many Caucasian rugs were made by Kurds living in that region.

In the past a number of names have been associated with Kurdish products that do not seem to have any application now. We are retaining the designations of Senneh, Bidjar, and Sauj-Bulak after the three areas associated with a particular type of rug; however, we are describing other Kurdish rugs simply as village products, although a number probably had a nomadic origin. This covers an enormous

variety of rugs, and if more information were available, one could probably localize these rugs more precisely to tribe or village. Unfortunately the literature gives us almost nothing, and the opportunity even now for amassing more information is limited, as travel throughout most of Kurdistan is restricted by the Iranian government.

Heading our list of discarded labels is one that is most venerable and useful from the standpoint of the merchant. Although many collectors and dealers have a precise idea as to what they mean by a Mosul rug, there is no agreement among them as to what this constitutes. Clearly it does not refer to rugs made in Mosul, an Iraqi city with no tradition of rug making. It similarly does not refer to rugs marketed in Mosul, although there is a tradition, difficult to refute or authenticate, that many rugs woven in Persia were at one time taken across the border (until 1919 Mosul was part of the Turkish empire) and marketed there under more favorable conditions than in Persia. Nevertheless, we know that since World War I the city has not been a sizable market.

Mumford[3] classifies Mosul rugs as Caucasian, then gives long descriptions that could apply only to Kurdish rugs. Jacobsen[4] notes that Mosul rugs are marketed in Hamadan and that Mosul is only a trade name. Other authors give varied descriptions and specifications; we are told by some that Mosuls are all wool and by others that the warp and weft are cotton. We are probably better off to abandon the term entirely.

Other names for various Kurdish rugs are Zenjan and Sauj-Bulak (Suj-Balaugh), two cities where rugs have been marketed but which are not associated with any particular type of design. Rugs from the Sauj-Bulak area, however, are distinguished structurally by their tight construction, depressed alternate warps, and red wefts.

The name Karadagh is often applied rather indiscriminately to Kurdish weaves, particularly if there are any design elements showing some Caucasian flavor; the term is more appropriately used to describe the tribal and village rugs from northern Persian Azerbaijan. Other Kurdish rugs may be labeled as Karaje, Gerous, and Miameh (after a large town about half way between Tabriz and Zenjan). Generally, unless some unlikely piece of information is known as to just where the rug was woven, it is best to avoid these names. If we abandon all these terms in favor of the simple description. "Kurdish Village Rug," we may be imprecise, but at least are not misleading.

THE RUGS OF SENNEH

The city of Senneh (modern Sanandaj), which includes a population of about 40,000 and is the provincial capital of Persian Kurdistan, lies about a hundred miles northwest of Hamadan. Its inhabitants are almost all Kurds of the Gurani tribe. The town boasts at least a two-hundred-year history as the source of a peculiar and readily identifiable fabric that is among the most coveted prizes for the rug collector. For reasons that have not been convincingly explained, in both pattern and construction the Senneh carpet differs greatly from that originating in any other part of Kurdistan, and, indeed, even the surrounding villages produce the typical crude Kurdish tribal weaves. The carpets of Senneh are among the most finely woven of all Persian rugs, with knot counts running as high as four hundred (which is probably as fine as we will ever find with the Turkish knot) and seldom below one hundred and twenty. The pile is closely clipped. The foundations are cotton, except for the best antique specimens, in which the warp is silk; the silk warps are often dyed, at times in stripes of red or green. The weft is spun very thin, in contrast to the usual Kurdish practice. The result is a thin fabric with a characteristic rough feel on the back, which is distinctive enough to allow identification of the rug blindfolded.

The colors of Senneh rugs have always been good, as synthetic dyes, usually shades of orange or violet, apparently arrived only after World War I. Designs have been consistent throughout the years. The Herati pattern, given perhaps its smallest and most finely delineated rendition, has always been most common, and, between the wars, nearly all Senneh rugs included this motif. Often there is a lozenge-shaped area in the center, with the Herati pattern on a different background. Some of the older Senneh rugs have floral patterns, at times suggestive of European designs; many of the finer Sennehs also have carefully drawn repeating Boteh figures.

Production of Senneh rugs has greatly declined

29. SENNEH KILIM, early 20th century, 4'7" x 3'9". Warp: C. /2\, white, 18/inch. Weft: W. /2\, variable number/inch. Average 40. Ends: upper—plain weave band and selvage. Lower—loose warp ends. Colors (6): black-brown, red, magenta, yellow, light green, light blue. Although the usual Senneh kilim is rectangular, this horse trapping shows typical border and field designs.

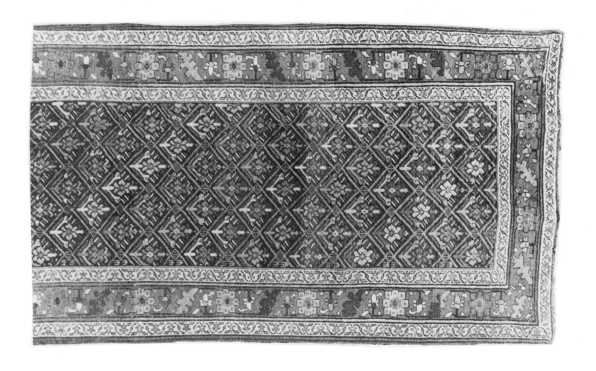

31. BIDJAR RUG (portion), 19th century, 12'8" x 4'7". Warp: W. /2\, light. Weft: W. /2\, light, 3 shoots. Pile: W. /2\. Knot: T-L, 80°, v. 6, h. 8, 64/sq inch. Sides: double overcast of pale red wool. Ends: .... Colors (10): pale red, dark and light blue, deep green, yellow green, yellow-orange, white, dark brown, pink, plum. Many wide Bidjar runners were woven in the late 19th century; most of them have various repeating designs.

30. SENNEH RUG, 19th century, 4'4" x 6'6". Warp: C. /4\, white. Weft: C. /2\, white, 1 shoot. Pile: W. /2\. Knot: T, alternate warps deeply depressed; direction of knot changes from one row to the next, v. 14, h. 14, 196/sq inch. Sides: double overcast of red wool over 4 warps. Ends: ....

during the last several decades, and certainly few new rugs of distinction are found from this area. The finest old pieces were probably made at least fifty years ago, and this may be noted as another variety of fine rug that has greatly deteriorated in the modern age.

SENNEH KILIMS

Unlike the above named carpets, the so-called Senneh kilim does not originate exclusively in the city of that name, but is woven in many parts of Kurdistan and varies accordingly in texture and weight. Weaving has apparently diminished during the last twenty years, but one may still find classic specimens of finely woven kilims that appear to have been derived from the Senneh rug. At times the pattern is so similar that one could hardly tell from a photograph whether the example was a pile or pileless carpet, as both designs and colors have a similar quality. In the intricacy of detail and fineness of weave, the Senneh fabrics are probably the best kilims made.

THE RUGS OF BIDJAR

The town of Bidjar lies about forty miles north and east of Senneh and numbers somewhat less than 10,000 inhabitants, although before World War I there were at least twice this many. During the war Bidjar was occupied first by the Russians and then by the Turks, who punished the town for alleged cooperation with the Russians.

Rugs are produced not only in Bidjar, but the fabric bearing this name is woven in about thirty villages in the vicinity. There is thus more variation in design and construction than one would find in Senneh rugs. The Bidjar is noted above all as being the stiffest carpet made, although the pile is no thicker than that in many other types. The difference is the degree to which the elements are packed together. Here we have an occasion in which the weft strands are literally compressed by long nail-like strips of metal, which are inserted between the warps and pounded with a hammer. The warp (with alternate strands severely depressed) is always of wool in the older rugs, although the new Bidjars are more likely to be cotton, and there are three wefts, one of which is very thick. This thick weft at times is nearly the diameter of a pencil, and its elastic quality allows the carpet to be packed more tightly. Later specimens have two wefts of about the same medium thickness and are not nearly so compact. The Turkish knot is always found in Bidjar rugs, and the count varies between about fifty

and one hundred to the square inch. A finely woven Bidjar is rare; many appear crude and irregular, as the combination of wool warp and heavy construction introduces a special hazard. The Bidjar is also among the hardest-weaving fabrics known.

Dyes used in the older rugs were invariably natural colors. Synthetics came into use only after the First World War when production declined. The Bidjar differs from the Senneh in the great number of patterns employed, as probably no other type of Persian rug has included so many designs. The medallion type is found at times with an open field, usually red or blue; or the field may contain a number of typical Kurdish figures. There are also repeating patterns, with the Herati quite common, also at times with a medallion. The Mina Khani design may well have originated in the Bidjar area, as it is almost certainly Kurdish, and the same may be said of the Weeping Willow pattern. The so-called Crab design is hardly less common, and even Shah Abbas motifs are abundant in Bidjar. Indeed, all the common Persian designs of the nineteenth century (excepting types associated with various nomadic tribes) are to be found in Bidjar, usually in a modified rectilinear adaptation, although there are examples of a simple curvilinear approach. A Bidjar rug thus could seldom be identified from design alone, as many of the same patterns could well have been from Hamadan or a wide area of Kurdish villages. Only around Bidjar, however, is the texture so heavy and inflexible.

One seldom finds a new Bidjar, and those that are encountered seem without distinction. Scatter sizes were more prevalent among antiques, but very large carpets may be found.

KURDISH VILLAGE RUGS

No detailed survey of the Kurdish village weaves has ever been attempted. Our ignorance is even more embarrassing in the light of the numerous and appealing rugs that fall into this category which we are consequently unable to localize or identify by tribal divisions. Indeed we know the names of a number of Kurdish tribes, as we have references to the Gurani, Herki, Senjabi, Jaffi, and Kalhors groups, and we are told that much of the production occurs in the vicinity of several villages, most prominently Qorveh, Songur, and Shirishabad.[5] Still we have no data on how we could distinguish between the weaves of these localities, and the patterns present no more hopeful an approach, as they show many diverse elements. We are unable even to tell which are the products of nomads and which are from the villages, although we often con-

32. BIDJAR RUG, 19th century, 4' x 6'10".
Warp: W. /3\, light. Weft: W. /2\, 3 shoots undyed,
1 very thick. Pile: W. /3\. Knot: T-L, 70°, v. 9, h.
9, 81/sq inch. Sides: .... Ends: .... Colors (7): red
field, bright yellow, dark blue, light blue, ivory,
dark brown, pink. Earlier Bidjar rugs often show
crudely rendered, simple designs, with exceptionally clear colors.

33. BIDJAR SAMPLER, 19th century,
3'7" x 4'5". Warp: W. /2\. Weft: W. /2\, dyed
red in some portions, 3 shoots, 1 thick. Pile:
W. /2\. Knot: T-L, 80°, v. 11, h. 10, 110/sq
inch. Sides: double overcast of pale red wool.
Ends: both ends have plain weave band and
selvage. At top there are 5 rows of Soumak
brocading in plain weave; at the bottom
there are 3 rows. Colors (9): ivory, light blue,
pale red, deep red, dark brown, red brown,
yellow, light green, pink. For some reason
there are a particularly large number of Bidjar samplers or "Wagirehs." Some of these
seem to contain elements of many rugs—perhaps the repertoire of a village or individual
weaver. This specimen probably includes
only elements of one rug; the entire design
could be reconstructed from the portions
depicted here.

Courtesy of the Oriental Rug Co., Berkeley,
California.

34. KURDISH VILLAGE RUG, early 20th century, 3'10" x 7'3". Warp' W. /3\, undyed. Weft: W. /2\, undyed, 2 shoots. Pile: W. /3\. Knot: T, v. 10, h. 7, 70/sq inch. Sides: heavy double overcast of dark goat hair over 10 warp strands. Ends: .... Colors (6): ivory field, red, apricot, light blue, yellow, dark brown. Many Kurdish village rugs have an unusually long and fleecy pile, often with rather oily wool. This piece is nearly as heavy as a Bidjar, although the warps are all on one level.

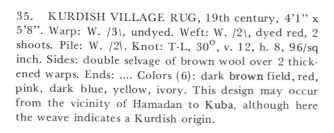

35. KURDISH VILLAGE RUG, 19th century, 4'1" x 5'8". Warp: W. /3\, undyed. Weft: W. /2\, dyed red, 2 shoots. Pile: W. /2\. Knot: T-L, 30°, v. 12, h. 8, 96/sq inch. Sides: double selvage of brown wool over 2 thickened warps. Ends: .... Colors (6): dark brown field, red, pink, dark blue, yellow, ivory. This design may occur from the vicinity of Hamadan to Kuba, although here the weave indicates a Kurdish origin.

veniently describe the most crude and irregular as nomad rugs. This may or may not be true. In any event, nomadism among the Kurds has decreased greatly since the mid-1920s, when Reza Shah instituted his settlement policies. Now almost all Kurds are village dwellers.

Village rugs generally range among the smaller sizes, with many long or wide runners. Materials are classically all of wool, with the pile of a particularly rich and durable texture, as Kurdish sheep are pastured at higher altitudes with harsh winters. The warp is of heavy wool, often with long, shaggy fringes, and the wefts are double, almost always undyed; the sides are usually double overcast, with a dark brown wool. Another type of Kurdish village rug is found with a cotton warp and weft, or with only a cotton warp. In construction these resemble rugs of the villages around Hamadan; at times there are rugs that could be classified under either label. There are many Kurds in the villages producing so-called Hamadan rugs, and a distinction in some cases is only a guess.

In design the village rugs are as varied as the rugs of Bidjar, and there is some apparent effect of geographic proximity to neighboring areas. Rugs from the northern parts of Kurdistan show a distinct Caucasian influence; others have an Anatolian cast.

One variety of Kurdish rug shows a peculiarity of weave not frequently encountered from other areas. This type, usually found in saddlebags or small rug sizes, has a rectilinear design woven with the knots staggered so that only alternate rows occupy the same two warps. (The lines thus do not diverge at the usual 45 degree angle.) Most of these rugs are made by members of the Jaffi tribe who live in the part of Iran adjoining Turkey.

36. KURDISH BAG FACE, 19th century, 20" x 29". Warp: W. /2\, undyed, light. Weft: W. /2\, undyed, medium brown, 2 shoots. Pile: W. /2\. Knot: T, in the field the diagonal lines move only 1 warp horizontally with each knot; v. 11, h. 5, 55/sq inch. Sides: .... Ends: .... Colors (7): dark brown, dark green, apricot, deep red, white, dark and light blue. The type of knotting used in the field provides rather unusual angles. Most rugs of this type are probably made by Jaffi Kurds, living near the border between Turkey and Iran. There are several other common designs woven in the same manner.

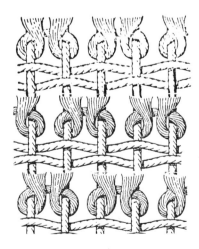

37. Unusual type of weaving found on one variety of Kurdish rug, Turkish knotted.

THE RUGS OF HAMADAN

Hamadan numbers well over 100,000 inhabitants and has been, at intervals, an important commercial and government center for at least three thousand years. Under various names, most notably Ecbatana, it was the capital of the Median Kingdom, and under the Persian Achaemenian dynasty it was a summer capitol because of its mild climate. Hamadan is situated on a plateau 6,000 feet high in the foothills of Mt. Alvand, with relatively cool summers and harsh, below-freezing winters. It lies on the route taken by various conquerors between Persia and Mesopotamia, and as a result has been occupied by numerous armies. It was sacked by Alexander and was one of the first Arab conquests

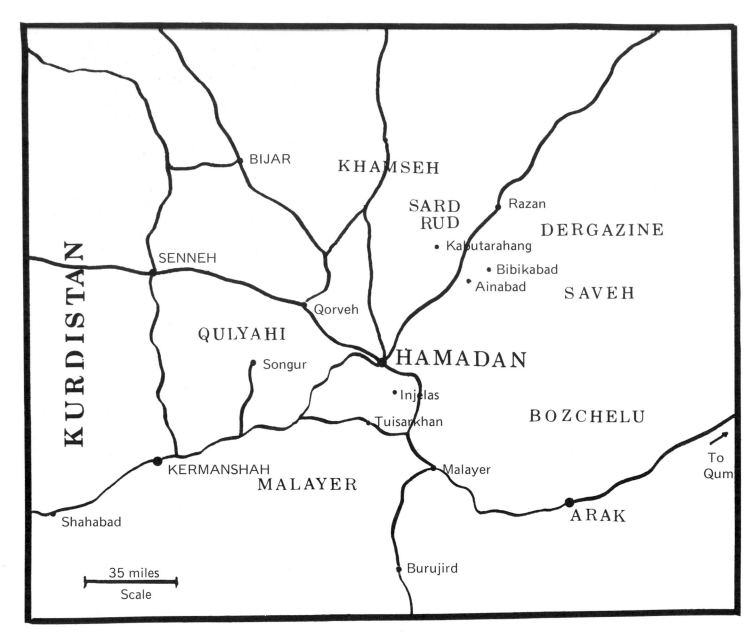

Map No. 3.   The Hamadan District and the Major Kurdish Weaving Areas

in Persia. In the eleventh century the Seljuks occupied the entire province of Hamadan as well as Azerbaijan. Although the latter area came completely under the sway of Turkish culture, Hamadan was less affected. The city inhabitants still speak Persian, but most villagers of the surrounding area speak Turkish. Villages to the north and west market their goods in Hamadan. The population of these villages includes many Kurds, and most Kurdish rugs, even those from Senneh and Bidjar, have found their outlet to Western markets through Hamadan. This has contributed to a general confusion between the two classes.

As a weaving center, Hamadan is without equal in the sheer bulk of its output, although the weaving originates mostly from the district's six-hundred villages. Probably more rugs of this type have been imported into the United States than from any other two areas combined, and for decades over three quarters of the scatter sizes have been from Hamadan, as well as most of the long runners and perhaps one quarter of the larger carpets. Most of these have been of low to medium quality, with only a small number of really fine fabrics, but there is a toughness about these rugs that has made them justly desired. This feature is accounted for by the quality of wool, which comes from sheep raised at high elevations.

There is no clear evidence as to when weaving began in Hamadan, although we may surmise that it has gone on for many centuries. We know that Shah Tahmasp, in the sixteenth century, presented a carpet from Dergazine to Suleiman the Magnificent of Turkey, and this would presuppose a level of excellence in the workmanship of at least one portion of the Hamadan area. There is no tradition, however, that any of the currently existing Sefavid period carpets were produced in the province.

Rugs from the city of Hamadan and those from surrounding villages represent an entirely different tradition, with the former only dating back to the period just before World War I. The village weaves are by far the most important, as they represent the output of what Edwards[6] estimates to be 30,000 looms, which, though not active continuously, account for the enormous quantities of Hamadan rugs. Weaving is only a sideline in most of the villages, and only under favorable market conditions are many looms in operation.

Each village has its own distinctive patterns, and anyone familiar with the market in Hamadan could well identify each as to district of origin. Such detail does not come within the scope of this book, although we will describe a few of the major areas. Our primary concern is to define a way to distinguish rugs of Hamadan from those originating in other parts of Persia. This is readily accomplished, as almost all the village rugs have only one weft strand between each row of knots. This feature is not unique, as some Baluchi rugs, many Afshars, and a significant number of tribal rugs from Fars also are single wefted, but these others may readily be distinguished by their designs and lighter weight. Bahktiari rugs have a greater similarity, as they are nearly as heavy as Hamadans, and they also employ the Turkish knot. Only their designs, in characteristic lozenge or panel shapes, are obviously different. Otherwise one can tell a Hamadan rug at a glance, as the single weft creates an easily recognizable appearance on the back of the rug. As every other warp strand is covered by weft, and the next row has those strands covered that were not covered in the preceding row, a checked pattern is created by the exposed portion of the warps. These are almost always (invariably in the newer rugs) of white cotton, and the knotting always Turkish. The weight actually approaches that of a Bidjar, although much of this comes in the long pile rather than the closely packed body of the rug.

DERGAZINE

The most important of the Hamadan weaving districts in bulk of output is Dergazine, which comprises about sixty villages located to the north and

38. HAMADAN RUNNER, mid-19th century, 3'1" x 6'8". Warp' W. /4\, undyed. Weft: W. /3\, undyed, 1 shoot. Pile: W. /2\. Knot: T, v. 9, h. 7, 63/sq inch. Sides: .... Ends: .... Colors (7): camel field, red, yellow, light green, light tan, dark brown. The camel colored field is now seldom encountered on rugs from the Hamadan area, although it was common during the 19th century. (The camel field Hamadan seems to have virtually disappeared from current production, although it was common and much desired among 19th century rugs of this area. Nevertheless, many similar rugs that are called Hamadans originate from other sources. Among these are many Serabs and a good number of Kurdish rugs with a camel field. This latter type is usually double wefted and therefore distinguishable on structural grounds. One may also find very large [over 20 feet] 19th century Hamadans [possibly from the Kabutarahang area] with a camel field and a plain strip along the sides and ends.)

east of the city. The name derives from the village of Dergazine. Traditionally the rugs from this district have been considered as among the best Hamadans; however, in recent years this reputation has deteriorated. The current rug of this label is a thick and coarsely woven fabric with synthetic colors and designs that have little relation to the tradition. Many small mats no more than several feet long are found in this class, as are various lengths of runners, often narrower than other Hamadan products. The dominant red of most Hamadan rugs is also less common here, as many show a white field with blue or green figures. The designs are quite simple, requiring almost no skill in execution; frequently there is a crude, repeated floral spray pattern. Older rugs from the Dergazine district are of much finer construction, and many show the classic anchor-medallion patterns common to other Hamadan weaves.

KABUTARAHANG

Kabutarahang is one of the largest villages of the Hamadan plain. Along with several other nearby villages, it is the only place in the vicinity to weave mostly carpet sizes. Production has been high, at least since the end of the nineteenth century, and the American market is particularly fond of these rugs.

In color the Kabutarahang usually shows a red or cream field, about which are arranged large floral sprays, much as one would find on a low grade Sarouk. There is often a small, lozenge-shaped medallion, but this is less and less common. For years these have been the best selling and cheapest Persian carpet, and many used specimens are to be found.

39. HAMADAN RUG, mid-19th century, 3' x 6'4". Warp: C. /5\, white. Weft: W. /2\, light brown, 1 shoot. Pile: W. /2\. Knot: T, v. 11, h. 9, 99/sq inch. Sides: .... Ends: .... Colors (8): pale red field, brick red, dark and light blue, dark and light green, ivory, dark brown. The medallion and anchor design occurs in many variations from numerous Hamadan villages. This is a particularly fine example.
(Examination of this rug reveals a level of craftsmanship from the Hamadan district that one can particularly regret being absent today. The figures on each side of both "anchors" appear as a brown-violet from several feet away, but on closer inspection they are found to be made up of blue and red knots, alternating in a checkerboard fashion. Certainly rug weaving in the Hamadan district could have taken a different direction when it expanded; unfortunately it followed a path in the direction of coarser, mass-produced rugs.)

MEHRIBAN

The area of Mehriban (not to be confused with Mehrivan, a village near Tabriz weaving Heriz type rugs) lies due north of Hamadan and comprises about forty villages. The designs of this area have developed without influences from the outside, and the rugs, even today, show little change from those made before the world wars. The colors, primarily indigo and madder, are among the best in the area, and the construction is tight. Most of these rugs are found in scatter sizes, with a few carpets. Typical among the designs is a medallion on a camel-colored ground. Mehriban rugs are noted for their durability.

KHAMSEH

The Khamseh area lies adjacent to Mehriban on the north and east, but rugs of this district are inferior in construction and color, as the dyes are now almost all synthetic. In design rugs of the two areas are similar, with the ground more often red in Khamseh rugs.

BIBIKABAD AND AINABAD

Near Kabutarahang, east of the Hamadan-Kazvin road, are the villages of Bibikabad and Ainabad, which today produce similar fabrics and which also weave primarily carpet sizes. The design of these rugs is usually built around the Boteh or Herati patterns, often with a medallion.

INGELES

The village of Ingeles (also Injilas) lies almost due south of Hamadan; it is the best known among a cluster of villages producing a similar type rug. Designs are limited to the Herati and an overall Boteh pattern, almost always on a madder field. The weave is light and the dyes good. Some dealers describe these pieces as "Sena-Kurds," a dubious title based on the notion that they are Kurdish rugs derived from Senneh patterns. Rugs are still produced in a variety of scatter sizes, and one may find long Ingeles runners.

BOZCHELU

The district of Bozchelu lies east and south of Hamadan. The only curvilinear designs of the Hamadan plain are woven here. This is a recent innovation, however, as rugs from the first part of the century had rectilinear patterns with a good deal of black (from the large number of black sheep) and madder. The present designs almost always show a floral medallion, and most are in scatter sizes.

OTHER VILLAGE RUGS

There are dozens of other well-defined weaves around Hamadan, and in passing we should mention Tafrish, Noberan, Kerdar, Tuisarkhan, and Damaq. Designs found within these and other villages are perhaps as numerous as those of the Kurds. Our identifications are thus incomplete, as a good many single-wefted rugs of cotton foundation—ones we can identify as to type—will surely fall into a village category we have not considered. We simply resort to the label of Hamadan village rug, with the awareness that this covers a broad area.

One other curious feature should also be noted in reference to the older Hamadans with field and borders of natural camel color. One is assured by dealers that these rugs (or at least the light brownish portions of them) are of camel hair, but this is seldom true. Camel hair provides a soft, luxuriant cloth for cloaks, both in the natural color and dyed black, and it is still used in garments worn by the Mullahs. Its suitability as a carpet material is less clear. Microscopic examination of many "camel hair" Hamadans reveals that sheeps' wool is used throughout. The color is obtained by dying ordinary wool with walnut husks.

RUGS FROM THE CITY OF HAMADAN

The birth of the city industry, which began in 1912, is described with great authority by Edwards,[7] who had a significant part in its beginning and in determining the type of fabric to be woven. The resulting rug, which has never rivaled the village products in output, has become a most respected and well-made carpet in the medium price range. It was determined that a Turkish knotted fabric with two wefts and about 10 x 11 knots to the inch would be most suitable, and the weight was set at approximately 12 pounds to the square meter (about the weight of a Bidjar). Warp and weft are both cotton, with wool for the pile coming from Kermanshah, where the best Kurdish wool is marketed.

As these rugs were made to order for European firms, the designs would seem to present a particular hazard. In other areas we have noted a deterioration in quality with the introduction of patterns drawn for their potential appeal to Western housewives. In this case, however, designs from earlier periods of Persian history were sought, including many curvilinear motifs from the Shah Abbas period. While these are not so finely executed as the designs from Kerman or Kashan, the carpets are extremely durable.

In Europe this type of carpet has gone under the name of Alvand, while in the United States the label of Kazvin has been used. (Few rugs actually have been made in Kazvin, which has led to some confusion over the name.) These rugs are still made in large quantities.

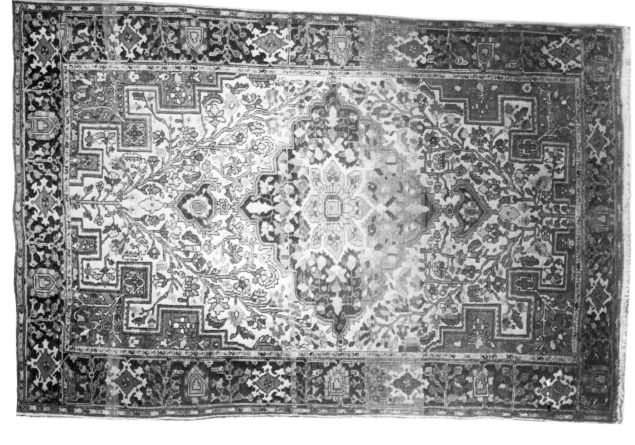

41. JOSAN RUG, 19th century, 4'2" x 6'3". Warp: C. /2\, dyed light blue, 2 shoots. Pile: W. /2\. Knot: T-L, 75°, v. 14, h. 11, 154/sq inch. Sides: double overcast of dark blue and brown wool over 2 warps. Even recent Josans often show a considerable likeness to late 19th century Sarouks.

40. HAMADAN SAMPLER (Waigereh), 19th century, 3'7" x 5'4". Warp: C. /4\, white. Weft: C. /4\, white, 1 shoot, loose. Pile: W. /2\. Knot: T, v. 8, h. 7, 56/sq inch. Ends: .... Colors (5): brown-black field, bright red, light green, pale orange, ivory. Samplers contain an assemblage of the border and field elements found on the rugs of a particular village or area.

MALAYER

Except for its size of nearly twenty thousand inhabitants, the town and district of Malayer could be described along with the Hamadan villages. Lying about fifty miles south of Hamadan and seventy-five miles north and west of Arak, Malayer produces carpets with some characteristics of both areas. Production is consistently high, and most of the rugs are marketed in Hamadan.

Villages north and west of Malayer, numbering over one hundred, produce rugs that are single wefted and resemble in all externals the Hamadan product. In several villages south and east of the town, a double wefted, finely woven rug is produced that resembles in design and color the earlier Sarouks of the present century. The best known of these villages is Josan, and the products of this area are often referred to as "Josan Sarouks" or "Malayer Sarouks." Even today the rugs resemble older Sarouks, although they are Turkish knotted and may be distinguished by this feature. The knot count may be well over one-hundred and fifty to the inch. Most come in scatter sizes, but one may also find larger carpets. Many of these rugs are in the old medallion designs that have had little use in the Arak area for several decades.

THE ARAK AREA

The province of Arak is undistinguished in its contribution to the history of Persia, as it contains little in the way of significant archeological sites, nor have any of its towns ever served as administrative or cultural centers. Perhaps this very lack of importance has been a blessing of sorts, as it was traversed by invaders only superficially, and it suffered little from either Seljuks or Mongols. Its harsh, dry summers and severe winters, on a rather bleak landscape, did not attract outsiders, and the population has remained essentially Persian in language and custom. The area has prospered agriculturally, however, and it is now one of the richest granaries in Persia. Arak has produced the greatest number of large carpets of any Persian province.

Weaving around Arak (formerly Sultanabad, and now a thriving city of over fifty thousand) has probably been significant since the beginning of the nineteenth century. The dating of older specimens is largely a matter of speculation. At first these fabrics were woven for use within Persia, becoming export items only later in the century. To this generation almost certainly belong the earliest of the so-called Feraghans (named for the plain of Ferahan, an area about 30 by 40 miles to the north and east of Arak), which were among the first and finest Persian rugs to be sent in great numbers to the West. These rugs were almost all woven in classical repeating patterns, with the Herati being most common, and the Mina Khani, Gol Hennae, and Mustaphi designs also frequent. The fabrics were Persian knotted on a cotton foundation, with the weft usually dyed light blue or pink. The pile was short, and the wool particularly soft. Most were relatively supple, a result of the warps being nearly parallel, which was quite different from the thicker Sarouks which followed. These later rugs had alternate warps deeply buried, and the fabric was thus thicker (although the pile was still short) and less flexible. Most of the old Feraghans are now heavily worn, and good specimens are much sought by collectors. The weave usually exceeded one hundred knots to the inch, which distinguishes them from later copies. Often the carpets were roughly twice as long as they were wide.

Dyes were among the best natural substances used in Persia, with madder and indigo as the basic repertoire. More green was used than in other carpets, and we also see considerable yellow and ivory. The Herati was usually rendered in red on a blue background, with the border on a light green. The Gol Hennae more frequently was drawn against a red background, with an occasional ivory. Some medallions are found, but these were more common on the smaller rugs, often set off by open fields of red, green, or ivory.

THE SAROUK CARPET

The next weave of the area to achieve distinction is known as the Sarouk, named for an obscure village twenty miles north of Arak on the western fringe of the Ferahan plain. Although most of these carpets were undoubtedly produced in other villages or in Arak itself, they are still known by the original name. They began to appear in quantity during the 1880s as a response to the stimulus of Tabrizi merchants and Western markets. (A few specimens date back to the early nineteenth century.) Their medallion designs seem to owe much to Tabriz, and early carpets of the two areas look superficially alike. The Sarouk soon became well established and was sought by both Americans and Europeans. The fabric was tightly woven, usually between 100 and 200 knots to the inch, with a velvet-like short pile and excellent wearing qualities. Most were in carpet sizes, and almost all had a central medallion that was originally quite rectilinear, but which gradually evolved into a more fluid and curved style as the weavers

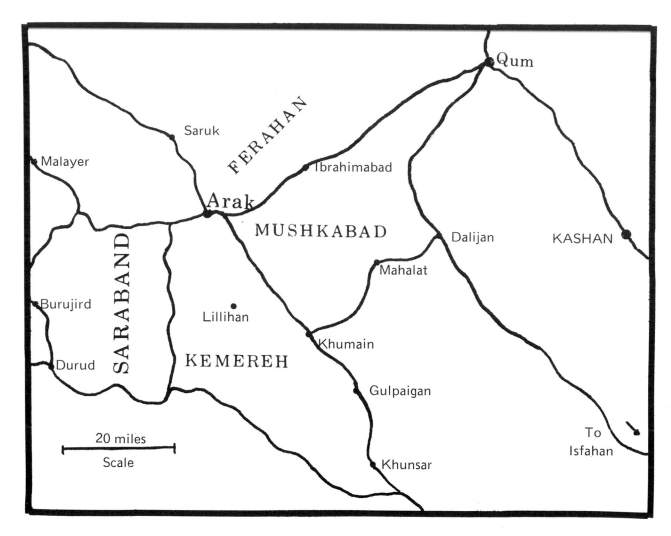

Map No. 4.   The Arak Weaving Area

gained proficiency with the scale-paper technique of weaving. The field colors were cream, indigo, or a pale red, the characteristic color of these older carpets, and floral motifs in the field showed various shades of orange, green, and brown. Earlier rugs had much color variation (abrash) throughout the field, but this decreased in the early twentieth century. Production continued until World War I, when the European market was closed, and the industry suffered a momentary decline. When it revived to meet the great American demand of the 1920s, the product was of an entirely different nature.

The rug industry of Arak was organized from the beginning on a factory basis. There was some production in individual homes, but the bulk of carpets, even in the larger villages, came from factories with ten to one hundred looms, giving the industry greater quality control. Many of the factories were owned by foreign firms; probably the

most influential was Ziegler and Co., a Manchester based firm of Swiss origin. At one point they controlled 2,500 looms, and other foreign firms had similar investments. During the 1920s virtually the entire industry passed into the hands of Persians.

THE MODERN SAROUK

Since World War I the tastes and needs of American housewives have dictated characteristics of weave, color, and design for Arak products. The same designs are produced in all the weaving districts around Arak, and we differentiate not by locality of origin, but by fineness of weave. There are at least four grades of Sarouk carpet, with the finest about 18 x 18 knots to the inch. Below these are carpets known variously in the trade as Arak, Sultanabad, Mahal, and Mushkabad, although no dealer is able to give a precise definition as to the specifications of each type. There is not even agreement as to whether the Mahal or the Mushkabad is the lowest grade, as neither term applies to place of origin. Mushkabad is the name of a nearby village that was formerly an important town. The name Mahal is explained variously—as an abbreviation of Mahalat, a district that now weaves only Sarouks, or as a derivative of an Arab word simply meaning "place."

42. FERAGHAN RUG, 19th century. The so-called "turtle" border on a green background is a classic feature of many Feraghans. Here the medallion and most of the field are covered by a fine rendition of the Mina Khani design.

Arak rugs show the same general characteristics whatever the density of weave, as all are woven on a cotton foundation with the weft strands usually dyed blue. The pile is long and thick, which appeals to the American housewife. Field colors are predominantly deep rose or maroon. For years they were some of the least honest shades available, as they were almost always the result of a heavy bleach and painting. The first rugs of the type had colors too bright for American tastes, and they were washed with a light bleach to subdue the tones. This often removed too much color or caused irregularities to show more prominently. The technique of repainting with a brush and suitable dyes was thus developed, primarily in New York. The indigo would remain virtually unbleached, but the rose would require repainting with a deep magenta. As this would often take the luster from the wool, various oils or glycerine would then be added. The result would have rich, luxurious colors and a brilliant sheen. The housewife would be sold a carpet that would wear less well and that often faded to expose irregularities in the dye application (a water-marked appearance around the figures on the field). This practice must be regarded as a low point in the merchandising of rugs. (A painted rug may be detected by examining the field shade on the front of the rug and comparing it to the back. If the back is lighter—the obverse of what would happen from fading due to light—then the rug was probably painted.)

Almost as appalling as the colors are the designs that have established themselves so perniciously. The modern Sarouk began with an overall field design of detached floral sprays, often clumped together in bouquet fashion, and it has changed little in the intervening fifty years. Thousands of rugs were produced in virtually the same design. The coarser weaves often had more variety of color and classical patterns such as the Herati and Gol Hennae, but the finer Sarouk adhered to isolated floral sprays with traditional borders. The artistic inspiration is certainly not Persian, nor related to the classic period, but was likely supplied by American merchants.

Fortunately, during the last several years, with the Persians gaining control of production and Europeans monopolizing the market, the tide has turned. There are again a number of rugs made in the older style of medallion designs and shorter pile. This provides some hope for the future, as Sarouks have always been well made, but they were too long a slave of foreign commercial enterprises. We may now expect a more interesting generation of rugs.

There are still a great number of the old type available in this country, however, especially of the larger sizes in which sales are slower. They are rich and lustrous. Many are called "Royal Sarouks," a dealers' term to suggest illustrious parentage. They little seem to deserve such a title, as they show neither honesty nor imagination.

LILLIHAN

The Lillihan is one fabric of the Arak area that deserves some special mention, as it differs from the others in weave if not design. It is the only single-wefted weave of the district, although in other ways it resembles a lower grade Sarouk. The colors are the same, and they were traditionally painted much as the Sarouk. Before World War II a large number of these rugs were imported, but new ones are less common.

Lillihans are made in the Kemereh district to the south of Arak, where Armenians inhabit a small cluster of villages. These people were allegedly transferred from their homeland around Kars and Erivan by order of Shah Abbas, who was concerned about the security of Persia's northwestern border

43. SAROUK RUG, 19th century, 4'2" x 6'5". Warp: C. /12\, undyed. Weft: C. /4-5\, undyed, 2 shoots, 1 tight and 1 loose. Pile: W. /2\. Knot: P-L, 70°, v. 14, h. 14, 196/sq inch. Sides: .... Ends: .... Colors (8): dark blue field, pale rose medallion, light blue, light green, deep red, yellow, dark brown, ivory. The early Sarouks, somewhat stiff and angular, were probably influenced by Tabriz rugs of the same period. By the early 20th century the designs had become more curvilinear.

44. MAHAL RUG, 19th century, 4'5" x 6'3". Warp: C. /6\, undyed. Weft: C. /6\, undyed, 2 shoots, 1 loose, 1 tight. Pile: W. /2\. Knot: P-L, 30°, v. 8, h. 8, 64/ sq inch. Sides: double overcast of dark blue wool over 4 warps. Ends: .... Colors (7): dark blue field, pale rose, light green, light blue, yellow, ivory, dark brown. When the more finely knotted Sarouks adopted the detached floral spray patterns popular on the American market, the coarser rugs of the Sultanabad area continued to rely more on traditional designs.
Collection of Emmett Eiland, Berkeley, California.

45. SAROUK RUG, Ca. 1930, 4'2" x 6'4". Warp: C. /12\, white. Weft: C. /4\, white and dyed blue, 2 shoots, 1 tight. Pile: W. /2\. Knot: P-L, 90°, v. 14, h. 14, 196/sq inch. Sides: double overcast of dark blue wool. Ends: .... Colors (9): painted red field, dark blue, 2 shades of light blue, pink, light green, medium brown, ivory, yellow. This is typical of the painted Sarouks that were, until recently, a significant part of the American market. Many thousands of rugs were made with virtually the same design.

with the Ottoman Empire. As Armenians inhabited both sides of this border, it was considered a security measure to force a migration of the Persian Armenians to central Persia, where they have since lived separately, but well integrated into the social and economic system.

There is one more village in the area that produces a distinctive fabric. The rugs of Reihan resemble the Lillihan in structure, but they have long used only one basic design, which has changed little in the last hundred years.

SARABAND

The Saraband is perhaps the most unvarying of all the rugs of Persia. Both its field and border patterns can well be illustrated by a single plate, and only a few other pictures would be necessary to show the occasional medallion types and those in which the field has indentations along the sides. To this we can add several variations in the corners (those with or without serrated diagonal lines) and the rare specimen with a completely open field, and we have virtually covered the type. Within these slender limits, the colors are hardly more variable. Red is dominant, typically a light madder. One will occasionally find a Saraband with a blue or even a cream field, but nearly always it is red. The inevitable repeating Boteh figures may be blue, white, or red, and those of every other row usually face in the same direction.

The Saraband area (or the Sarawan district) begins some twenty miles southwest of Arak, although it is separated from this city by formidable mountains and is more accessible from Burujird to the north. About three hundred villages weave the Saraband, and they differ from the populace of the surrounding area by being predominantly Turkish. The Turkish knot is used on a cotton foundation with double wefts. The weavers are probably an offshoot from the Seljuk migrations that gave their Turkish language and customs to Azerbaijan and most of Hamadan.

Sarabands vary considerably in dimension, with a number of scatter sizes and less common larger pieces. They are readily available on the market today in any quality from the most crude to a good medium weave. These are mostly marketed in Arak and Burujird; some are found in the bazaars of Hamadan.

One sees many references to the so-called Mir-Saraband, which classically is a finely woven antique with red and white Boteh figures on a rich blue background. These are now rare and much sought by collectors. Jacobsen[8] notes that they were woven in the town of Mirabad. Edwards[9] suggests that they were likely from Mal-e-mir, the district's administrative center, although he repeats a story that the name derived from the fact that a number of "mirs" (descendants of the prophet) lived in the area, and that the carpets were woven for their homes. Others explain the term as deriving from various Emirs who ordered carpets.

KASHAN

Kashan is a city of 50,000 inhabitants, lying half-way between Tehran and Isfahan on a route little used today. The main highway has been constructed to the west, on the other side of the Kuh-i-Sefid ridge, a barren and extensive volcanic outcropping that reaches its greatest height a few miles north of Kashan. The ridge prohibits trunk roads into the city. Kashan may be reached only over a poorly maintained gravel road that follows a former caravan track. Thus the city has been removed from the major commercial routes of Persia. During Sefavid times, however, its functions as a trade center were much like those held by Tehran today, for while it was not at a crossroads, it was the largest city on the northwestern arc of the interior trade route, and virtually all traffic between Isfahan and the East passed through it.

At this time Kashan developed a reputation as one of the finest weaving centers of the East, and likely the Vienna Hunting Carpet and other great works of the Sefavid period were produced there. It was especially known for its work in silk, as much of the limited croplands around the town have been devoted to sericulture. This crop is well suited to these lands, for, more than any other major Persian town, Kashan is an oasis, surrounded by gravel plains too arid for dry farming and standing near no river. The area receives its water from abundant and perennial springs in the Kuh-i-Sefid, which issue five miles north of Kashan around the village of Fin. There the water is first directed through a series of pools in a magnificent garden built by Shah Abbas and still maintained. These springs supported one of the earliest known settlements on the Iranian plateau, and excavations may be seen near the town. Despite the vicissitudes of the silk industry, such as economic depression and diseases of the silkworm, the water continues to support a flourishing sericulture on the sloping plain surrounding the town.

The splendid heritage of weaving silk continues today in Kashan, and until the last two dec-

46. KASHAN RUG, late 19th century, 4'4" x 7'1". Warp' C. \12/, white, machine spun. Weft: C. \6/, dyed light blue, 2 shoots, machine spun. Pile: W. /2\. Knot: P-L, 90°, v. 18, h. 18, 324/sq inch. Sides: double overcast of lavender silk. Ends: .... Colors (7): pale red field, dark blue, light green, medium brown, pale yellow, 2 shades of light blue. The design is more curvilinear than Color Plate II, but the very short pile and soft merino wool are the same.

ades, when silk began to be used extensively in Isfahan, the city held a virtual monopoly in Persia on the production of this type of rug. Before the turn of the century Tabriz offered some competition, with silk rugs that were woven in a wide variety of designs, from Turkish prayer rugs to Sefavid motifs, but these have not been made since the 1920s. The Tabriz can usually be distinguished by the use of Turkish knots.

Silk is not ideally suited for floor covering, as the pile becomes matted down and wears poorly; consequently most of the rugs are small enough to be used as wall hangings or other types of coverings, although one will occasionally find a large carpet. The medallion design is not so common in these as in the wool carpets, and frequently one sees variations on the tree-of-life theme.

The more abundant wool rugs of Kashan are relatively less distinctive. Still they are among the most tightly woven rugs of Persia, averaging about 14 x 14 knots to the square inch. Many of the older specimens are considerably finer, and only the finest Kermans, the best Qums, and the new Nains and Isfahans are comparable in construction. As would be expected, these are woven on a cotton foundation, except for a few antiques with a silk warp.

The wool employed in Kashan has always been among the best, and the rugs often show a rich surface sheen. The weaving tradition of the Sefavid era was halted by the disasters of the Afghan invasion; rugs were likely not made in quantity between 1723 and the late nineteenth century. About 1890, however, expanded international trade brought into Persia European textiles that forced Kashan woolen goods from the market. Until that time the city had imported wool from other localities (even Australian wool processed in Manches-

47. QUM RUG, Ca. 1960, 3'6" x 5'4". Warp: C. \9/, white, machine spun. Weft: C, machine spun. Pile: W. /2\. Knot: P-L, 90°, v. 14, h. 14, 196/sq inch. Sides: double overcast of red wool. Ends: plain weave of white cotton and loose warp ends. Colors (11): cream field, dark and light blue, red, green, bright yellow, dull yellow, medium brown, black, pink, and gray. This is a rectilinear adaptation of an old Persian design found in 19th century carpets from Sultanabad and Tabriz. The designers of Qum rugs produce perhaps the most eclectic array of patterns of any Persian city.

Courtesy of the Oriental Rug Co. of Berkeley, California.

48. ISFAHAN RUG, date 1962, 4'9" x 6'11". Warp: C. /8\, machine spun. Weft: C. /4\, dyed light blue, machine spun, 2 shoots. Pile: W. /2\. Knot: P-L, 90°, v. 18, h. 18, 324/sq inch. Sides: double overcast of red wool. Ends: loose warps, braided together at one end. Colors (11): red, maroon, pink, light, medium and dark blue, yellow, green, olive green, light brown, ivory. Contemporary Isfahans usually feature medallion designs, but occasional repeating patterns of scrolling vines are also found.

ter) and had woven fine materials for Persian use. Unable to compete with these imports, the Kashan weavers were left with large stocks of merino wool that had no market. A revival of carpet making was in order, and the industry expanded at a spectacular rate, also including the nearby villages.

Merino wool continued to be imported for Kashan carpets until the early thirties, when the international depression adversely affected the rug market. Thereafter selected wools were purchased from Sabsawar, Isfahan, and Kermanshah; after 1940 the final processing was taken over by local mills. The quality of the wool is still superb, although many regard the merino carpets as superior. The early designs, however, were crude in comparison to the later work. The first carpets had much the same appearance as Sarouk products of the time, with stiff and rectilinear drawing. This soon gave way to styles suggestive of the Kerman tradition, with naturalistic floral medallion designs. The field, though sometimes open, has usually been covered, with the ground color in bright madder red or, less commonly, indigo. Some pieces with a cream ground are also found. Since World War II many Kashans have shown strong Sefavid influences like the modern Isfahan. Still the designers demonstrate less imagination than in other weaving centers, and one finds hundreds of Kashans in the same limited number of designs. Particularly common is the small lozenge-shaped medallion on a red field, produced in all sizes and grades with remarkably little variation from one rug to the next.

Work in Kashan is carried out in the homes rather than in factories, with each house having a pair of looms working from the same pattern. The weaving is done almost exclusively by women. Quality is usually maintained at the same level, whether the rugs originate in the city or a surrounding village, although there are some villages that specialize in a much cheaper grade of rug. (These may appear on the market under the name *Aroon*.)

Currently two factors threaten the reputation of the Kashan rug. The jufti knot is endemic in Kashan, with its resultant weakening of the fabric, and the dyes have become predominantly synthetic, especially the red. This is all the more to be regretted in that otherwise the craftsmanship of Kashan is so superlative.

With the development of commercial interest in Kashan rugs, weaving also expanded in and around Natanz, another town of prominence during Sefavid times. Natanz, with a population of about 5,000, stands where the road southward from Kashan splits toward Isfahan and Yezd. As the in-dustry developed only after 1925, its distinctive but variegated output has not established itself as a separate class of rug; the equally finely made products of Natanz are still grouped with those of Kashan.

QUM

The city of Qum lies about ninety miles south of Tehran; it probably would be better known as a regional center were it not for this proximity. Nevertheless, within the last fifty years it has succeeded in establishing a well-accepted category of carpets, although there was probably no previous tradition of weaving. While technically similar to the rugs of Kashan, the products of Qum usually are not designed around a central medallion, but consist of a uniformly distributed pattern, most often a single motif or two interlocking motifs repeated over the entire field. The Boteh is frequently found, but, unlike the Saraband, in vertical rather than diagonal orientation. In the borders there is less reliance on serially repeated forms than in most Persian rugs, and a broader range of variation is exhibited. Other common field patterns are the so-called Zili Sultan (with a vase and floral spray repeated over a cream field) and panel designs adapted from old Persian garden rugs. Positive identification of Qum rugs is complicated by their resemblance to Kashans and some Isfahans, although the latter are seldom found in repeating designs. Recently silk Qums have been woven.

For commerce Qum is actually better situated than Kashan. Not only is it a more populous town, but it also commands a far larger agricultural area. There is a modern highway from Tehran, which provides a superb market for the produce of Qum.

In addition to economic advantages, Qum contains the Shrine of Fatima, which is excelled in national esteem only by that of her brother in Mashad. The Shrine of Fatima is visited more often by pilgrims because of its central location and easy accessibility. Fatima's remains are said to lie beneath one of Persia's most elegant Mosques, which boasts a golden dome and a complex of graceful minarets. Included within the sanctuary walls is the most important theological institute of the Shi'ah sect and headquarters of the college of the "mujtihid," learned doctors of Islam who are granted powers by the Persian constitution to veto any ordinance of the land they deem incompatible with the faith. The shrine has been the center of the city's existence for centuries, and Qum's recent integration into the secular economy, through the new highway and nearby oilfields, has done little to alter this. In consequence, outside of the splendid religious architecture, there is little about Qum of interest other than to the pious. Considering the strict orthodoxy of its inhabitants on matters of religion, the versatility in rug design seems all the more remarkable, for rug production is concentrated entirely within the city itself, almost exclusively in the homes of the weavers.

ISFAHAN

Among the cities of Persia, Isfahan is almost universally described by travelers as the most elegant and entertaining. Its flowering in the seventeenth century as the Sefavid capital is associated with the high point of Persian art since the Islamic Conquest. From those achievements the traditions of succeeding periods have evolved, and today Isfahan still shows the results of a conscious effort to maintain standards of excellence in its crafts. In carpet weaving the city has become known as the origin of the finest fabrics currently made.

Isfahan has long been a prosperous city, as we note from references by Arab geographers and travelers during the ninth and tenth centuries. By the time it was made the national capital by Shah Abbas, it was the largest Persian city. Its central location made it safer for the court than the relatively exposed Tabriz. Under later Sefavids the city flourished, with the arts blossoming under a lavish royal patronage. There is considerable evidence that many of the finest Sefavid carpets were woven there. Descriptions by European travelers during the seventeenth century are so numerous and detailed that we can localize the exact area where carpets were made for the royal court. These sources say little about the designs, but evidence bearing on this is amply provided by the surviving court buildings, many of which are lavishly decorated with the same stylized floral elements we find in carpets from the period. One cannot examine the Ali Kapu without a strong sensation that the class of silk rugs enriched with strands of gold and silver (the so-called Polonaise rugs) were of the same time and artistic tradition, and this coincides with the many contemporary references by Europeans to such carpets with metal threads. The Chehel Sootun Palace displays ornamentation just as clearly related to another class of carpet now usually attributed to Herat — even a casual glance at its ceiling discovers stripes that could serve as borders to these rugs. Elements suggestive of the vase carpets are nearly as abundant.

The era of opulence came to a rather inglorious end with the Afghan invasion of 1722, when the last Sefavid was unable to defend the empire against an enemy that was outnumbered and would seemingly have been easily defeated. The Afghans began their reign mildly, but when an insurrection was feared in Isfahan, the city was burned and pillaged by the invaders. This scourge was not lifted until Nadir Shah purged the country of its affliction several years later. When he became Shah in 1736, he moved the seat of government to Mashad. Isfahan thus ceased to be a capital, and for the next two hundred years its fortunes followed a course of decay until, by the end of the Qajar dynasty, its monuments were crumbling, and it had assumed a distinctly provincial status. Fortunately the process was reversed by Reza Shah Pahlavi, who began the task of restoring the buildings and much of the grandeur of the former capital. Now Isfahan is easily the most beautiful and gracious city in Persia.

The Rugs of Isfahan

The carpet industry of Isfahan has echoed the general recovery in the city's status, and while it was practically nonexistent during the early part of the century, it is now responsible for many of the most esteemed modern rugs. There are no rugs we can definitely attribute to Isfahan during the two centuries after the Afghans, who destroyed the court manufactories, but the 1920s witnessed a reawakening of interest coincident with the vast expansion of carpet weaving throughout the country. Thereafter we note two distinct phases in the development of the Isfahan carpet. Until the Second World War, Isfahan fabrics were almost all in carpet sizes of only moderate quality. The design and workmanship were excellent, but the quality of the product was reduced by the use of poor dyes. These rugs were intended to compete in the European markets with the better-known weaves of Tabriz and Kerman. When the war effectively shut off the European market, the industry faced a crisis. This was resolved by increasing the quality of the weave (up to 26 x 26 knots to the inch) and improving the quality of the materials. The wool was mostly imported from Sabsawar and Kermanshah, and the dyes improved considerably. Designs showed an influence not so much of current Persian products, but of the Sefavid period, and this trend was accentuated by the establishment of a design institute in Tehran. There the best draftsmen of the country were recruited to bring increasing refinement to the modern adaptations of these patterns.

This improvement occurred at the same time as a local Persian demand expanded, and today many Isfahan rugs are woven for the domestic market. Most of them are small or medium-size pieces from 4 x 6 to about 8 x 10 feet, and are of exceedingly elaborate and complex floral designs. In compliance with current tastes, cream fields and light blues are common, often with a heavy use of bright red. Usually the rugs are woven in pairs, and it is not unusual in the United States to find them chemically treated. This reduces the brightness of the colors and makes the white more of a cream shade.

Despite the commercial success of the Isfahan rug, little of this wealth has filtered down to the weaver, which explains how such a finely woven fabric is still economically feasible there. The general populace is wretchedly poor, and a visitor to the city can immediately sense a level of poverty much lower than that of Tehran or Shiraz. Even the shopkeepers seem busier than elsewhere, spending much of the day actively working at some craft. The metal shops bordering the Maydan are a scene of great activity, and, unlike at Tehran, one can see considerable work progressing in the bazaar. In contrast to conditions before the war, when an estimated 2,000 looms were located in separate houses, most weaving today is done in small factories, where the work can be exactingly inspected. A large part of the work is by special order and is undertaken only after the customer has approved the design.

Recently there has been a tendency to use silk warps in the finer grades; many rugs are woven either entirely of silk or with a yarn blended of silk and wool. The dyes are mostly synthetic, but are of a fine quality, and some of the better carpets will show over twenty distinct shades, including excellent light blues, deep reds, and many varieties of green.

The medallion design is still favored, but there are occasional overall patterns. Scenic rugs, apparently because they bring a higher price for virtually no greater effort, are becoming more common. Hunting scenes suggestive of Sefavid court pieces are popular, and some of these approach eight hundred knots to the inch. The rug stores of Tehran display large stocks of these rugs, and when present in number they illustrate the limited imagination that the designers bring to their task of adapting older motifs. The workmanship of these carpets is so exquisite that it seems a pity for so many of them to be made in virtually the identical patterns. After examining the very choicest specimens, one can see how the exigencies of mass production have robbed the others of a certain grace and spontane-

ity. Despite this uniformity, the Design Institute has contributed much, if only in making available the unmatched material of the classical carpets. Since most of these are housed in museums and collections outside the country, they are otherwise unavailable to the local craftsmen.

The Isfahan rug may be so similar in construction to those of Kashan, Qum, and Nain that one cannot make a positive distinction between them. Usually, however, the design will give some hint as to origin.

NAIN

Nain is a town of about 6,000 people on the rim of the Great Desert, northeast of Isfahan. It has been a textile center for many years, but changes in fashion before World War II brought about a decline in demand for the fine woolen fabrics produced there. The carpet industry began in the late 1930s and after the war developed rapidly in a most unexpected direction. Instead of producing coarse and readily marketable rugs with designs suited to American tastes, the weavers of Nain began to make what is one of the most finely knotted new carpets available. With knot counts between 350 and 800 to the inch, they compare favorably to the best antique pieces. The foundation is usually cotton, but, as in Isfahan, silk is now frequently used for the warp. The closely clipped pile is softer than most Persian wools, and silk Nains are occasionally found. One characteristic that may be used to identify a Nain is the outlining of the design in silk in an otherwise wool rug. This is less commonly found on Isfahan rugs.

In design Nain rugs closely resemble those of Isfahan, as they also include elements from the Sefavid period. Shah Abbas motifs and medallion designs are common, often on an ivory field. Carpet sizes are rare, with the most common pieces being 5 x 7 feet or smaller. Few have been imported into the United States, as they are among the most expensive modern rugs, and the short pile has a limited appeal to American buyers. More receptive markets have been found in Europe and Tehran.

JOSHOGAN

Rugs known by this name are quite different from those described by many earlier writers as Joshogans. Apparently the term was formerly used as a nonspecific label for floral rugs of no discernible origin. More recently, however, we have used

50. ISFAHAN MEDALLION RUG, Ca. 1930, 4'9" x 7'. Warp' C, machine spun (2 threads Z-plied strands). Weft: C, machine spun, dyed blue, 2 shoots. Pile: W. /2\. Knot: P-L, 90° /2\. h. 18, 324/sq inch. Sides: double overcast of pale red wool. Ends: ivory plain weave bands, with adjacent warp ends knotted together. Colors (8): ivory field, pale red, dark blue, 2 shades of light blue, medium and light brown, light yellow. The modern Isfahan medallion design almost always represents an adaptation of Safavid motifs, with scrolling vines and realistic floral figures.

49. ISFAHAN PICTORIAL RUG, Ca.1950, 3'3" x 6'. Warp: Silk, /5\, ivory. Weft: C. /2\, undyed, 2 shoots, 1 straight and 1 loose. Pile: W. /4\. Knot: P-L, 90° /2\, v. 24, h. 24, 576/sq inch. Sides: double overcast of blue wool. Ends: narrow ivory plain weave bands and loose warp ends. Colors (17): 4 shades of green, light, medium and dark blue, deep red, red, pink, light and deep yellow, 2 shades of light brown, dark brown, mauve, ivory. Pictorial designs are common on modern Nains and Isfahans, often of hunting or animal scenes.

it only for rugs produced in and around the village of Joshogan, which lies 75 miles north of Isfahan in the valley of the Kuh-i-Varganeh. There are less than 10,000 people now in the village, but the tradition of rug making goes back at least several hundred years. References to Joshogan rugs occur in journals of the Sefavid era, and many seventeenth century carpets of the royal court are alleged by various authors to have been woven there. A. U. Pope[10] is particularly lavish in attributing many of the period's great carpets to this village, but the evidence for doing so is indeed meager, and one must be cautious of any use of this name for pieces earlier than the last hundred years. It is likely, however, that there was production in the late eighteenth century, and an example from this era in the Victoria and Albert Museum closely resembles the current fabric.

Only one design is clearly attributed to Joshogan during recent times. A small medallion may or may not be present, and the size or arrangement of the lozenge-shaped floral bunches may differ, but the essentials are usually so similar as to make identification certain. Red is by far the most common background, while the designs are outlined in dark and light blue, white, orange, green, and yellow. One occasionally finds a Joshogan with a cream or blue field. The background of the border is usually cream.

In construction the true Joshogan also shows little variation. The warp and the two wefts are cotton, often with the wefts dyed light blue. The pile is of medium length and the knot Persian. Older specimens have a count exceeding 100 to the inch. Those woven just after World War II showed a great decrease, while the most recent rugs have

51. JOSHOGAN RUG, 4'1" x 6'9". Warp: C. /4\, undyed, white. Weft: C. /2\, dyed blue, 2 shoots. Pile: W. /2\. Knot: P-L, 75°, v. 12, h. 12, 144/sq inch. Sides: double overcast of dark blue wool over 2 warps. Ends: .... Colors (7): dark blue field, red, ivory, light blue, apricot, light green, dark brown. The same basic design has been used in Joshogan rugs for at least several hundred years. They vary considerably in knot density.

again returned to the fine weave, at times exceeding 150 to the square inch. The rugs called Joshogans by the older books (Mumford, Hawley, Dilley) are noted to have Ghiordes knots, and although these were apparently of diverse origins and designs, one will occasionally find a rug in the Joshogan design with this construction. This represents a case in which the design has been borrowed by another area, and such rugs may have been woven in the Hamadan villages or even Tabriz. Some Bahktiari rugs, often quite large, are found in this design, but these, and other copies, may be identified by details of construction.

Most Joshogans are woven in scatter sizes, although there are a few larger pieces, usually with much coarser knotting. Europe has provided the best market for these rugs, and much of the current production goes to London. Altogether the Joshogan is still an honest fabric, with a design spanning a tradition of several centuries and construction that has, if anything, improved in fineness during the last decade. The colors and wool are similarly of high quality.

BAHKTIARI RUGS

The Bahktiaris are a large and powerful tribe of over 400,000 who inhabit an area west and south of Isfahan along the eastern slopes of the Zagros Mountains. They have long played an important part in the history of Persia. Generally they have been more prosperous than other tribal groups. Aside from the roughly twenty percent who are still seminomadic, most Bahktiaris live sedentary lives in farming villages. The land is rich and relatively well watered.

Some question has existed as to just who makes the rugs known as Bahktiaris. The weaving is generally not done by Bahktiaris at all, but by villagers of Turkish descent who inhabit the Chahar Mahal, which is the part of the Bahktiari domain bounded by the Ziandeh River on the north, the Zagros to the west and south, and the Isfahan Plain to the east. The rug making takes place in approximately twenty villages in the vicinity of Shahr Kurd, which is the principal market place and weaving center. The great bulk of the Bahktiaris to the north and west apparently do not weave commercially salable rugs, although much wool must come from this source. Sheep all along the eastern Zagros produce a heavy, lustrous wool that makes excellent carpets.

In older Bahktiari specimens the warp and weft were both of wool, but newer rugs have a cotton foundation and are generally more coarsely

52. BAHKTIARI RUG, Ca. 1940, 4'6" x 6'6". Warp' C. /3\, undyed. Weft: C. /3\, undyed, 1 shoot. Pile: W. /2\. Knot: T, v. 8, h. 6, 48/sq inch. Sides: heavy double overcast of dark brown wool over 12 warps. Ends: loose warp ends. Colors (6): red field, dark blue, light blue, apricot, dark brown, ivory. The majority of Bahktiari rugs come either in this design or one in which the field is broken up into small square compartments containing simple, rectilinear floral elements.

knotted. The Turkish knot is almost always used, and the weft crosses only once between each row of knots. (This has also changed recently in some rugs to a double weft.) The pile is thick, and the sides are finished with a double overcast of thick yarn. The newer rugs are similar in weight and texture to contemporary rugs from Hamadan, although they are readily distinguishable by pattern.

Most commonly Bahktiari patterns involve the use of rectangular or lozenge-shaped panels, but there is some borrowing from neighboring areas which use medallion designs. Almost always the drawing is rectilinear, as scale paper is not used.

Color Plate I. SAROUK PRAYER RUG, late 19th century, 4'6" x 7'6". Warp: C. /12 , undyed. Weft: C. /4–6\, dyed blue, 2 shoots. Pile: W. /2\. Knot: P-L, 70°, v. 12, h. 12, 144/sq inch. Sides: double overcast in blue wool. Ends: narrow woven band with loose warp ends. Colors (8): dark blue field, light blue, rust red, deep red, deep green, yellow, dark brown, ivory. The stiff, stylized flowers are suggestive of "art nouveau," with hanging lamps and ornate candlesticks.

Color Plate II. KASHAN RUG, late 19th century, 4'4" x 7'1". Warp: silk, /4\, white. Weft: C. /2\, undyed, white, 2 shoots. Pile: W. /2\, very soft and lustrous, probably English-processed Australian wool. Knot: P-L, 90°, v. 18, h. 18, 324/sq inch. Sides: double overcast of violet silk. Ends: loose warp ends. Colors (8): pale red field, dark blue medallion, light blue, light green, yellow, pale rose, dark brown, ivory. Late 19th century Kashans are particularly finely clipped, with soft, English-processed wool. The designs, which resemble medallion types from the Sultana-bad area, soon evolved into floral forms that were more curvilinear and realistic.

Color Plate III. KURDISH RUG from vicinity of Sauj-Bulak, early twentieth century, 4'9" x 8'. Warp: W. /3\, light brown. Weft: W. /2\, dyed red, 2 shoots. Pile: W. /2\. Knot: T-L, 30°, v. 8, h. 6, 48/sq inch. Sides: double selvage over 2 thickened warps. Ends: upper—narrow band of selvage from warp ends. Lower—several extra rows of weft, loops. Colors (7): black-brown field, deep red, pink, yellow, light blue, light green, ivory. Sauj-Bulak rugs have long, fleecy pile and are relatively stiff. As in this example, the designs may show a particular asymmetry.

Color Plate IV. NORTHWEST PERSIAN RUG, 19th century, 4'3'' x 7'. Warp: W. /3\, undyed, light brown. Weft: W. /3\, 1 shoot, undyed. Pile: W. /2\. Knot: T-L, 60°, v. 12, h. 12, 144/sq
inch. Sides: .... Ends: .... Colors (9): medium blue, red, deep burgundy, light blue, turquoise, buff
yellow, rose, brown, ivory. The "weeping willow" pattern is usually found on Bidjar rugs, but
there is some question as to the attribution of this piece. The single weft and border design suggest
an origin around Karadja.

Dr. G. Dumas—H. Black collection.

Color Plate V. BIDJAR RUG, 19th century, 4'6" x 7'10". Warp: W. /3\, light brown. Weft: W. /2\, undyed, 2 shoots. Pile: W. /2\. Knot: T-L, 80°, v. 9, h. 10, 90/sq inch. Sides: heavy double overcast. Ends: .... Colors (7): dark blue field, light blue, red, light green, ivory, dark brown, pink. The Herati pattern here is rather crudely rendered, but the borders show a gracefulness characteristic of the best older Bidjars. Most of the border figures are not outlined, which is unusual in Persian rugs in general but occurs fairly often in this type.

Color Plate VI. SILK QUM RUG, Ca. 1960, 4'6'' x 7'2''. Warp: S. /3\. Weft: S. /2\, 2 shoots.
Pile: S. /2\. Knot: P-L, 90⁰ v. 18, h. 20, 360/sq inch. Sides: double overcast of dark blue wool.
Ends: plain weave bands of ivory silk. Colors (8): dark blue field, medium and light blue, white, 2
shades of gold, red, mauve. During the last decade Qum has probably produced more silk rugs than
any other area. The design of this piece is an adaptation from late 19th century Tabriz types.

Color Plate VII. QASHGAI RUG, late 19th century, 4'1" x 5'10". Warp: W. /2\, light. Weft: W. /2\, dyed red, 2 shoots. Pile: W. /2\. Knot: P-L, 45°, v. 10, h. 10, 100/sq inch. Sides: double overcast of light and dark wool. Ends: .... Colors (6): blue field, red, ivory, medium blue, yellow, brown-black. The clear, brilliant colors, tight construction, and design motifs identify this as a Qashgai. Because of the depressed alternate warps these tend to be less pliable than Khamseh rugs of the same period.

Color Plate VIII. BALUCHI RUG, 19th century (?), 5'3" x 8'7". Warp: W. /2\, dark; 12/inch. Weft: W. /2\, ground weave of dark wool in portions with weft float brocade. Weft discontinuous in other parts of rug where tapestry kilim technique is used with warp sharings and embroidered outlining. Colors (8): rust red, light, medium, and dark blue, blue-green, yellow, apricot, white (cotton). The Baluchis make numerous pieces in various flat weaves, often combining several techniques. This example was purchased in Afghanistan, although the exact origin as to subtribe is uncertain.

Courtesy of the Oriental Rug Co., Berkeley, California.

Most common in the repeating lozenge design is the tree pattern; this is found with minor variations in countless rugs. Along with another pattern of small, square panels, the design graces most of the shops of Isfahan, and one can see such excesses as the corridor in one of the larger Isfahan hotels where over fifty of these rugs of identical basic design line its great length. In recent years more variation has been provided by occasional pictorial rugs, usually of scenes that could well derive from European post cards.

Weaving has probably gone on in the Chahar Mahal for centuries, but older Bahktiari rugs are rare. They were not imported into the United States until the 1920s. The scarcity of these rugs may at least partly be a result of the geographic isolation, as only recently has the area become accessible by motor. Neither Mumford nor Hawley made any mention of these rugs, and examples are not to be found in historical collections.

VERAMIN

Many older rugs labeled Veramin would appear suspect as to attribution, for the town of this name lies southeast of Tehran; yet the rugs alleged to be from Veramin are clearly Kurdish in design and weave. There is no real inconsistency, however, as the rugs are products of the Pazekis, a once-powerful tribe which now consists of a few thousand families living around Veramin and Khar. Many of them speak Kurdi, and, although of mixed origins, they are predominantly Kurdish. These Veramin rugs are all wool, with an almost invariable use of the Mina Khani design. This was carefully drawn, often on an ivory or dark blue field, usually with relatively narrow borders. These pieces are seldom large and were never plentiful. They have virtually disappeared from the market.

More recently another type of rug has emerged from the Veramin area. This strongly resembles the Qum, with a cotton foundation and Persian knots. The old designs are still found, along with others using Sefavid motifs.

THE RUGS OF KHURASSAN

Carpet weaving in the province of Khurassan poses an intriguing question in the history of the art. We have statements by Arab travelers (e.g., Mukadassi) as early as the tenth century that the Qainat was known for its elegant carpets. There are miniature paintings attributed to the court of Shah Ruhk in Herat from the fifteenth century, showing carpets in rectilinear design. We have, in addition, the numerous Sefavid carpets that are described almost unanimously by art historians as probably having been produced in Herat; their origin somewhere in Khurassan is virtually certain. Herat was at that time capital of the province and only later was taken by the Afghans. We have a further tradition that a large number among the first wave of mid-nineteenth century Persian exports were from Khurassan, particularly many of the long narrow carpets with a Herati pattern on a dark blue ground.

Although exact localization of various types of rugs is uncertain, the nineteenth century travel literature provides us with more information on Khurassan than other areas. The British travelers Fraser[11] (1822) and Conolly[12] (1838) assure us that carpets of both wool and silk were woven in Herat, while the former source notes the area around Qain as producing numuds (felt carpets). The Herat fabrics were described as having "brilliant" colors, and both observers noted that production had apparently decreased from a former time. Mashad, the city accounting for most of the recent production, was listed only for its manufacture of numuds, and it probably did not have a carpet weaving industry before 1880. Since that time the entire province has devoted a large portion of its energies to rug weaving, and the resulting fabrics have become known for their vivid colors and soft wool, if not for durability.

THE SHRINE CITY OF MASHAD

Next to Isfahan, Mashad is described as the most beautiful city in Persia, and as a religious shrine it is by far the most important. It is the burial place of Ali-al-Riza, the eighth Imam, and of Harun-al-Rashid, Caliph of Baghdad. Nadir Shah was born in the vicinity and built a mausoleum there, while the most spectacular mosque was built by order of Jawar Shadh, wife of Tamerlane's son Shah Rukh. The city has had a most eventful history. Exposed on Persia's eastern frontier, it is the logical first step for any invader from the East. It was taken by both Seljuks and Mongols, and occupied and retaken several times by Uzbegs and Afghans. It survived many disasters, but was always rebuilt, and its legacy of architectural landmarks is spectacular. The area composing the shrine itself occupies several square blocks within the city, and there are numerous sacred colleges. Well over 170,000 pilgrims a year come to Mashad, where

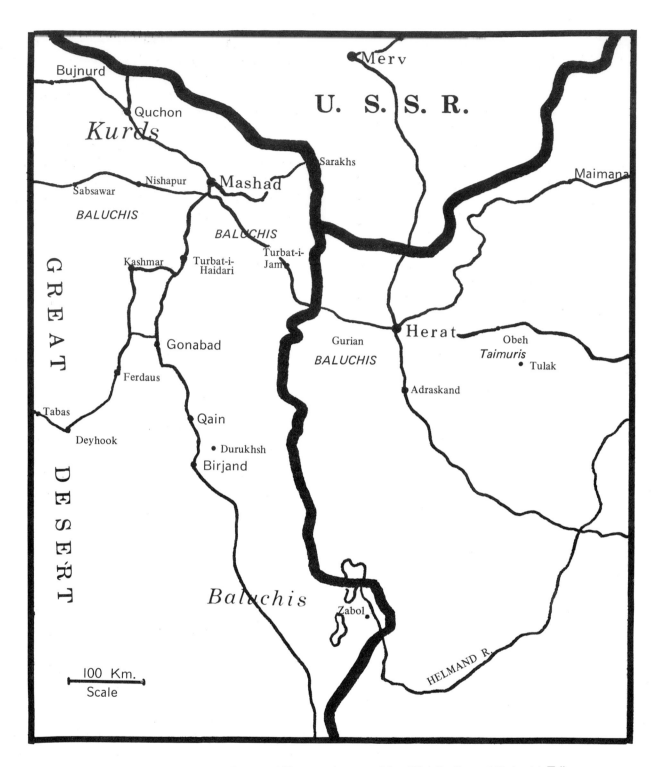

Map No. 5.   Rug-Weaving Areas of Eastern Iran and the Distribution of Baluchi Tribes

they swell a population that exceeds 150,000. Indeed an atmosphere of the shrine pervades the entire city.

The area around the town is rich in agriculture and is one of the best wool-producing regions of Persia. Sabsawar, Nishapur, and Quchon are important markets for wool, much of which is sent to other parts of the country. Of the two shearings, the spring clipping provides the longest fibred wool. The autumn wool has a distinct softness, and its former use in Mashad carpets is one of the factors that decreased their durability.

Mashad provides an outlet for the fabrics of the entire province, including Turkoman rugs from the north made by Tekke and Yomud tribes that have migrated from the Soviet Union, and Baluchi rugs made by nomadic tribes to the south, east, and west. Among city and village rugs marketed in Mashad are the local products (both the Persian-knotted Farsibaff and the Turkish-knotted Turkbaff), those of Birjand, and various towns of the Qainat. They are sold in the West under a variety of labels, often not corresponding to place of origin so much as to grade. The Turkbaff weave was introduced in the late nineteenth century by weavers and merchants from Tabriz. These weavers brought with them the Tabrizi technique of tying the knot with a hook. Rugs made by this method are tightly woven and generally more durable than the Farsibaff, which has traditionally been made with a jufti version of the Persian knot, an accepted standard in Mashad. The Farsibaff technique is more widely used, and Mashad is the only place in Iran where the two types of knots are used by weavers working in close proximity, at times within the same factory. Before World War I many of these Persian-knotted rugs employed a technique of varying the number of wefts, which made the carpet readily recognizable. Between most rows of knots there would be one or two very thin weft strands, but after every three or four rows there would be a band of many wefts (up to ten). This would produce a ribbed appearance horizontally along the back of the rug and cause portions of the pile to stand together on the front. The modern products are usually double wefted, although I have recently seen in the Mashad bazaar several obviously new rugs made in the old manner.

The dyes of Mashad have traditionally been dominated by cochineal. It is used in virtually no other part of Iran, except for the province of Kerman, and is a distinguishing feature, particularly when it appears as a deep magenta. Often it is used so lavishly as as to give a purplish cast to the entire rug.

There have been relatively few small rugs produced in Mashad, and even the carpet sizes have ranged from medium to large. Usually these pieces are slightly more squarish than in other areas, with many 10 x 13 foot specimens. Production has again reached a high level after a slump following World War II. At that time the European market was virtually nonexistent, and Mashad carpets sold poorly in the United States. Even now they are not popular. When they are seen, they are often called Isfahans, or Isfahan-Mashads. There seems to be no

more sense to such a label than to call them Sarouks or Hamadans, but many dealers cling to the practice.

In design the early Mashad rug was most often a medallion type, with curvilinear forms resembling those of Kerman, but readily distinguishable by differences in the rendering of floral motifs and by the generally darker colors. Large rugs with a finely drawn Herati pattern were also common. During the last decades, however, Mashad weavers have turned increasingly to copying the designs of other areas. Now we find Mashad renditions of Kerman and Arak rugs that are virtually indistinguishable from their prototypes.

CARPETS FROM THE QAINAT

The Qainat is a mountainous area about 200 miles long by 60 miles wide which extends in a southeasterly direction from Juymand to about one hundred miles south of Birjand. On the west these uplands fall away and blend with the Great Desert, while they merge with the hills of Afghanistan to the east. Carpets likely have been woven in the area for many centuries, with the most probable centers of production being around Gonabad, formerly a large town with a number of subsidiary villages, Qain, the town from which the region derives its name, and Durukhsh, a town in the hills north of Birjand.

Today little weaving takes place in Gonabad, although there is a tradition that the old Herati design carpets were woven in nearby villages. Qain, now a town of only about 5,000, has similarly turned to other activities, despite its long association with carpet weaving. Many older carpets in elaborate repeating Boteh designs are alleged to have been made there.

Durukhsh and its surrounding villages still weave a sizable number of carpets. The older pieces featured bold medallions on plain fields of cochineal or cream, although new rugs resemble the output of Birjand. In construction they have been similar to the Mashad Farsibaff, with jufti knots.

Birjand is now the most important town of the Qainat, with a population over 10,000 and a thriving carpet industry. This dates only from the beginning of the present century and was developed on a factory system both in the town and outlying villages. By the thirties Birjand had a considerable market in Europe and produced a large number of carpets which were generally preferred to those of Mashad. When the European market was devastated by the war, the industry suffered, and only in the early 1950s did recovery begin. Now a number of tightly woven carpets originate there, most of which still are sent to Europe. Medallion designs are most common.

In the United States the name of Birjand is often not used strictly to label rugs from the town, but refers to a quality of carpet. These are the lowest grade exported from Khurassan and are comparable to the coarser carpets of Arak.

KURDISH RUGS OF KHURASSAN

Seemingly out of place among the weaves of Khurassan are rugs from the villages around Quchon, some eighty miles northwest of Mashad. These are woven by a thriving colony of Kurds (nearly 40,000), descendants of tribesmen who were originally transplanted from their native Kurdistan by Nadir Shah in 1740. Acting as an effective buffer against incursions by the Yomud Turkomans, the Kurds maintained many of their old traditions, including particular rug designs. Occasionally one may see rugs which appear Kurdish, but are woven with the softer wool of Khurassan. It is of further interest that the designs have changed little, despite a separation of several hundred years from the rest of the Kurdish people. Quchon rugs are also found in adaptations of Turkoman patterns, with large, crudely drawn guls. They are Turkish knotted and still made exclusively of wool.

THE GABA RUG

During the last several decades a large number of so-called Gaba rugs have appeared in the Western markets, usually in small sizes, with natural shades of ivory, black, gray, and brown. The field is almost always an off-white shade, and the designs are simple and rectilinear. A few of these rugs have originated from the Tabriz area (often in the Bahktiari panel design), and a larger number come from Fars. Most of them, however, originate in the villages around Mashad and from nearby Baluchi tribesmen, and they are consequently distinguishable from other varieties by their use of Persian knots. The warp is usually of white wool, with thick cotton wefts, and the designs are suggestive of simplified Baluchi patterns.

BALUCHI RUGS OF KHURASSAN AND AFGHANISTAN

Rugs of the Baluchi (also Belouch, Beloudge, and other spellings) tribesmen are so distinctive as to be recognizable at a glance, and anyone remotely familiar with oriental rugs could hardly mistake a typical example; yet a misconception of their origin exists in the minds of many dealers and in most rug books. This derives from the fact that there is an area called Baluchistan, the southeastern-most portion of Iran and western Pakistan, which is inhabited by nomads and villagers of Indo-European origin. These people do not, however, make pile rugs. Rugs of this name are made several hundred miles to the north in Khurassan and northern Afghanistan by displaced Baluchi tribes, most of whom have lived there since the reign of Nadir Shah, when they were forcibly resettled. Subsequent migrations have also taken place.

The first historical references to Baluchis occur in the tenth century, when they inhabited the area south of Kerman. Probably under pressure from the Seljuk migrations, they subsequently moved to the east into Seistan and their current homeland, where most of them have remained. Today Baluchistan is among the most underdeveloped parts of Persia, with traditional village life having changed little for the last thousand years.

The groups actually making rugs probably number no more than 30,000 persons, with about 12,000 in Iran and the remainder in Afghanistan. (There are approximately 200,000 Baluchis in southern Iran and perhaps another 70,000 in southern Afghanistan, but these people make only crude, flat woven fabrics.) The major production area in Iran is around Turbat-i-Haidari, where elements of the Bahluli, Baizidi, Kolah-derazi, Jan Mirzai, Rahim Khani, and Kurkheilli tribes market their products.[13] (Bogolubov's[14] 1908 Russian publication on Turkoman rugs depicts two Baluchi specimens purchased at Turbat-i-Haidari.) Also important as a market center, for rugs of the Kolah-derazi and other tribes, is Kashmar, while around Sarakhs are collected rugs from a number of small groups, including Brahui elements (a people living among the Baluchis, but speaking a Dravidian language).

Baluchis also weave rugs in Seistan, particularly around the Helmand delta. These rugs are marketed in Mashad, usually under the name of Zabol, the major town of the area, and they have evolved into a very distinctive type during the last few decades. The designs are imaginative and include elements adapted from the Turkomans, particularly the Ersaris, while the colors are more

53. MASHAD MEDALLION RUG, Ca. 1920, 8'6" x 12'6". Warp: C. /3\, white. Weft: C. /2\, white and dyed blue, 2 shoots. Pile: W. /2\. Knot: P-L, 90°, v. 12, h. 12, 144/sq inch. (Many jufti knots.) Sides: double overcast of red wool. Ends: plain weave of white cotton and loose warp ends. Colors (11): cochineal red field, dark blue, 2 shades of light blue, light green, apricot, orange, yellow, medium brown, pink, ivory. For at least the last century medallion rugs of this type have been produced in Mashad. The earlier pieces were thinner, had softer wool, and the red was more likely to be a deep magenta. Later examples are thicker and have rather hard synthetic dyes.

54. BALUCHI RUG, early 20th century, 3'9" x 6'3". Warp: W. /2\, light. Weft: W. /2\, dark, 2 shoots. Pile: W. /2\. Knot: P, v. 9, h. 9, 81/sq inch. Sides: double selvage in checkerboard pattern over 4 warps, with red, dark blue, and blue-green alternating. Ends: band of slit tapestry kilim followed by plain weave with a few rows of weft float brocade) and loose warp ends. Colors (8): brick red field, deep pink, apricot, light and dark blue, blue-green, yellow, ivory. Rugs with relatively lively colors are made around Zabol, often in designs that appear to be borrowed from Ersaris in northern Afghanistan.

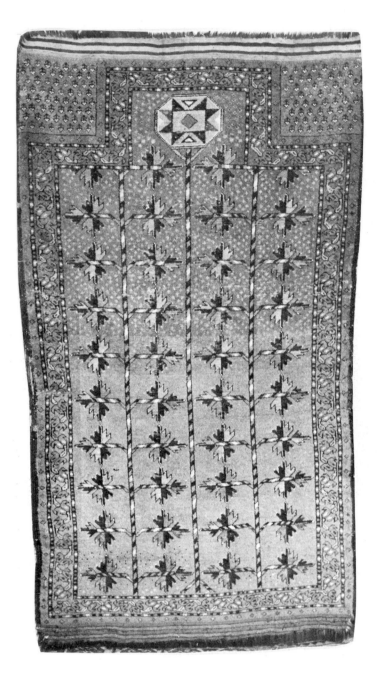

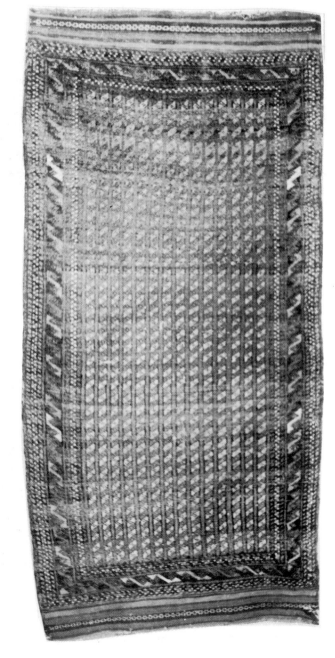

55. BALUCHI PRAYER RUG, 19th century, 3'5" x 6'4". Warp: goat hair, /2\. Weft: C. /2\, unbleached gray, 2 shoots. Pile: W. /3\ and C. /2\ for white. Knot: P, v. 9, h. 8, 72/sq inch. Sides: double selvage of dark brown goat hair over 4 warps. Ends: plain weave bands with blue and faded yellow stripes. Colors (6): camel colored field, medium blue, rust red, faded yellow, dark brown, white (cotton). Although apparently an older rug, this piece is peculiar in having a cotton weft and white cotton used in the pile. The leaf figures are often more clearly arranged around a central "tree-of-life."

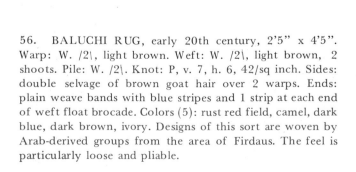

56. BALUCHI RUG, early 20th century, 2'5" x 4'5". Warp: W. /2\, light brown. Weft: W. /2\, light brown, 2 shoots. Pile: W. /2\. Knot: P, v. 7, h. 6, 42/sq inch. Sides: double selvage of brown goat hair over 2 warps. Ends: plain weave bands with blue stripes and 1 strip at each end of weft float brocade. Colors (5): rust red field, camel, dark blue, dark brown, ivory. Designs of this sort are woven by Arab-derived groups from the area of Firdaus. The feel is particularly loose and pliable.

57. BALUCHI RUG, 19th century, 3'2" x 6'1". Warp: W. /2\, light brown. Weft: W. /2\, undyed natural gray, 2 shoots. Pile: W. /2\. Knot: T-L, 30°, v. 8, h. 8, 64/sq inch. Sides: double selvage of dark brown goat hair over 4 warps. Ends: plain weave bands with multicolored stripes. Colors (8): light yellow-green, light blue, mauve, gray, reddish-purple, gray-brown, red-orange, white. Some Turkish knotted rugs are woven by Baluchis south of Herat, in the Adraskand Valley and south of Gurian. Most of these rugs show a strong use of latch hooks in the design, and many are relatively brightly colored. Another group, however, shows an exceedingly dark tonality, with black, dark brown, and dark blue.

Dr. G. Dumas—H. Black collection.

58. TEIMURI PRAYER RUG from Afghanistan, 19th century, 2'9" x 4'3". Warp: W. /2\, light. Weft: W. /2\, undyed, 1 shoot. Pile: W. /2\, Knot: P, v. 9, h. 7, 63/sq inch. Sides: double selvage of dark brown goat hair over 3 warps. Ends: plain weave bands elaborately embellished with weft float brocading. Colors (5): dark brown field, medium blue, apricot, medium brown, ivory. Teimuri rugs, which are marketed in Herat along with many Baluchi products, are indistinguishable from Baluchis in structure. However, these particular design elements are characteristic.

varied and lively than those of other Baluchis. These rugs are usually a little larger than most Persian Baluchis, and have slightly longer pile.

In Afghanistan small groups of Baluchis live among the Turkomans in the north, but the most important tribes are the Jaqub-Khani, living around Zurabad, and the Dokhtar-i-Ghazi, who live north of Herat. (Prayer rugs of this latter group are characterized by three dome-like arches across the top, standing above longitudinal panels.) Other smaller tribes live around Gurian, Adraskand, and Tshakansur.[15]

A number of other peoples, not of Baluchi origin, also weave similar rugs. The Taimuris of Afghanistan (and related Taimanis and Djamshidis) inhabit an area around the town of Obeh and Tulak, where they have long woven rugs of a distinct type. These peoples are of mixed Turkish and Iranian origin.

Along the eastern rim of the Great Desert in Iran live small tribal groups of Arab origin, many of whom still speak Arabic. Firdaus is the primary market for their rugs, although rugs are also to be found in Tabas. These are virtually indistinguishable from products of the Baluchis, but are somewhat more loosely woven.

The designs of Baluchi rugs are often said to resemble those of the Turkomans, at least in spirit. Frequently one sees small gul or medallion-like figures arranged diagonally across the rug, with color variations, but no change in basic pattern. There is a great variety of these figures, which also may occur in combinations. Usually one of the border stripes is wider than the others, often with a meandering vine pattern similar to that of Yomud rugs, although again the variation is enormous. The minor border stripes are usually simple, with latch hooks or small turrets. Occasionally classical Persian patterns are found (modifications of the Herati and Mina Khani), and in more recent rugs of obvious Baluchi origin there are Turkoman guls. The prayer rug usually displays a squarish mihrab, often with a tree of life pattern in the field.

The color tonalities of Baluchi rugs were formerly somber, until the introduction of bright, synthetic dyes. Classically the Baluchi was woven with deep blues, rust reds, dark brown and black (natural dark wool, which also could be further darkened with indigo), occasional bits of yellow, orange, and green, and a very sparing use of white in outlining. Camel shades (occasionally actual camel hair) are more frequent in early twentieth-century rugs, particularly from the Herat area, while those rugs with a blue background were most likely woven around Turbat-i-Haidari.

59. BALUCHI RUG, late 19th century, 3'11" x 6'10". Warp: W. /2\, medium brown. Weft: W. /2\, dark brown, 2 shoots. Pile: W. /3\. Knot: P, v. 8, h. 6, 48/sq inch. Sides: double overcast of dark brown goat hair over 4 warps. Ends: long plain weave bands of brick red. Colors (5): brick red field, dark blue, dark brown, rust red, ivory. This somberly colored rug was probably woven in the vicinity of Turbat-i-Haidari.

(The main border, which is relatively common on older Baluchi rugs, is suggestive of Yomud borders, and the guard stripes [turret-like figures in white] are found on numerous Turkoman rugs, particularly Salors and Tekkes. The field elements, however, are not Turkoman, although similar figures are found from the Teimuris in Afghanistan. Occasionally one finds large rugs [up to 7 x 12 feet] with these motifs.)

In materials the rugs are all much the same. The warp and weft are wool, or frequently goat hair mixed with sheep's wool. The side selvage, woven around three or four thickened warp strands is usually of coarse goat hair, while cotton is used rarely in the decorative brocading of the kilim strips at the ends. Camel hair is found in the very finest Baluchi "Balishts," a type of pillow woven with pile on one side and a plain weave back, usually about 32 x 16 inches. These, and the small dowry rugs, are among the best Baluchi pieces, and the very finest may occasionally contain silk.

In the late nineteenth century rugs from various tribes could still be distinguished by design, as each family wove a certain pattern and no other. During recent years, however, there has been much borrowing from one area to the next, with the demands of commerce determining what will be produced. Now it is often next to impossible to recognize the exact origin of a rug, although other factors may provide some clues. Rugs of the most western Baluchis (marketed in Mashad) are the most finely woven and are likely to be somewhat long and narrow, while many from around Gurian and Adraskand are larger, reaching sizes up to 7 x 12 feet. Some of the latter type are Turkish knotted, which is relatively unusual for a Baluchi. (These rugs often have lighter colors and feature stiff figures ornamented with latch hooks.) There are typically two wefts between each row of knots (occasionally one), and alternate warps are very slightly depressed. The ends usually show a long woven band, which may be decorated with plain weave stripes, a simple kilim-woven design, or more complex figures in weft float brocading. Often these are finished with great care. The Baluchi rug feels more flexible than the Turkoman, which results from the relatively coarse knotting and looseness of weave.

Recent Baluchi Rugs

Baluchi rugs have undergone considerable change since World War II, with a dramatic brightening of color. The new rugs may be cotton warped, and the dyes are almost always synthetic. Designs have changed little, but the bright colors create an entirely different effect.

THE RUGS OF KERMAN

With sixty thousand inhabitants and numerous surrounding villages, Kerman is one of the major rug producing areas of Persia. It has probably had a less eventful existence than any other center of comparable size, and the arts have been allowed to flourish and expand with relatively little interference from the outside. This can be accounted for by its geographical isolation, which kept the city outside of the usual commercial channels (except for the ancient caravan route to India, which decreased in importance as the sea routes were opened) and the arid climate that has made Kerman the poorest of the five major provinces of Persia. The city existed for centuries in provincial isolation, with its basic Persian population little disturbed by the repeated invasions that devastated other parts of the country. The Seljuks, conquerors of the area in the eleventh century, showed no desire to settle there, as they did in Azerbaijan and Hamadan, and the Mongols did not venture that far south. There was indeed little incentive for them to do so, as Kerman was in no sense wealthy. Under the Sefavids, the province enjoyed an undisturbed tranquility, and even the Afghan invasion was not a disruptive factor. The only major siege of the city occurred in 1794, and the army of Aga Mohammed Qajar did considerable damage. The city slowly recovered but remained relatively poor. In more recent times it has been important almost exclusively as a carpet center, entering only peripherally into the political and social movements that have brought about much change in Persia.

Development of the carpet industry is poorly documented in Kerman, as elsewhere, although we have clear documentation that weaving occurred during Sefavid times. Some of the best wool in Persia—a soft, white wool—is produced in Kerman; there were such limited opportunities for attracting money from the outside that turning the wool into a medium of exchange was virtually inevitable. Kerman fabrics of various types have thus developed to meet the prevailing styles demanded by commerce. In Marco Polo's day, the fabrics apparently were not rugs, as he makes no mention of them, while describing other types of cloth in detail. Chardin, who was in Kerman in 1666 and 1672, describes local carpets, as did the chronicle of Shah Abbas, the "Alamara-i-Abbasi." Carpets were shipped from Kerman to India during this time, and quite possibly they influenced the weaving of that country. We do not know what effect the Afghan invasion had on Kerman's industry, but we may surmise that it induced a decline. Still, carpet weaving must have continued at some level during the eighteenth century.

Fraser,[16] who provided an extensive survey of Persian commerce in 1821, assures us that carpets were one of Kerman's most important products, and he comments particularly upon the renown of Kerman wool. Sir F. J. Goldsmid, in his book *Eastern Persia*,[17] describes the carpet industry in 1871 as though it were an established part of the city's heritage.

> The curiosities of Kerman are the carpet and shawl manufactories. . . . The former, once the most celebrated in the East, have much diminished in number since the fatal seige, from which date all the calamities of Kerman. In the governor's private factory alone are the finer qualities produced. The white wool of the Kerman sheep, added perhaps to some quality of the water, gives a brilliancy to the coloring unobtainable elsewhere. In pattern the carpets are distinguishable from those of the North and West both by this purity of color, and a greater boldness and originality of design, due probably to a slighter infusion of Arab prejudices on the subject of the representation of living forms. Not only flowers and trees, but birds, beasts, landscapes, and even human figures are found on the Kerman carpets. . . .

> . . . we proceeded to the workshops, entering by a hole in the wall, just big enough to admit a man, but certainly not large enough to pass a chair; and the first thing that struck us was the utter want of ventilation, there being absolutely no way of purifying the air, which was close and smelt most unwholesome. About sixty or seventy men and boys were seated in three rooms . . . . The emaciated bodies of the children were especially noticeable, and their arms seemed to be almost withered away, but there is no "Factory Act," in Persia. We were informed by the proprietor that the hours allotted to sheer work averaged fourteen a day . . . .

> From the shawl manufactory we went some little distance to that of the no less celebrated carpets. These are manufactured in a way reminding one strongly of the gobelin tapestry made at present, or rather before the war, in Paris. The looms are arranged perpendicularly, and the workers sit behind the loom, but in this case, unlike the Gobelin, they have the right side of the carpet toward them. The manufacture of carpets differs from that of shawls in this particular that each carpet has a painted pattern, designed and drawn out by the master of the manufactory, which is pinned to the center of the carpet, and which the workers can consult if necessary, from time to time. Advantage, however, is rarely taken for this facility of reference, for the boy who sits nearest the pattern reads out in a monotone any information required concerning it. The carpets are made entirely of cotton [editor's note: clearly an error], woven in by the fingers into the upright web. Their manufacture is tedious and costly to the extreme, but they are beautiful and soft and durable. The man whose manufactory we visited was said to be without rival in Persia . . . . We saw a beautiful carpet he was making for the Shrine at Mash-had, which was to cost . . . 200 pounds, being eleven yards long by about two and a half broad; than which nothing could be more beautiful.

We could conclude from these comments that carpet weaving must have been well developed during most of the nineteenth century, as in 1821 and 1871 foreign travelers seemed aware of Kerman's reputation. Production, was probably on a relatively modest scale, however, as the shawl industry was

initially much more important, rivaling that of Kashmir. When machine manufacture of these fabrics became a reality, the local industry suffered greatly, but this decline coincided with the increased demand for carpets, and the artisans of one craft were thus easily able to change to another, with the result that the carpet industry showed remarkable growth within a few years.

Originally the industry was under local control, but in the early part of the century the Tabrizi merchants became more aggressive in commissioning weavers. By the highpoint of 1929, most weaving in Kerman was under the control of outside firms, generally American. When the depression struck in the early thirties, and the United States could no longer purchase large numbers of carpets, the weaving industry suffered greatly in Kerman, as ninety percent of its production had gone to America. Foreign firms liquidated their assets and left the remaining resources, such as they were, to the Persians. Fortunately, the policies of Shah Reza Mohammed had brought about a great change in Persia, and the economy had begun to prosper. A market for Kerman products slowly developed under the patronage of local merchants. When the Western market again opened after World War II, the industry in Kerman was far less dependent on the outside, and prices were accordingly higher. This has, in part, brought about an improvement in the wretched living conditions of most Kermanis, who were among the lowest paid and most poorly treated weavers.

Traditional Kerman Rugs

The rugs of Kerman have always been among the most easily recognized fabrics of Persia, with curvilinear, graceful floral designs in a brilliant variety of colors. They have been woven in virtually all sizes up to the largest carpets, with a size of about 4 x 6 feet being most common and probably the one eliciting the most exquisite workmanship. The foundation is always cotton, differing from other Persian city rugs in that there are three wefts between each row of knots, one of which is exceedingly thin. (This does not strengthen the fabric, but is a matter of tradition.) Alternate warps are depressed, while the pile is short on the older specimens. Kermans have at least four grades of knot density, with the finest over 18 x 18 to the inch, and the others counting approximately 16 x 16, 14 x 14, and 12 x 12. The Kerman virtually always has over 140 knots to the inch.

The dyes of Kerman are probably the most varied and imaginative in all Persia. The number of

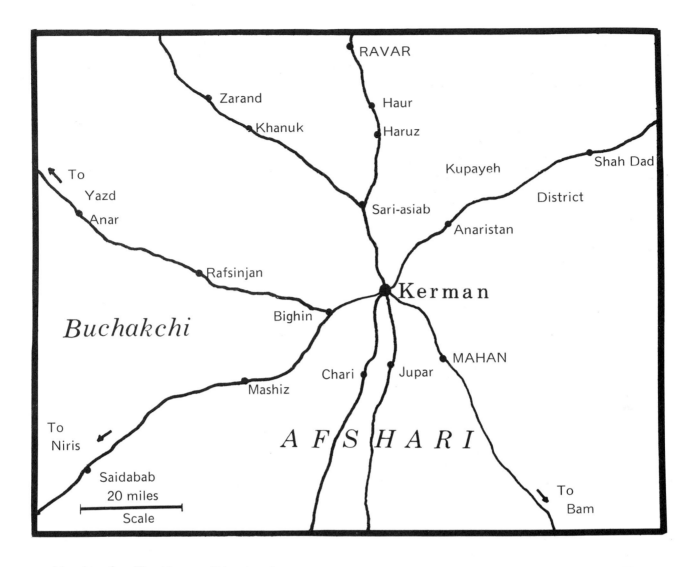

Map No. 6.   The Kerman Weaving Area

shades available is enormous, and one may find considerable variation within one rug. Cochineal has traditionally been used for the reds, with only a subsidiary use of madder. This provides shades from the most delicate pink to a deep magenta, and is characteristic of the Kerman carpet just as deeper shades of the same dye are associated with the works of Mashad. The blues are from indigo, and again a variety of shades is available. Synthetic dyes have done less well in Kerman, probably because the dyers themselves have been important artisans.

Much could be said praising the design of Kerman rugs. Consistently, from the 1870s through the 1930s, the Kerman was exquisitely conceived and executed, with a more thorough development of design than one finds elsewhere. Many of the finest rugs involved elaborate overall or panel de-

signs, and there were many adaptations from various shawl patterns. The designers were encouraged to be inventive by their status in the city; they were among the most respected local artisans. They have probably contributed more to the art than all designers from the rest of the country combined, and many of the best from Kerman were enlisted in the founding of the Institute of Design in Tehran. While individual rugs of other cities might be more appealing than the finest Kermans, the general level of excellence has been unapproached. The American tradition of bleaching these rugs is most regrettable.

Modern Kerman Rugs

Since the 1930s the Kerman rug has undergone considerable change. The current product is

60. KERMAN RUG, late 19th century, 4'1" x 5'10". Warp: C. /6\, undyed. Weft: 3 cotton wefts—2 are /4\, undyed, straight; 1 weft is /2\, dyed light blue, thin and loose. Pile: W. /2\. Knot: P, left warp depressed 85°, v. 16, h. 16, 256/sq inch. Sides: double overcast with blue wool. Ends: loose warp ends. Colors (7): cochineal red, pink, dark blue, light blue, dark brown, light brown, ivory. By the late 19th century the typical Kerman medallion designs were made in abundance, and, although they became more realistically floral, they changed little until the 1920s. In more recent years the medallion has tended to become smaller with more use of the open field.

61. KERMAN RUG, late 19th century, 4'3" x 7'1". Warp' C. /6\, undyed. Weft: C. 2 strands undyed /4\, both pulled tight and following same path; a third shoot /2\, very thin and loose. Pile: W. /2\. Knot: P, left warp depressed 85°, v. 18, h. 18, 324/sq inch. Sides: double overcast of blue wool. Ends: loose warp ends. Colors (8): cochineal red, pink, dark blue, light blue, light green, dark brown, medium brown, white.

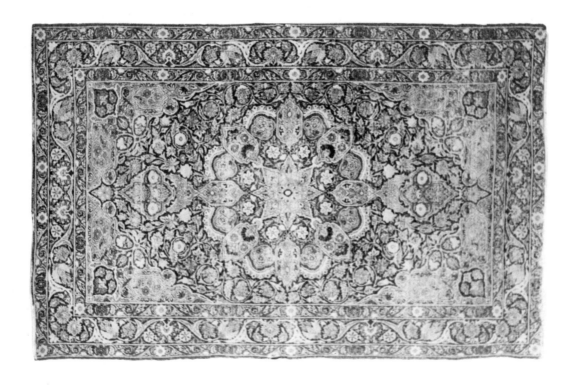

scarcely recognizable as issuing from the same looms that produced the intricate, closely clipped masterpieces of the nineteenth century. The American taste for subdued colors, a rather simple design, and a thick pile has been met by a fabric that conforms in all essentials and which is the only type of new Kerman now found in America. The elaborate floral designs were replaced by the detached floral sprays common in Sarouks, and this eventually evolved toward the open field of pastel rose, blue, or green so common now. The colors at first were merely treated with a bleach, but even untreated carpets now show very light colors. The resulting carpet is unobtrusive and would seem designed to compete with the better machine-made fabrics, which it resembles; yet Kermans are among the most expensive carpets currently imported.

Kermans made for domestic consumption, mostly in Tehran, are of an entirely different sort. While the American type rarely counts over 150 knots to the inch, those woven for wealthy Persians count as high as 18 x 18. These have a shorter pile and intricate designs, often with an open field. This is almost always in a vivid cochineal, and the general tone is much brighter.

An important malady afflicting the current Kerman fabrics is the jufti knot, which has seriously undermined the reputation of the entire local industry. Within the last thirty years it has become endemic in Kerman, and it is found to some extent in nearly all modern carpets.

RAVAR

In the rug trade there has long been a tradition that the choicest Kermans are those from the village of Ravar, or, as it is erroneously and more commonly known, Laver. Often this designation is quite arbitrarily applied to particularly finely woven rugs, especially those in a prayer format with a tree-of-life design. While it is difficult to determine in retrospect whether any given specimen was actually woven in Ravar, those that we know have been made there are not notably fine. Indeed, the earliest examples are perhaps more rectilinear and stiff than Kermans of the same period. The pile is also more likely to be medium long on these rugs, while the reds may verge more toward magenta.

YEZD

Yezd is an ancient and industrious city situated along the edge of the Great Desert, about halfway between Isfahan and Kerman. It has a long history of artistic achievement, particularly in fabrics other than rugs, and Yezdi merchants carry on active commercial operations throughout the country. Yezd is the home of most of the few remaining Zoroastrians in Persia; its architecture has taken some of its flavor from this heritage. In the surrounding area are ruins of burial towers, and travelers have long found Yezd one of the most exotic cities of Persia.

Yezd has a long tradition of carpet weaving. Fraser[18] mentions carpet production there as early as 1821; but prior to World War II these rugs were uncommon and of obscure repute in the West. Most were in carpet sizes, with the Herati pattern rendered on a blue field. The borders were distinct from those of other areas weaving a Feraghan-like carpet, and the floral elements may be more naturalistically drawn. The reds are dyed with cochineal, and the wool has a texture similar to that of Kerman.

During the last several decades the traditional style has given way to designs that are in all respects nearly identical to the modern Kerman. Indeed, craftsmen from Kerman were imported, and they have established the familiar medallion designs. Most of the rugs are made in the style currently demanded by Persian tastes, with open red fields and generally bright colors. Few Yezd rugs are brought to the United States.

RUGS OF THE AFSHARI

The Kerman province produces more than the city rug of that name, as the areas to the south and west are inhabited by nomads who weave brightly colored rugs of geometrical designs. The most important of these are the Afshari, although there are many smaller tribes, including the related Buchakchi and dozens of other obscure groups. The Afshari have a well-documented history in this region. There is evidence that they were forcibly settled in southern Kerman under the reign of Shah Tahmasp. Previously they had been one of the Azerbaijani Turkish tribes which had supported the rise of the Sefavid dynasty under Shah Ismail. To Tahmasp, Ismail's son and successor, they represented a potential source of disturbance, and a large portion of them were forced to relocate in the south.

In migratory habits the Afshari resemble the nomads of Fars, as they have traditionally spent summer and winter at different altitudes, providing year-round pasture for their flocks. The terrain consists of roughly the same divisions into "garmsir," "mu'tavil," and "sarhad" (see p. 83), the sarhad constituting an area about 50 by 150 miles south and west of Kerman. In the winter the tribe migrates toward the warmer hills bordering the Persian Gulf. Because of the Iranian government's settlement policy, probably over two thirds of the 40,000 Afsharis are sedentary, having settled among the Persian villagers of the same area. There has been frequent exchange in design between the two groups, and both make rugs of the same general appearance. The horizontal loom is standard, and the warp and weft have traditionally been of wool. Recently, however, cotton has been used with increasing frequency, particularly for the weft. This practice started in the villages, but now many of the nomads use cotton, which is still less common in Fars. Earlier Afshar rugs were often single wefted, but now two wefts between each row of knots is standard.

Formerly the knot could be used to distinguish village and tribal rugs, but this feature is less reliable now, as there has been extensive intermarriage. The tribal rugs were traditionally woven with the Turkish knot, while the Persian villagers used the Persian knot. The weave is generally of medium fineness, with some recent coarsely knotted fabrics, but the pile is seldom long. In weight and feel the rugs are lighter than most of the Fars group, and one could almost mistake the older pieces for some of the finely woven Caucasian fabrics.

Afshari products are seldom larger than about 5½ x 7 feet, and they tend to be more squarish than Fars rugs. Some specimens show a striped kilim band at the ends, at times with a few rows of brocade. The sides are double overcast, often with yarn of varying colors. In design there is great variation, and many motifs found elsewhere are given a fresh approach. The Boteh is drawn in large, angular figures, usually against a light background. (Generally Afshari rugs could be described as lighter than their neighbors from Fars.) Another common design consists of lozenge-shaped panels, arranged diagonally across the rug, filled with stylized flowers and remotely suggestive of Kerman patterns.

The medallion rugs are even more clearly influenced by the products of Kerman, as here we have a central figure in an open field, with corner pieces resembling a quarter of the medallion. These are often enclosed by jagged white lines, and the red or blue field shows a few stylized flowers, usuall arranged stiffly in rows.

Afshari rugs are marketed in Kerman, in the towns of Saidabad and Baft to the south, and in Shiraz. Production is currently good, with most of the rugs being sent to Europe. Dyes and wool re-

62. AFSHARI RUG, late 19th century, 3'6" x 4'5".Warp: W. /2\, light. Weft: W. /2\, dyed red, 2 shoots. Pile: W. /2\. Knot: T, v. 8, h. 8, 64/sq inch. Sides: double overcast of dark blue wool. Ends: .... Colors (6): dark blue field, red, yellow, light green, ivory, dark brown. Often Afshari rugs appear in crude, rectilinear adaptations of Kerman city rugs. This piece is certainly suggestive of the Kerman medallion and corner designs.

63. AFSHARI RUG, early 20th century, 3'8" x 4'11". Warp: W. /2\, dark brown, light, and mixed. Weft: C. /2\, undyed and blue, 2 shoots. Pile: W. /2\. Knot: P-L, 60°, v. 8, h. 7, 56/sq inch. Sides: double overcast of dark blue wool. Ends: several rows of red wool plain weave remain; loose warp ends. Colors (9): dark blue field, red, apricot, rust red, ivory, light green, medium and dark blue, dark brown. Repeating figures are common on Afshari rugs, particularly large, elaborate Botehs.

main of high quality, and, like the rugs of Fars, they represent an essentially honest native art, not directly under the influence of foreign tastes.

THE TRIBAL AND VILLAGE RUGS OF FARS

The province of Fars lies south of Isfahan and west of Kerman, bordering the Persian Gulf to the south. It includes an area of over sixty thousand square miles and is inhabited by an estimated one million people of diverse origins. Throughout the province there are remnants of past grandeur, as Fars was at one time the center of the Persian Empire, the home of the Achaemenian and Sassanian kings. Persepolis is found among dozens of ruined cities, and from remains of ancient waterways one would assume that the area once was rich and prosperous.

Fars, indeed, is still potentially a fertile land, as it is better watered than most of Persia, with three major rivers—the Zuhreh, Shahpur, and Qara Agach—emptying into the Persian Gulf. Although the land is carved into a heavy relief of hills and valleys, much of it is capable of agricultural development at a higher technological level than is now available to the inhabitants. Basically the land falls

into three climatic categories, each significant in the yearly migration of the nomads who make up a large portion of the population. First there is the "garmsir," or hot district, which comprises the coastal plain along the Persian Gulf, extending inland where the hills become steeper and cooler. Vegetation is sparse, and in summer the heat is severe. At about 3500 feet the terrain changes, and we enter a climatic zone that the Persians call the "mu'tavil," which extends to an elevation of about 6000 feet. Most of the cities (Shiraz, Niris, and Firuzabad) are in this region, along with the larger villages. There are some oak forests, among the last in Persia, and many wild fruit trees. The climate is bearable in the summer and not especially severe in winter.

The upper climatic zone is the "sarhad," or cold country, which extends to eight and nine thousand feet, with the mountain summits above 12,000 feet. Summer temperatures are quite comfortable, and grass is abundant, providing excellent pasture for the flocks. In autumn the nomads descend through the "mu'tavil," which is more of a traffic corridor than an area of long occupancy, to the "garmsir," where the flocks find grass while snow covers the upper slopes. About four months of every year is spent on the trail, and some migrations cover a distance of over 300 miles. All the truly nomadic peoples make such moves, and year after year they return to the same areas, often inhabiting the same portions of land that other tribes occupy at different times. Even the migration corridors are clearly defined, with each tribe exercising certain rights which have grown up through tradition and warfare.[19]

Although urban dwellers make up about one-quarter of the population of Fars (with Shiraz numbering 130,000), we are little concerned with this group, as rugs are only marketed and not woven in the cities. Many of the early rug books insist that rugs named Shiraz are actually made in Shiraz, and Dilley[20] alludes to specimens dating from the city's brief reign as Persia's capital under Karim Khan Zand. In other rug books one may find the fanciful name of "Mecca-Shiraz," along with accounts of how rugs were taken to the sacred city during pilgrimages and sold there. Likely this is an invention of the dealers to give an added aura of mystery to their wares. Rugs so designated are all the products of nomadic tribes or the villagers of Fars.

There are two major tribal divisions in Fars, the most important being the Qashgai, numbering about 250,000 members. The lesser group is the Khamseh Federation, a loosely knit alliance of 70,000 Arab-, Persian-, and Turkish-derived nomads, which has lost most of its social and political meaning as an organization. Defining the areas inhabited by each is difficult, as they differ in summer and winter. Basically the Qashgai can be said to occupy areas west of Shiraz, migrating south of the city in winter and north during the summer. The Khamseh make similar moves in the area east of Shiraz. (Refer to map.)

THE QASHGAI

These nomads speak a Turkic dialect similar to that of Azerbaijan, and there is some evidence indicating them as remnants of Seljuks who entered Fars from the north in the thirteenth century, possibly to avoid the Mongols. The Qashgai have a reputation as the best weavers of Fars, and although output must be only about 20 percent of the current total for the area, their rugs are in demand.

Qashgai men have long been known as fierce, bloodthirsty warriors, but the women of the tribe appear even more formidable. Clad in great multi-layered garments of perhaps a dozen colorful fabrics, their proud, imperious bearing leaves no doubt as to who actually owns the world. Although their

lot has not been easy, particularly in recent years, and they live on the brink of destitution, they stride through the bazaars with a primal elegance. This same intense pride seems to be reflected in their weaving.

The Qashgai are divided into a number of sub-tribes, with the Qashguli, Darashuri, Shishbuluki, Farsimadan, and Gallanzans being the most important. Women of all these groups still weave rugs that have traditionally been Turkish knotted. Today, however, there has been enough intermarriage with Persian villagers that the Persian knot is used in perhaps 30 percent of the rugs. Qashgai products are also double wefted, while those of the Khamseh were formerly single wefted, but this distinction is also vanishing; single wefted rugs are now less common from any source. The knotting is consistently among the finest of Fars weaves, while the foundation is less likely to be of dark wool or goat hair than the Khamseh rugs. Some newer Qashgais are woven on a cotton foundation.

In design Qashgai rugs are rectilinear, with patterns often involving three medallion figures arranged longitudinally. Another layout, with a small central medallion and similar figures in the corners, is also common. The rug merchants of Shiraz can often tell at a glance exactly what subtribe produced any given rug, but it is difficult for the outsider to make these distinctions. Perhaps rugs of the Qashguli are easiest to identify, as they are often the most finely woven and are more likely to have red wefts and sharply depressed alternate warps. In design they frequently have an overall pattern of elaborate Boteh figures or a mihrab (often a double mihrab) with a profusion of floral elements. (These are obviously related to the earlier "mille fleurs" rugs in many major collections, although they are not necessarily of the same origin.) Even new Qashguli rugs are quite expensive in Shiraz, and they are made in insufficient numbers to be found frequently abroad.

Shishbuluki rugs are also of exceptional quality. Often these have a central diamond-shaped medallion with surrounding animal or floral figures in concentric lozenges. Qashgai rugs in general have a lighter color tonality than others from Fars, with white and yellow employed much more commonly.

THE KHAMSEH FEDERATION

This group differs from the Qashgai in that its component tribes are of multiple origins and speak different languages. The Arab and Baseri tribes constitute the largest groups, apparently inhabiting the same area since the Arab Conquest of the seventh

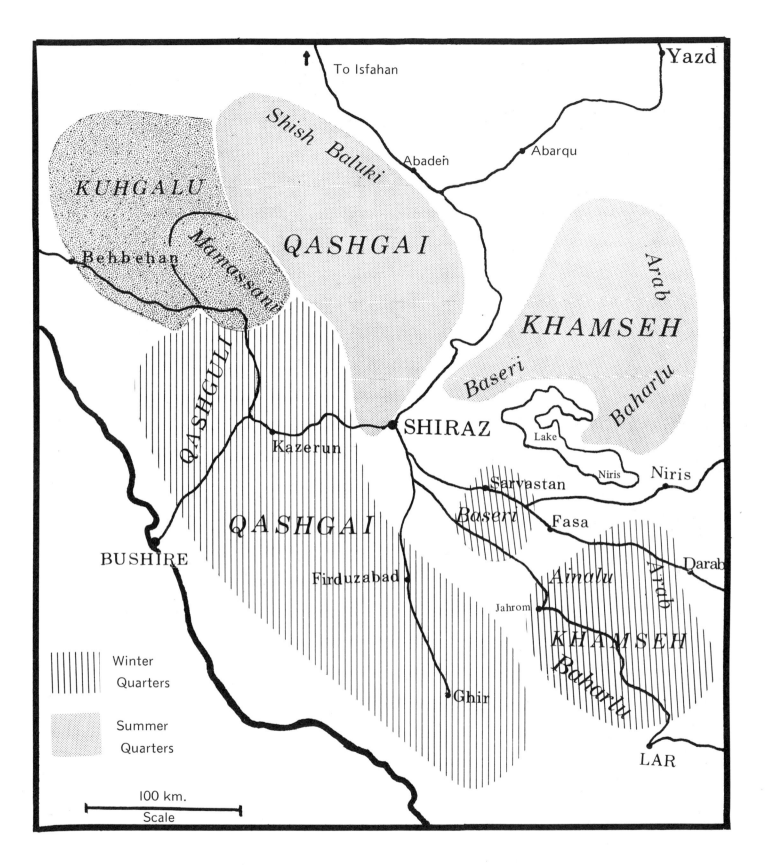

Map No. 7.   The Weaving Tribes of Fars. (Names of nomadic tribes and subtribes are in italics.)

century; they speak a corrupt Arabic. The Ainalu and Baharlu tribes speak a language similar to the Qashgais. The Ainalu have a tradition of an eighteenth-century migration from Turkestan, but the origins of the Baharlu are unknown. The Nafar are a minor tribe of Turkic and Luri origin.

64. SHIRAZ RUG, 19th century, 5'1" x 8'3". Warp:
W. /2\, medium to dark brown mixture. Weft: W. /2\,
dyed red, 2 shoots. Pile: W. /2\. Knot: T, v. 10, h. 9,
90/sq inch. Sides: double overcast in multicolored
wool over 5 warps. Ends: .... Colors (7): dark blue
field, red, yellow, light green, light blue, dark brown,
ivory. The great variety of floral and animal figures
occupying the field is typical of Qashgai rugs.

65. QASHGULI SAMPLER, 20th century, 1'5" x
2'8". Warp: C. /5\, white. Weft: C. /2\, white, 2 shoots.
Pile: W. /2\. Knot: P-L, 80°, v. 9, h. 11, 99/sq inch.
Sides: double overcast of red and green wool mixed
together. Ends: loose warp ends, with adjacent warps
knotted together. Colors (14): dark blue field, medium
blue, 2 shades of light blue, orange, deep yellow,
bright yellow, blue-green, dark green, olive green, deep
red, rust red, ivory, and dark brown. The upper stripe
includes a very common major border, while the
second, wider band provides enough of the Herati for
the entire pattern to be reconstructed. The realistic
floral figures are often found on Qashguli bags, while
the Boteh figure is of the sort one finds repeated on
large rugs.

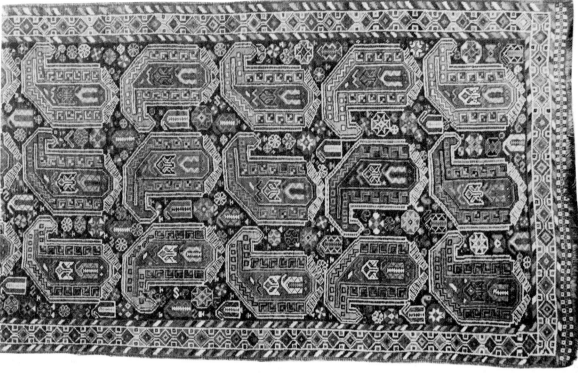

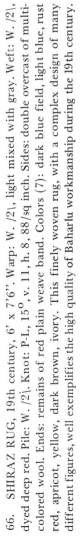

66. SHIRAZ RUG, 19th century, 6' x 7'6''. Warp: W. /2\, light mixed with gray. Weft: W. /2\, dyed deep red. Pile: W. /2\. Knot: P-L, 15°, v. 11, h. 8, 88/sq inch. Sides: double overcast of multi-colored wool. Ends: remains of red plain weave band. Colors (7): dark blue field, light blue, rust red, apricot, yellow, dark brown, ivory. This finely woven rug, with a complex design of many different figures, well exemplifies the high quality of Baharlu workmanship during the 19th century.

67. BAHARLU RUNNER, 19th century, 3'5'' x 15'4''. Warp: W. /2\, dark wool. Weft: W. /2\, dark wool, 2 shoots. Pile: W. /2\. Knot: T, v. 8, h. 8, 64/sq inch. Sides: double overcast of light blue and rust red wool. Ends: brown plain weave bands. Colors (7): dark blue field, rust red, brick red, light blue, yellow, ivory, dark brown. This same type of large, elaborate Boteh is relatively common on Baharlu rugs even today. These have often been labeled as Qashgais in the West.

Courtesy of the Oriental Rug Co. of Berkeley, California.

68. BASERI RUG, early 20th century, 5' x 10'6".
Warp: W. /2\, gray brown. Weft: W. /2\, dark wool dyed
red, 2 shoots. Pile: W. /2\. Knot: P, v. 7, h. 8, 56/sq inch.
Sides: double overcast of dark brown wool. Ends: plain
weave band of red wool; warps selvaged at top and left
loose at bottom. Colors (5): dark blue field, deep red, yellow, ivory, dark brown. Baseri rugs resemble those of the
Arab Khamseh tribe in structure, although the designs
are simpler. Relatively few rugs of this type are made today.
Courtesy of the Oriental Rug Co. of Berkeley, California.
(Baseri rugs present a particular problem of identification, as many of them resemble Kurdish rugs made farther to the north. However, they are usually Persian
knotted, like this specimen, which is very rare for a
Kurdish rug, and they are somewhat looser in construction. This layout, with lozenge-shaped panels, resembles
work by the Afshari and Bahktiari, and is much less
common in Fars rugs.)

At least 40 percent of the rugs of Fars are
produced by these tribes, although their quality is
well below the Qashgai both in tightness of fabric
and execution of design. Generally the colors are
also deeper, with very sparse use of yellow and
white. Arab rugs are probably the darkest of all,
with a loose weave and long pile that give the design
a rather muddied appearance. They are woven with
the Persian knot, often with only one weft between
each row of knots. The designs usually involve a
row of three medallion figures along the length of
the rug, with the field covered by small animal or
floral figures. They are the lowest quality of Fars
nomad rugs. Baseri rugs are of similar weave, usually with a shorter pile, while the designs often involve larger figures.

The Baharlu and Ainalu make few rugs today,
but antique pieces are found that are quite comparable to Qashgai work. (In the United States
many of these are labeled as Qashgais.) Despite the
Turkic origin of these tribes, most of the rugs are
apparently Persian knotted; they may be either
double or single wefted. Baharlu rugs of the late
nineteenth century may be found in particularly
large sizes (Qashgai rugs seldom exceed 10 feet),
and a few Baharlu runners may be found. These are
often covered by large, elaborate Boteh figures, usually more stiff and angular than those employed by
the Qashgai.

CURRENT STATUS OF THE NOMAD

The Qashgai and particularly their Luri neighbors to the west, the Boir Ahmedi, were a source
of great concern to Reza Shah during the twenties.
They accepted little direction from the central
government and, having a long tradition of bandit-
ry, raided and plundered villages more or less at
will. On several occasions Persian army detachments
were destroyed by these rebellious horsemen. This
situation was not to be tolerated for long by some-
one so truculent and inflexible as the late Shah.
After considerable difficulty, the tribesmen were
overcome and disarmed, and an enforced settlement policy was put into effect. Although such a
solution may again be needed (to further develop the province), in this instance it was brought
about in such an abrupt and arbitrary manner as to
cause great suffering among the tribesmen. Some
groups were forced to settle in the "Garmsir,"
which resulted in great loss of life among their
flocks during the searing, hot summer. Those who
remained in the colder highlands had similar trouble

69. SHIRAZ RUG, late 19th century, 4'8" x 7'4". Warp' W. /2\, medium to dark brown. Weft: W. /2\, medium brown. Pile: W. /2\. Knot: P, v. 9, h. 7, 63/sq inch. Sides: double overcast of red and blue wool over 6 warps. Ends: .... Colors (7): dark blue field, rust red, light green, light blue, dark brown, apricot, ivory. This rug was woven by the Arab Tribe of the Khamseh Federation. Recent Arab rugs are of an inferior quality, with a coarse weave and dark, muddy colors.
Courtesy of the Oriental Rug Co. of Berkeley, California.

in the winter. Disease and starvation became rampant, and by the time of the Shah's abdication in 1941, the situation seemed bleak. As this event coincided with a general lessening of control by the central government, the nomads were quick to take up their old ways again. Within a year many had returned to the custom of taking their flocks from winter to summer pasturage, but large groups remained settled so that there are now fewer nomads than before the Shah's program.

Gradually, during the last thirty years, the settlement policy has been reasserted by the government, only now there is no effort to bring about precipitous change. The central authority has been so firmly established that government permission must be obtained before a migration is begun. The nomadic way of life is slowly being replaced.

VILLAGE RUGS

Increasingly the rugs of Fars are village products, and this has led to some change in the basic fabric. For the first time the cotton foundation is coming into wide use, with the effect of making the rug somewhat straighter. (Often one finds a wool warp and cotton wefts.) Synthetic dyes have almost completely replaced vegetable products. A visit to the Shiraz dyers (where wool even for the tribal rugs is processed) reveals the familiar boxes from Bayer and Hoescht. More large rugs are being made now, with 7' x 10' and 6' x 9' sizes popular in the West. As horizontal looms are still used, which makes larger rugs awkward, there are few pieces beyond these sizes.

Kilims from Fars are currently found in sizable numbers from all of the weaving tribes. These are mostly woven with the common slit-tapestry technique, but about ten percent employ warp sharing. Perhaps the colors are brighter than those of pile fabrics, with a heavy use of vibrant, synthetic orange and red.

GABA RUGS

The so-called Gaba (or Gabeh) has been produced in increasing quantity during the last several decades. Despite an absence of demonstrably old

70.   LURI RUG, 20th century, 5'8" x 8'3". Warp: W. /2\, dark brown and gray brown. Weft: W. /2\, gray brown, 2 shoots. Pile: W. /2\. Knot: T-L, 30°, v. 7, h. 7, 49/sq inch. Sides: double over-cast with alternating blue and red brown wool. Ends: plain weave bands, turned under at bottom and loose warp ends at top. Colors (6): red violet field, medium blue, ivory, green, yellow, blue-black. This is most likely a product of the Mamassani, who inhabit an area west of the Qashgai. Courtesy of the Oriental Rug Co. of Berkeley, California.

specimens, I am assured by sources in Shiraz that this is a traditional tribal type. These rugs are wo-ven with naturally colored wools, in shades of ivory, brown, gray, and black. The design is usually simple and sparse, with very coarse knotting. I have found no village named Gaba, and local sources indicate that the term refers to grade and color scheme, much as "farsh" and "ghali" describe other types of rugs.

Gabas are made in many parts of the province and by both nomads and villagers. Most are Turkish knotted, however, which distinguishes them from the Persian knotted Gabas from Khurassan. The Fars products are also woven on a wool foundation, usually dark, and the fabric is soft and pliable. Occasionally small patches of dyed color are found, usually orange or red.

RUGS OF THE LURI

In an area north and west of the Qashgai sum-mer quarters, extending into the valleys south of Isfahan, a number of villages are inhabited by Luri, a people of Persian descent and language. In Fars the most important of these tribes is the Mamassani, while the more numerous Kuhgalu range farther to the north; scattered elements are found as far as Kurdistan. Their output of rugs has probably never been large, and most of them, particularly the bet-ter grade, are marketed in Shiraz.

In construction these rugs resemble other vil-lage products of the area, although the foundation is more likely to be of dark wool, with two wefts between each row of Persian knots. Some Luri rugs are woven with a rectangular medallion and anchor-like hooks at both ends, but we also see a design with jagged lines defining large lozenge-shaped areas along the length of the rug. These products usually lack the multiple small figures associated with Qash-gai rugs, for example, displaying simpler, broad expanses of color.

The Luri who live nearer to Isfahan weave a particularly coarse fabric on a cotton foundation, usually with thick, red-dyed wefts. Many of these rugs have panel designs and bear a superficial re-semblance to Afshari weaves.

YALAMEH

The so-called Yalameh rug, which has established an identity in Western markets only during the last several decades, is produced both by Persian villagers and Qashgai elements in an area south of Abadeh. The designs are distinctive, featuring lozenge-shaped panels, latch hooks, and relatively unbroken expanses of color, with few subsidiary figures. The colors are somewhat unusual for Fars, with considerable yellow and green.

These rugs may be woven with either a Persian or Turkish knot, the foundation is often of dark wool, and they tend toward the larger sizes (around 6 x 10 feet). Some of the most recent village examples have a cotton foundation.

NOTES

1. Edwards, A. C., *The Persian Carpet*, Duckworth, London, 1953, pp. 54-6.

2. *Ibid*, p. 67.

3. Mumford, J. K., *Oriental Rugs*, Scribners, New York, 1900, p. 103.

4. Jacobsen, C., *Oriental Rugs*, Tuttle, Rutland, Vt., 1962, p. 228.

5. Edwards, *op. cit.*, p. 126.

6. Edwards, *op. cit.*, p. 190.

7. Edwards, *op. cit.*, pp. 96-8.

8. Jacobsen, *op. cit.*, p. 255.

9. Edwards, *op. cit.*, p. 144.

10. Pope, A. U., *A Survey of Persian Art*, Vol. III, London, 1938-9, pp. 2386-7.

11. Fraser, J. B., *Narrative of a Journey into Khorassan*, London, 1825, p. 31 (Appendix B).

12. Conolly, A., *Journey to the North of India*, London, 1838, Vol. II, p. 11.

13. Edwards, *op. cit.*, pp. 185-6.

14. Bogolubov, A. A., *Tapisseries de L'Asie Centrale*, St. Petersburg, 1908.

15. Wegner, D., "Nomaden und Bauern-Teppich in Afghanistan," *Baessler-Archiv*, Neue Folge, Band XII, pp. 146-7.

16. Fraser, *op. cit.*, p. 31 (Appendix B).

17. Goldsmid, F. J., *Eastern Persia, an Account of the Journeys of the Persian Border Commission*, 1870-2. MacMillan, London, 1876, pp. 101, 186-7.

18. Fraser, *op. cit.*, p. 31 (Appendix B).

19. Garrod, Oliver, "The Nomadic Tribes of Persia Today," *Journal of the Royal Central Asian Society*, Vol. 33, pp. 32-46.

20. Dilley, A. U., *Oriental Rugs and Carpets*, rev. ed. by M. S. Dimand, Lippincott, New York, 1959, p. 50.

VI   TURKISH RUGS

American and European dealers visited the commercial centers of Turkey several decades before Persia was easily accessible. Consequently, the earliest rug books describe Turkish rugs more thoroughly than others. The information, however, was gleaned from the markets of Istanbul and Smyrna, not from the rug makers. Thus, although there is widespread agreement on the origin of certain designs, we find most of our present data are speculative and based on oral tradition. Little documentation exists on the production of Anatolian village and nomad rugs during the period emphasized by this survey, while rugs made after World War I until the present are mostly commercial products of minimal concern to us.

To many connoisseurs the apogee of the oriental rug is found in the Ghiordes, Kulah, and Ladik prayer rugs of the eighteenth and nineteenth centuries. Therefore, although these rugs are seldom available on the current market, we will give them considerable attention. Other major varieties from the same period will be described; however, rug weaving was so universal throughout Anatolia that we cannot make any pretense to completeness. Many types of obscure origin and unusual design defy classification.

Several other types of Turkish rug are generally thought to predate those under consideration by one or two centuries. The Sultan's court manufactories obviously influenced many village rugs. Examples of another class have been found in the churches of Transylvania; they bear an obvious relationship to later rugs, although we cannot specifically locate their place of manufacture.

THE LAND AND THE PEOPLE

Modern Turkey is a nation of thirty-one million people and a rapidly expanding economy. In the 1920s, under Kemal Ataturk, the land emerged from a long period of feudal stagnation and oriented itself toward western Europe and a basically democratic political system. The temporal power of the Mohammedan religion was fragmented, and the manner of living changed drastically in everything from clothing to the alphabet. The twentieth century has witnessed a sweeping revolution.

Geographically the country is enormously varied, ranging from the Aegean coast, with its moderate climate and rich, fertile river valleys, to the harsh angular mountains that blend with the Lesser Caucasus to the east. In between are a multitude of distinct regions. The major portion of the central Anatolian plateau consists of rolling hills with heavy rainfall and plentiful grasslands. In some areas the drainage converges into large lakes, leaving the surrounding terrain a damp marsh during the winter and a dustbowl during the dry season. Toward the east the elevation gradually rises, and the climate becomes more severe and arid; yet in one area south of the Tarsus Mountains the summers are as humid as on the Egyptian delta. The terrain, indeed, is so diverse as to justify the claim that nearly every European zone can find its counterpart somewhere in Turkey.

Historically the area has been subjected to a variety of influences that have left their marks upon the land and the Turkish character. Some of the earliest known inhabited sites have been found in southern Anatolia. Between the eighteenth and thirteenth centuries B.C. a strong imperial force, the Hittites, was based in central Anatolia. This was the first power to control large areas of the peninsula; even today the basic racial stock is similar to the sculptored likenesses found among the Hittite ruins. This empire was replaced by a number of lesser kingdoms. There was a heavy influx of Greek settlers, particularly around the Aegean coast. Troy was one of these smaller states; other Greek colonies were Smyrna, Ephesus, and Pergamum (modern Bergama). During the height of the Persian Empire under Cyrus and Darius, Anatolia was contested by the Greeks, and it passed several times from one sphere of influence to the other.

The next great empire to annex Anatolia was Rome, bringing the region under the influence of Christianity. Paul of Tarsus was of Anatolian birth, and the early church probably became more firmly established in Anatolia than any other area. The Emperor Constantine even moved his capital east to the city on the Bosphorus named for him. For nearly the next millennium the Byzantine empire continued to control an area around the city, although Anatolia began to break up into smaller segments, at times under the control of Persia. During the eleventh century, the Seljuks arrived from the east, and their continued migrations into Asia Minor gradually changed the complexion of the countryside. Chris-

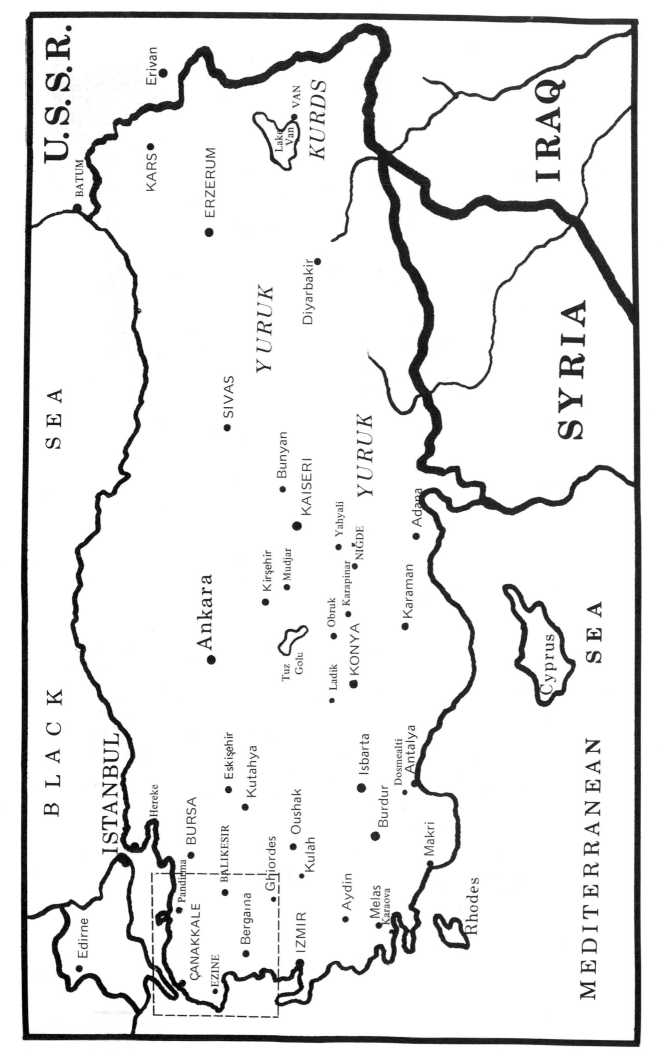

Map No. 8. Turkey, Areas of Rug Production

tianity was supplanted by the Turks' militant Mohammedanism; the language began a slow change from the commonly spoken Greek. For the last 850 years Anatolia has been controlled by descendants of these Turkish migrants, as the name of the country implies.

The basic peasant stock is Turkic elements mixed with the Mediterranean race that has inhabited the peninsula since Hittite times. The people are rather fair skinned, with dark eyes and hair, medium height and stockiness. They are virtually indistinguishable from many Balkan peoples; yet within their midst several ethnic groups retained separate identities through hundreds of years of Turkish rule. This was true to a large extent of Greek communities, which coexisted with an intact language and religion. Although persecuted at times, they occupied a well-defined place within the society. Those of Greek origin who adopted Islam were assimilated into the Turkish social fabric; the others remained separate. After the dissolution of the Turkish Empire, many of these peoples migrated to Greece and few now remain in Anatolia.

The other distinct people, important from a rug-making point of view, were the Armenians, who for at least four millennia inhabited an area in eastern Anatolia and the Lesser Caucasus. Although these people are Christian, they never lost their identity while the area was controlled by the Christian Byzantines. Despite conquest by a long list of invaders (Persians, Medes, Assyrians, Romans, Turks, and Mongols), they survived as a separate group. Even today their homeland is partitioned between Russia, Iran, and Turkey. Within the Turkish Empire the Armenians constituted a merchant class who were usually well tolerated. But in World War I they made the mistake of siding with the Russians; the Czarist military collapse left them helpless, and they became the victims of widely publicized atrocities. Most Armenians left Turkey, with large numbers settling in Greece and eastern Europe. Armenians had always been weavers; thus Turkey was deprived of some of its most skilled artisans. Probably many of the great Anatolian rugs were woven by Armenians and Greeks.

In southeastern Turkey lives another notable minority, one that has remained unassimilated despite its Moslem religion. The Kurds, whose population in Turkey exceeds three million, speak a language related to Persian. At times they have constituted a powerful force. Their numbers are divided between Turkey, Iraq, and Iran, and there has been considerable agitation for a separate national identity. Most of this dissidence has been directed toward the government of Iraq, although fewer Kurds live there than in the other two countries. Kurdish rugs, which vary greatly from Anatolia to the Kurdish areas of Iran, will also be discussed under Persian rugs.

Other groups not welded into the fabric of modern society are the nomadic tribes, of both Turkoman and Kurdish origin, who until recently lived much as they had for the last millennium. Most estimates place the number of people living a wandering, pastoral life at about two million. As in Iran, they range throughout the country. The government has exerted pressures to gradually suppress this way of life, and the army keeps careful control over the movements of each tribe.

CHARACTERISTICS OF THE TURKISH CARPET

Turkish rugs of the nineteenth century and before—the period involving our major interest—are distinguishable from Persian rugs of the same period, although the reasons for this are often not readily apparent and can be defined only in subjective terms.

Perhaps the most immediate clue is the difference in colors. The shades in Turkish rugs are on the whole brighter, the combinations blending in a characteristic harmony. One could describe the rugs as lighter than most of the classic Persian types (the dark field is almost unknown in Turkish rugs); yet they are less inclined to use pastel shades. Earth tones of brown, beige, and rust are employed perhaps more subtly, as in many antique specimens from Kulah and Melas, and green is relatively prominent. The use of a large central prayer niche of a solid color gives many Turkish rugs a dominant tonality, with the border colors playing a subsidiary role.

Nearly all Turkish rugs are rectilinear; yet there is a plastic element at times suggesting curvilinear forms. Another feature distinct from the Persian weaves is the rarity of repeating patterns, such as the Herati and Mina Khani. Most Turkish rugs have a single, over-all design.

In construction the older Anatolian rugs are almost uniformly of wool, with occasional use of silk and cotton. The weft and portions of white pile in many Ghiordes rugs are of cotton, and commercial pieces, particularly in larger sizes, were woven on a cotton foundation by the late nineteenth century. Otherwise the earlier rugs are all wool, varying greatly in texture in different regions. A characteristic feature is the use of a single shoot of unplied wool for the weft, which crosses two or more times between each row of knots. Rugs from other areas usually employ wefts twisted of two or more threads. The knotting, with very few exceptions, is Turkish, and seldom exceeds 150 to the square inch; more commonly it is below 100. Generally the later rugs are less finely woven, but in itself this is a poor measure of age.

In the following sections we will consider each major type individually, noting features that may be used for identification. In some cases reliable data are scarce.

THE GHIORDES PRAYER RUG

Few types present more frustrating problems than the Ghiordes prayer rug, as much that has been written about it is clearly fictitious or at best questionable. Most major museums and many private collections boast examples of these rugs. Some connoisseurs rank them among the finest products in the history of weaving. Since the late nineteenth century they have consistently brought high prices, and most rug books include descriptions of their origins and development. When we examine these data, however, the picture suddenly becomes confused.

Sources basically agree in attributing these rugs to the vicinity of Ghiordes (modern Gördes), an Anatolian town of less than 10,000 population to the west of Oushak. Our suspicions are initially aroused, however, by comments in the older rug books on the town's history. Hawley[1] notes that "Ghiordes. . . is on the site of the ancient Gordium where tradition says that the father of Midas dedicated his chariot to Jupiter, and Alexander severed the bark which bound the pole to the yoke." Lewis[2] also mentions that "it is the ancient Gordium from which was named the Gordian knot that Alexander the Great cut." Indeed, virtually every author to comment about the town (Mumford, Jacobsen, Schlosser, and many others) repeats the same misinformation. On reading such unanimity of opinion, one would be tempted to accept such an assertion without question and proceed to other matters; if, however, one were to consult a source no more remote than a good encyclopedia, the story would appear in a different light. Gordium, the capital of ancient Phrygia, lies at the junction of the Sangarius and Tembris rivers, about fifty miles WSW of Ankara. The ruins have been extensively excavated, and the site is not currently inhabited. On consulting a map of Turkey, we find that this location is approximately 400 miles to the east of Ghiordes and appears to have no connection with it. What, then, might we conclude from such an inconsistency?

The author has found such researches disturbing in a number of ways. First, we become suspicious of the possibility that other "facts" we have previously accepted without question from the literature are no more valid. Second, we wonder where such misinformation gets started. Is it invented by dealers or the imaginative writers of rug books? Third, and more specific, we wonder whether the "authorities," who, decade after decade, have made such obvious mistakes, are any more exact about other data they provide for the Ghiordes prayer rug. Our doubts are reinforced by a technical examination of rugs with a Ghiordes design; they reveal such diversity that we can scarcely believe all the rugs to have been made in the same place. We find warps of wool, silk, and cotton; wefts of dark wool, red-dyed wool, silk, white or blue cotton, and linen. The ends and sides are similarly varied, while colors include virtually anything to be found in the Middle East; even the wool differs greatly from one rug to the next. One might wonder whether we have adequate information to sort out this tangle.

Fortunately we may be fairly clear on certain points. We know, for example, that the typical Ghiordes design elements (e.g., the open field mihrab with pillars or a hanging lamp) are found on Ottoman court rugs of the sixteenth and seventeenth centuries; clearly these rugs influenced the later village weaves. We also have a clear tradition that rugs have been woven in the Ghiordes area at least since the eighteenth century. We are just as certain, however, that from the late nineteenth century there have been numerous copies from other areas, as a great enthusiasm developed for these rugs after they were featured in several major European exhibits. There were copies from Kayseri, Bursa, Istanbul, Panderma, Hereke, Corfu, Tabriz, and numerous missions and orphanages throughout Anatolia. Even Europe contributed to the production, with Italian and Bulgarian examples in the familiar patterns. Usually these were represented merely as new rugs, but in many cases there were efforts to artificially produce a look of great age. Some of these specimens, which were chemically washed, heated and singed, or otherwise damaged, were then treated to elaborate repairs, as if to indicate their owners at a remote time had thought enough of them to invest greatly in their restoration. Only a small percentage of the rugs one sees with Ghiordes designs are the genuine article; copies from Kayseri are probably the most common. Distinguishing the real Ghiordes from the fake is, moreover, often quite difficult, although several criteria provide a reasonably consistent guide.

71.   GHIORDES PRAYER RUG, late 18th century, 6'4" x 4'8". Warp: W. /2\, undyed. Weft: W. /1 , undyed or red, 2 shoots. "Lazy lines" prominent. Pile: W. & C. (white). Knot: T, alternate warps depressed 45°, v. 14, h. 10, 140/sq inch. Sides: ... Ends: ... Colors (10): dark blue field, 2 shades of light blue, red, deep green, 2 shades of olive, white, dark brown, deep yellow. Although there is much controversy around the dating of these rugs, this specimen would generally be described as late 18th century. The foundation is all wool, and the mihrab is generally uncluttered with the floral figures found in later pieces.   Courtesy of the Oriental Rug Co. of Berkeley.

72.   GHIORDES PRAYER RUG, 19th century, 4' x 6'7". Warp: W /2\, undyec. Weft: C. /2\, undyed, 2 strands, both loose. Pile: W. & C. (white). Knot: T, alternate warps slightly depressed, v. 11, h. 8. 88/sq inch. Sides: double selvage of white cotton over 2 thickened warps. Ends: ... Colors (7): red field, pink, light blue, light green, apricot, dark brown, ivory. The stripe border and cotton wefts are both typical of later Ghiordes rugs, while the field has shrunk and is invaded by floral elements.

73.   GHIORDES RUG, mid-19th century, 4'2" x 7'4". Warp: W. /3\, light. Weft: C. /1 , white, 2 strands, with prominent "lazy lines." Pile: W. /2\ & C. (white). Knot: T, v. 7, h. 6, 42/sq inch. Sides: double selvage of white cotton over 2 thickened warps. Ends: .... Colors (7): red, pink, dark brown, ivory, olive, light blue, yellow. The "double mihrab" design is usually found on later examples, although this border is most common on the earlier prayer rugs.

The earliest Ghiordes rugs (eighteenth century or before) arc gencrally more curvilinear and show a relatively greater proportion of the surface occupied by the mihrab, which is usually dark blue, red, or ivory, and may have columns, less commonly a hanging lamp, and usually cross panels at both ends. In construction these rugs show a white wool warp (except for a few specimens with a red or blue dyed warp) and wool, single-shoot, untwisted wefts, often dyed red. Alternate warps are moderately to severely depressed, while the sides have a weft selvage; the ends may show a narrow plain weave band in red or dark blue. The knotting is usually between 120 and 200 to the square inch.

In the nineteenth century there were several changes in both construction and design. The warps, still of white wool, are more nearly at the same level, and the wefts are often of a darker wool. By late century there were rugs with cotton wefts that also frequently used white cotton for portions of the pile. The mihrab became relatively smaller as the borders increased in number, often in the form of numerous small stripes. The mihrab was also more likely to have small figures or hooks protruding from the sides into the field, and the hanging lamp became more prominent, at times accompanied by other figures arranged along the base of the field. To this generation belong a number of double-mihrab rugs and the variety known as the "Kiz Ghiordes," which was allegedly woven by young girls as a part of their dowries. Some of the rugs show an added silk fringe, at times extending up the sides for a few inches; obviously this was added at a later date.

One may observe frequent zigzag lines on the back of these rugs. These lines were also prominent, for a different reason, in the earlier carpets. Formerly that portion of the weft that crossed the mihrab was made to match the general color of the field. A weft of dark wool, for example, would be used for a blue mihrab rug and one of red-dyed wool for a crimson field. This was accomplished by zigzag weaving along the side of the mihrab so that the remainder of the rug would have wefts of the usual color.

Dealers and writers of rug books have attached a number of rather fanciful names to the Ghiordes, although they seem only to deepen the confusion. *Tchoubouklou* (or *Shobokli*) is a term referring to those rugs with a stripe border, while the reason for labeling a rug as a *Basra* (or *Bastra*) Ghiordes, apparently after the name of an Iraqi city, is far from clear. *Medjedieh* Ghiordes is a term that dealers use to describe a late nineteenth-century type with sparse design elements on a red or white field, often with no distinct border. These rugs were allegedly woven in conscious imitation of the European styles favored by Sultan Abd ul-Mejid (1839-61).

Apparently some rugs in the old patterns have been woven in very recent times, as there are fine examples from the early twentieth century. However, most rugs of the area had by then become strictly commercial. Among the late nineteenth-century weaves are some very large rugs (up to room size) in the old prayer patterns and familiar colors,

but with a coarser texture. During the 1920s many large and undistinguished rugs were produced around Ghiordes, with designs supplied to appeal to foreign tastes. These rugs resemble in many ways the later commercial Oushaks.

Determining the place of origin for Ghiordes copies may be next to impossible, although there are several well-defined groups that we can identify with some certainty. Among the wool rugs, those of Tabriz are characterized by a more naturalistic rendition of the floral elements, and these are to be considered as adaptations rather than copies. Silk copies were made in Kayseri, Hereke, Panderma, and no doubt in other places. Those of Kayseri, which were more often mercerized cotton than silk, usually have thick cotton wefts and sides with a weft selvage woven over four or five thickened warp strands. Hereke rugs are usually more finely woven. Few of these pieces approach the color combinations of the originals, in which the field gives a predominant tone to the entire rug. Without a subtle blending of color, the designs themselves are of little interest, and most copies may be seen at a glance to be inferior rugs.

74. GHIORDES RUGS, "Mejedieh." a) 4' x 6'1". b) 3'9" x 5'9". Both of these pieces have wool warps and cotton /2\ wefts. The first has a cochineal red field and 77 knots to the inch; it is certainly older and probably dates about 1880. The second piece has a bright red field, probably synthetic, and 45 knots to the inch. Both are the so-called "Mejedieh" Ghiordes, which represents an encroachment of European styles into Turkish decor.

KULAH

Kulah lies about fifty miles south of Ghiordes and also numbers about ten thousand inhabitants. The area has long produced rugs of several distinct types, most notably a prayer rug that is often mentioned with the Ghiordes as among the most successful of Turkish weaves. The two types are similar in construction, with a wool warp and weft, but the knotting is usually much looser and the wool softer in the Kulah. The wefts differ in being plied of two or three strands, and they are often undyed.

The colors are much more mellow and subdued in the Kulah, with yellow, brown, the more solemn shades of red, and minor use of green and white. The mihrab also is relatively longer, and a cross panel usually is found only above the arch. The borders are variable, but in later pieces often consist of thin, relatively simple stripes rather than the intricate floral forms of the early rugs. There are many rugs with double-mihrab designs (called "hearth rugs"), but perhaps the most distinctive feature of many Kulahs is the manner in which the ground is filled. Whereas the Ghiordes usually has an open field of solid color, the Kulah is likely to show repeated floral forms or even portions of landscape, with figures of houses and trees. Many of the older books call these "cemetery rugs" (*Mezarlik Kulahs*), suggesting that a burial place is depicted, but this seems most unlikely. Many of the rugs have columns along the sides of the mihrab, but the hanging lamp is not so prominent.

Several other types of rug also originate in the Kulah area, many showing an extremely coarse weave. During the 1920s a heavy commerical carpet resembling the Oushak was woven. Now there is a small output of prayer rugs in bright colors, and occasional specimens may be found in the old designs. One also finds in Kulah new copies of Bergama designs with the typical red and blue tonality.

LADIK

Ladik rugs are classified with the Kulah and Ghiordes as the apex of Anatolian village prayer design. There are several Turkish towns known by the name of Ladik, but the one associated with rug weaving lies north and west of Konia in a region where much wool is produced.

In construction the Ladik is like many Konia rugs, with a warp of naturally colored wool and a weft of natural, dark brown, or red-dyed wool. Alternate warps are slightly to severely depressed, and the knotting is among the tightest found in all Anatolian rugs. In shape the Ladik prayer rug is often quite long in relation to its width.

In color the Ladik is characterized by its vibrant shades of red and blue, often as subtly blended as in the Ghiordes but with more somber effect. The border usually consists of two subsidiary stripes of running vines and a wider stripe in which the Rhodian lily alternates with a characteristic rosette, on either a light or dark ground.

The field may be open or interrupted by a hanging lamp or stylized flowers, both of which suggest a later origin. The arch consists of a series of step-like progressions toward the top; frequently with each step a latch hook extends into the area above the niche. The cross panels, which may be at either or both ends of the niche, are generally the deepest found in any Anatolian prayer design. They classically show reciprocal vandykes, with straight stems culminating in a tulip-like flower. Often the color of the cross panel matches that of the mihrab, and this imparts a particular tonality to the rug.

Production of these rugs probably covered a period of several hundred years, decreasing sharply before World War I. There are many modern copies, although most are woven in other areas, such as Kirsehir.

A surprising number of Ladiks are dated and apparently were woven during the eighteenth century, although the authenticity of many pieces has been questioned. Another class of prayer rug, with columns dividing the field, is often given the name of Ladik, but most examples seem related to earlier western Anatolian types and are clearly influenced by Ottoman court pieces.

As in the case of Ghiordes, the history of Ladik has been romanticized in several rug books. Its earlier name of Laodicea is often thought to refer to the more important location of the same name—one of the seven cities to which St. John addressed the Revelations. But we speak of another city entirely; the modern name for it is Eskişehir.

KONIA

Konia (the ancient Iconium) is one of the largest cities of Asia Minor. Its population is nearly a hundred thousand, and the surrounding province is one of the richest regions for the production of soft, luxurious wool. Ancient carpet fragments from the mosques of Konia suggest that weaving has thrived here at least since the twelfth century. A variety of designs come from the Konia area, including many nomad rugs usually labeled as Yürüks. The older pieces featured earth shades of brown, beige, dull

76. KULAH RUG, early 19th century, 4'3" x 6'9". Warp: W. /3\. Weft: W. /2\, 2 shoots, undyed. Pile: W. /2\. Knot: T-L, 30⁰, v. 8, h. 6, 48/sq inch. Sides: double overcast of dull yellow wool over 2 warps. Ends: .... Colors (6): field of burnt gold, dark brown outlining, light blue, bright red, light green, ivory. Among Kulahs the double-mihrab rug is probably as common as the prayer rug.

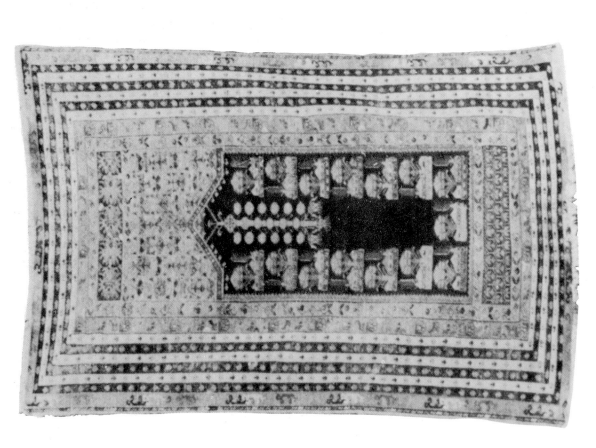

75. KULAH RUG, 19th century, 3'10" x 5'8". (Technical data unavailable.) The Kulah is usually more loosely woven and pliable than the Ghiordes, with soft, muted colors. The stripe border is a relatively late feature, and the landscape elements in the field are alleged to depict a graveyard. Among Collection of Chris Alexander, Berkeley, California.

78. LADIK PRAYER RUG, 19th century, 3'5" x 5'8". Warp: W. /3\, light. Weft: W. /1 , medium brown and light brown, 2 shoots. Pile: W. /2\. Knot: T-L, 20-30°, v. 9, h. 8: 72/sq inch. Sides: double selvage over 2 warps in alternating colors. Ends: ... (rewoven areas at both ends). Colors (8): red field, light blue and medium blue, yellow, ivory, pale gray, salmon, dark brown. This piece dates to about same time as Fig. 77, but the configuration of the mihrab is different and the field somewhat wider.

77. LADIK PRAYER RUG, 19th century, 3'4" x 5'10". Warp: W. /2\, undyed, light. Weft: W. /1 , dark brown, 2 shoots. Pile: W. /2\. Knot: T-L, 20°, v. 8, h. 8, 64/sq inch. Sides: ... Ends: ... Colors (6): red field, dark blue, light blue, dark brown, yellow, ivory. The relatively deep cross-panel with tulip-like floral figures is common on earlier Ladiks and becomes smaller and simpler during the 19th century. Earlier Ladiks are likely to have an open field.

79. KONIA PRAYER RUG, mid-19th century, 4'3" x 4'10". Warp: W. /2\, **light** brown. Weft: W. /1 , dyed brick red, 2-3 shoots. Pile: W. /2\. Knot: T, v. 7, h. 6,42/ sq inch. Sides: double selvage of red wool over 3 thickened warps. Ends: upper—plain weave band, ends selvaged, with terminal portions loose. Lower—plain weave band. Colors (5): brick red field, deep yellow, light blue, dark blue, dark brown. Older Konia rugs are characterized by their fleecy wool and loose weave. The design elements are diverse and the colors usually subdued.

yellow, and rust red, with an emphasis on lightness and restraint in color combinations. Most of the village rugs have red wefts and loose, fairly coarse knotting; the nomad pieces often have a foundation of dark wool or goat hair.

Ladik rugs as described above are the best-known local type from the province, but several others are notable. The towns of Karapinar and Tashpinar are the homes of recognizable rugs. The Karapinar fabric is heavy, with bold, simple designs, strongly resembling Caucasian fabrics. The Tashpinar, however, is somewhat tighter, thinner, and more likely to show crude but realistic floral forms. Even recent examples may have eight or nine different colors, which is unusual for Anatolian rugs. Many other distinct types are woven around Konia, including designs with crude columns (clearly descended from eighteenth and nineteenth century column rugs) and others with a characteristic extra border of turret-like figures at both ends.

A great number of small mats (yastiks) are also woven here, and kilim production is probably the highest in Anatolia. In the trade Turkish kilims of diverse origins have carried the name of Karaman, after a town somewhat south and east of Konia. Obruck is also a production center, particularly for prayer kilims in the slit-tapestry technique, with additional brocading, and large kilims woven in two longitudinal panels.

OUSHAK (Uşak)

Oushak is one of the larger towns of western Anatolia. Its tradition as a weaving center goes back at least three hundred years. Although it is not our intention here to survey the classic weaves, many of them now in museums, we shall record a number of recent products from both the town and surrounding villages that are distinguishable as specific types. Most common of these is the easily recognized commercial carpet of the late nineteenth century, with subtle reds and blues and large-scale floral designs. By the 1920s these had changed drastically in color to vivid reds, turquoise, and green.

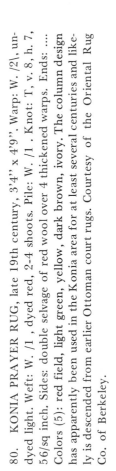

81. DEMIRCI RUG, 5'7" x 4'9", mid-19th century. Warp: W. /2\, undyed light. Weft: W. /2\, dyed red-orange, 1 shoot alternating with 2 shoots. Pile: W. /2\. Knot: T-L, 30°, v. 9, h. 7, 63/sq inch. Sides: double selvage of red wool over 2 thickened warps. Ends: very narrow plain weave band in pale red with loose warp ends. Colors (11): 3 shades of red, 3 shades of blue from very light to medium, light and olive green, white, yellow, field and outlines in brown. In the trade these rugs are often called "Komurdju Kulahs," but the colors, except for the dark ground, are similar to those of Oushak. New examples of these rugs do not appear on the market, and production apparently stopped early in the 20th century.

80. KONIA PRAYER RUG, late 19th century, 3'4" x 4'9". Warp: W. /2\, undyed light. Weft: W. /1, dyed red, 2-4 shoots. Pile: W. /1 . Knot: T, v. 8, h. 7, 56/sq inch. Sides: double selvage of red wool over 4 thickened warps. Ends: .... Colors (5): red field, light green, yellow, dark brown, ivory. The column design has apparently been used in the Konia area for at least several centuries and likely is descended from earlier Ottoman court rugs. Courtesy of the Oriental Rug Co. of Berkeley.

The construction was often quite coarse, with knotting at times less than thirty to the square inch, but the wool has been of good quality and the pile thick and luxuriant.

The development of Oushak designs can be traced back to the medallion and star Oushaks of the seventeenth and eighteenth centuries. Until very recently the floors of the larger Istanbul mosques (such as the Süleymaniye and Sultan Ahmet mosques) were covered with hundreds of older rugs, often several deep. For some reason most of these came from the Oushak district, and they were obviously acquired and gradually replaced over a period of centuries. A piece of apparent eighteenth century origin might lie next to an early twentieth century weave, a graphic illustration of the way colors and designs evolved over the decades. Rug making has decreased greatly in the Oushak area, but some small pieces are still woven in the villages, usually with a dominant bright red.

DEMIRCI

The villages around Demirci have long produced a rug that for some curious reason has been most often described as a Kulah, or "Komurdju" Kulah. (They are so labeled in the catalog for the 1968 Textile Museum exhibit of Turkish rugs.) Actually they bear little resemblance to Kulah rugs in design or construction, as the wefts are single plied, usually dyed red. The weft is often found to cross only once between each row of knots, or alternate rows are single and double wefted, a technique most unusual among Turkish rugs. The colors are similar to those of the Oushak area, with strong reliance on red and blue, although many of these rugs show a vibrant yellow, usually in the border. The field is often dark brown.

Demirci rugs are virtually all in scatter sizes, although there are a few runners. Some have design elements that may be traced back to the so-called Transylvania rugs of the sixteenth and seventeenth centuries. Production of hand-knotted rugs has almost ceased in the area, although in the town machine-made rugs are produced.

BERGAMA

About twenty miles from the Aegean stands the ancient city of Bergama (formerly Pergamum), which in the past has been a great center of learning and commerce. During the centuries of Greek primacy in western Anatolia, the city's population was far greater than its current twenty thousand inhabitants, and ruins are found on all sides of the present site. A wide variety of rugs are labeled in the books as Bergamas—the name seems to have become a catch-all for otherwise unclassified Anatolian weaves. Some rugs bearing the label are clearly of eastern Anatolian origin, while others show the texture and colors of rugs from the southern coast of Asia Minor. One must accept the label with caution.

Actually, the situation need not be so confusing. The northwestern coast of Asia Minor is readily accessible to travelers, and enough rugs are still made there in traditional village designs that one can identify with some certainty most antique specimens.

Rugs from the immediate area around Bergama are now usually small and adhere fairly rigidly to the traditional color scheme of brick red, dark blue, and white, although older specimens may also have small amounts of green and yellow. The woven bands at the ends are red, blue, or red and blue striped, with the warp ends often braided together. The wefts are red, usually crossing twice between each row of knots.

Several subvarieties of Bergama rugs are made in nearby villages. The so-called Yagci-bedir resembles the classic Bergama and has the same color scheme; most are in prayer designs, with numerous narrow border stripes. They are made to the west of the city, around the town of Dikili and in smaller villages along the Aegean coast. The town of Kozak, north of Bergama, also produces a type recognizable to the Istanbul dealers. These rugs are somewhat heavier and more variable in design.

The Yuntdag area, south of the city, produces rugs of several types, with the same compartment designs found in many antique pieces. The rugs are larger and heavier than the typical Bergama, occasionally having cotton wefts. The colors are the brightest from this area; recent examples feature pernicious shades of aniline orange and green.

The relation between recent Bergamas and Turkish rugs of the sixteenth and seventeenth centuries has long intrigued observers. Many Bergamas have design elements found in the so-called Transylvania rugs, while other examples clearly reveal elements of the column prayer rugs. A few of the older rugs also show peculiar technical characteristics, such as an occasional use of red or blue dyed warps; some nineteenth century Bergamas had beads, buttons, or other small colored objects sewn onto the ends. Generally the designs have become simpler over the decades and the rugs smaller. A wide variety of flat woven fabrics is made around Bergama, usually in some form of brocading rather than the slit tapestry technique more favored to the east.

82.   BERGAMA RUG, probably 18th century, 5'9" x 6'1". Warp: W. /2\, undyed. Weft: W. /1 , dyed red, 2 strands, both loose. Pile: W. /2\. Knot: T, v. 7, h. 7, 49/sq inch. Sides: double selvage in dark blue wool over 3 thickened warps. Ends: .... Colors (5): brick red, light and dark blue, white, dark brown. This design, in much more regular form, is found on many 19th century Bergama rugs, but the rampant asymmetry here suggests an earlier origin.

83.   BERGAMA RUG, early 20th century, 3'4" x 4'6". Warp: W. /2\ light. Weft: W. /1 , dyed red, 2 shoots. Pile: W. /2\. Knot: T, v. 5, h. 6, 30/sq inch. Sides: double selvage of red wool over 3 warps. Ends: plain weave bands of red and loose warp ends. Colors (4): red, medium blue, white, dark brown. This design, which bears an obvious relationship to the central field design of the Ghiodes rug in Fig. 73 (and which can also be traced to much earlier Transylvanian types), is most common around the town of Bergama itself. Like many rugs of the Aegean area, its basic form has changed little during the last several centuries, and new examples are still found.

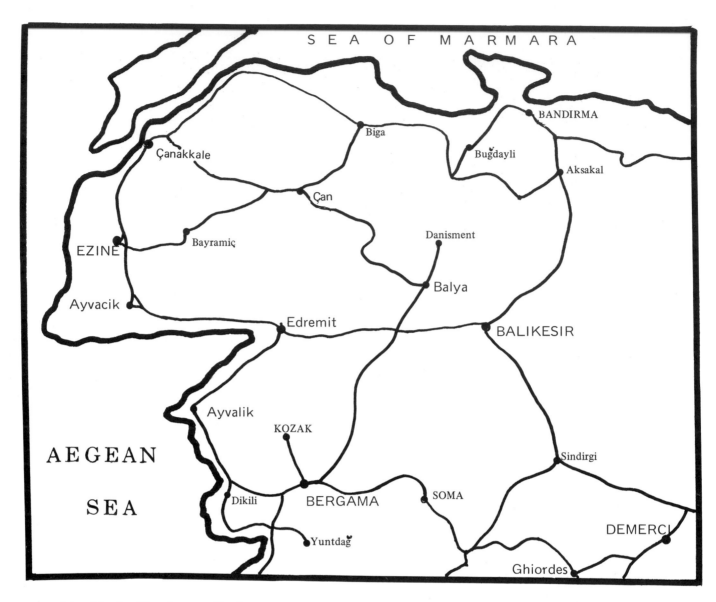

Map No. 9   The Aegean Region

ÇANAKKALE

Çanakkale rugs are almost universally labeled as Bergamas in the United States and Europe, but, since they are made in an entirely different area over a hundred miles to the north and west of Bergama, they would seem deserving of a separate identity. They are also among the most illustrious Turkish rugs in ancestry. Comparison of recent and antique specimens leaves little question that the so-called large-pattern Holbein rugs of the sixteenth and seventeenth centuries were woven in the Çanakkale area. Perhaps nowhere in Anatolia has there been such a continuity of design at a village level; one can see rugs in late Renaissance paintings that resemble the products of today.

The villages weaving these rugs are situated somewhat inland from Çanakkale and Ezine. The former is a town of some importance within a few miles from the ruins of Troy. Here one can also catch a ferry boat across the Dardanelles.

Çanakkale rugs are more loosely woven than those of Bergama. The weft is almost invariably dyed red (crossing two to five times between each row of knots), and the ends show wide plain-weave bands, usually of red but occasionally with terminal stripes of yellow or black. The sides are double selvaged in red or blue yarn, but the general color scheme, while relying on these two colors, has more variability than the Bergama. Green, apricot, and yellow are more prominent, while some rugs show much white.

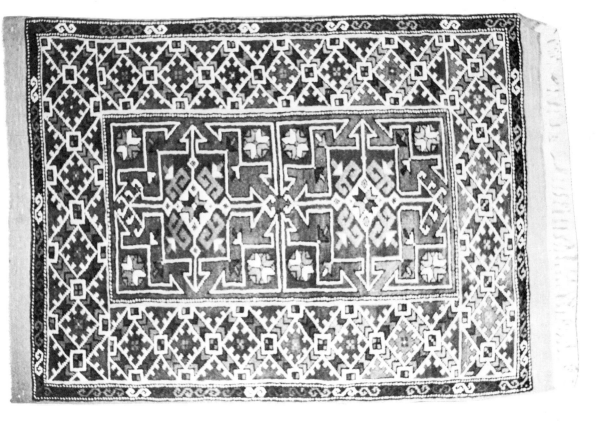

85. EZINE RUG, early twentieth century, 4'4" x 2'9". Warp: W. /2\, undyed, light. Weft: W. /1 , dyed pale red, 2-5 shoots. Pile: W. /2\. Knot: T v. 5 h, 7, 35/ sq inch. Sides: double selvage of light blue over 3 warps. Ends: red plain weave bands with loose warps. Colors (6): rust red, light blue, dark blue, ivory, yellow, dark brown. As with other northwest Anatolian designs still in use, this is visibly descended from earlier "large-pattern Holbeins."

84. YAGCIBEDIR RUG from Bergama area, 3'5" x 4'8". Warp: W. /2\, light. Weft: W. /1 , dyed red, 2 shoots. Pile: W. /2\. Knot: T, v. 6, h. 7, 42/sq inch. Sides: double selvage of blue wool over 3 warps. Ends: 3-4 inch band of plain weave in red and blue stripes, with loose ends braided together. Colors (5): red, medium blue, white, dark brown, rust red. These rugs are made in small villages to the west and south of Bergama, and most are in prayer designs with relatively simple borders.

86.   EZINE PRAYER RUGS, 20th century, a) 2'8" x 4'; b) 2'6" x 3'6". Warp: W. /2\, light. Weft: W. /2\, dyed red, 2 shoots. Pile: W. /2\. Knot: T, a) v. 7, h. 6, 42/sq inch; b) v. 8, h. 6, 48/sq inch. Sides: double selvage of red wool over three warps in a), 5 warps in b). Ends: a) red plain weave band; b) red plain weave with stripes of black and yellow. Colors: a) (5) ivory, medium blue, apricot, red, yellow; b) (7) brick red field, medium blue, yellow-orange, white, bright red, green, black. Small prayer rugs in numerous designs are still made around Ezine, with the designs becoming progressively more simple. Arranged horizontally across the middle of (b) are three large knots with the yarn left several inches long (lying the same direction as the mihrab). This is fairly typical of rugs from the Aegean area.

There are at least six major designs from the area. The commonest one is built around a central rectangle, with two squares above and below. Rugs from around Ezine often have two star-like medallions. The borders have undergone much more change than the field patterns, as the original Kufic figures on the earliest rugs have evolved into progressively simpler forms.

Çanakkale rugs are larger than other western Anatolian types, at times reaching sizes up to 7 x 11 feet. Recent specimens often have poor dyes that run. I have long been aware that the Turkish dealers have many of these rugs treated to appear as antiques. This seemed difficult to accomplish without ruining the rug, but on my last trip to Istanbul I learned otherwise while touring the processing plant. Soon after the rug is doused with water and bleach, it is quickly placed into a centrifuge. This removes the water before there can be much run-

ning; then the rug is transferred to a large, wooden cylinder that acts like a clothes dryer. One could wish that such impressive technology could be expended by the dyers!

MELAS

The Melas prayer rug features a characteristic mihrab with indentations along the sides, setting off a lozenge-shaped area on top. The colors are almost always earth tones, with rust red, tawny shades of brown, and a subdued mauve, which are remarkably similar from rug to rug. Another common type of Melas (from the nearby town of Karaova) shows panel or stripe designs and a more frequent use of green, while other Melas rugs show a close enough resemblance to these two types to make identification relatively simple.

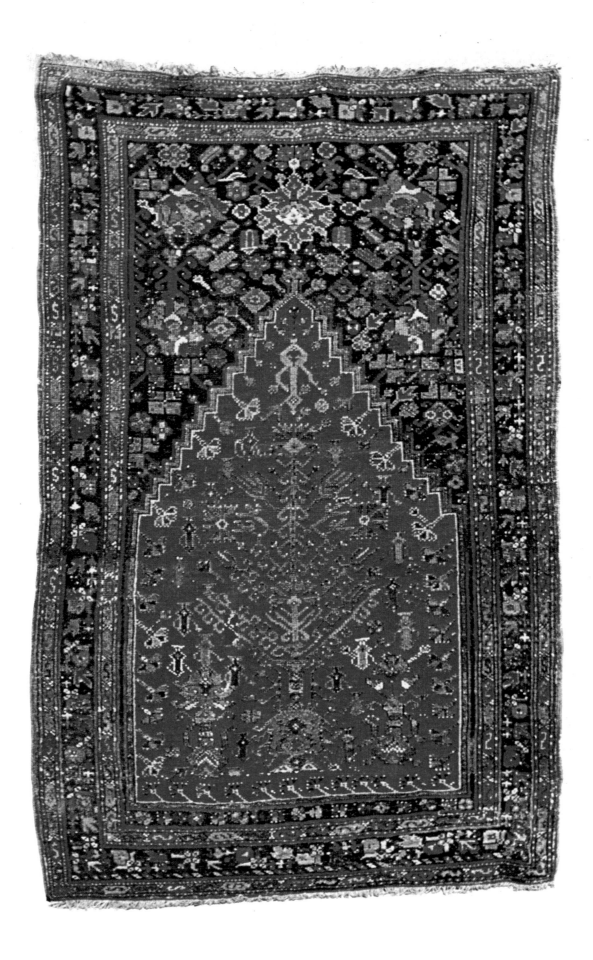

Color Plate IX. OUSHAK PRAYER RUG, mid-nineteenth century, 5' x 7'10". Warp: W. /2\, undyed light. Weft: W. /2\, dyed red, 2 strands, both loose. Pile: W. /2\. Knot: T, alternate warps very slightly depressed, v. 6, h. 5, 30/sq inch. Sides: double selvage of red wool over 2 thickened warps. Ends: very narrow plain weave band with loose warp ends. Colors (7): rust red field, light and dark blue, yellow, dark brown, ivory, pink. The evolution of the floral motifs found on Oushak rugs can be traced back at least several centuries.

Color Plate X. BERGAMA RUG, probably eighteenth century, 5'3" x 7'4". Warp: W. /2\, undyed. Weft: W. /1, dyed red, 2 shoots. Pile: W. /2\. Knot: T, v. 8, h. 7, 56/sq inch. Sides: double selvage over 8 warps, with red and blue forming a sawtooth pattern. Ends: bands of blue plain weave survive at both ends. Colors (5): brick red, dark and light blue, dark brown, ivory. The design shows an obvious relationship to the so-called "column Ladiks," and can be traced back to Ottoman court rugs of the sixteenth century.

Color Plate XI. EZINE RUG, late 19th century, 6'5'' x 4'8''. Warp: W. /2\, undyed. Weft: W. /1 , dyed red, 2-5 shoots. Pile: W. /2\. Knot: T, v. 5, h. 6, 30/sq inch. Sides: double selvage of red wool over 4 thickened warps. Ends: plain weave band of red with a few terminal rows of black wool remaining. Loose warp ends. Colors (6): ivory field, medium blue, brick red, yellow, light green, dark brown. This design occurs virtually unchanged in rugs dating back at least several centuries.

Color Plate XII. ÇANAKKALE RUG, late 19th-century, 6'3" x 9'10". Warp: W. /2\, undyed. Weft: W. /1, dyed red, 2-4 shoots, all loose. Pile: W. /2\. Knot: T, alternate warps very slightly depressed, v. 8, h. 6, 48/sq inch. Sides: double selvage in red wool over 3 thickened warps. Ends: upper—4 inch band of red plain weave, selvage, and loose ends. Lower—4-inch band of red plain weave, looped warp ends left free. Colors (6): brick red, blue, light green, yellow, dark brown, ivory. This type of rug would ordinarily be called a Bergama in the trade, although it was made considerably to the north in a village near Çanakkale.

Color Plate XIII. KIRSEHIR PRAYER RUG, 19th century, 3'8" x 5'3". Warp: W. /2\, light. Weft: W. /1 , dyed red, 2 shoots. Pile: W. /2\. Knot: T-L, 30°, v. 9, h. 8, 72/sq inch. Sides: double overcast in light green wool over 2 warps. Ends: narrow woven bands of light green wool. Colors (9): green field, carmine, apricot, yellow, mauve, dark brown, 2 shades of light blue, ivory. 19th century Kirsehirs have never received proper recognition for their variety of design and subtle blending of many colors; better examples certainly bear comparison with Ghiordes and Ladik rugs. The colors often include a relatively heavy use of green and yellow.

Color Plate XIV. TURKISH PRAYER KILIM (slit-tapestry technique), 19th century, 5'1" x 6'6". Warp: W. /2\, light, 10/inch. Weft: W. /1, dyed in various colors, 24/inch. Some figures outlined in brocade. Sides: continuous weft. Ends: adjacent warps knotted together. Colors (9): ivory field, 2 shades of mauve, red, brick red, medium blue, medium brown, pale yellow, light green. From the design and colors this would seem to be from western Anatolia, although kilims in general can seldom be given a precise localization.

Collection of Emmett Eiland, Berkeley, California.

Color Plate XV. "VERNEH" RUG, early 20th century, 5'7" x 6'. Warp: W. /2\, dyed red, 20/sq inch. Weft: W. /2\, dyed red. (Design woven in weft float brocade.) Sides: double selvage of red wool, with two loops over 3 warps each. Ends: plain weave of red wool, with adjacent ends knotted together. Colors (7): rust red ground weave, light green, light blue, yellow, white (cotton), black, and mauve-brown. This is one type among several that are usually labeled as "vernehs," an obscure term of uncertain origin. Certainly most of them are of Eastern Anatolian origin, although some may have been woven in the Caucasus. They are often, but not necessarily, made in two pieces, and usually their age is exaggerated. They still turn up occasionally in the Istanbul bazaar, either on a dark wool or a red wool foundation.

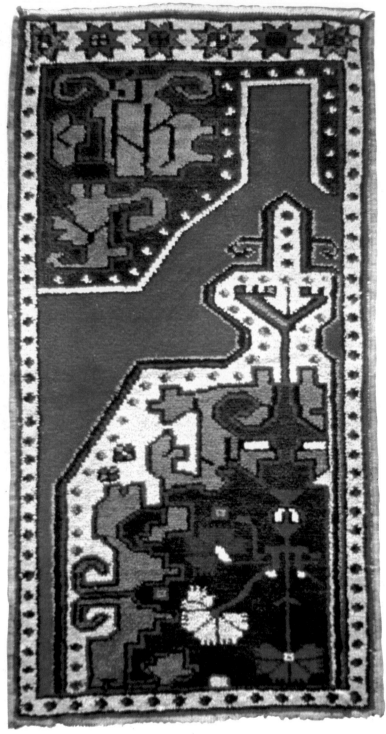

A

B

Color Plate XVI. TURKISH "SAMPLERS" from the Konia area. a) 1'9" x 3'4"; b) 2'7½" x 3'4¼". Warp: a) C. /6\, white; b) W. /2\, light. Weft: a) C. /2\, gray; b) W. /1, dark, 2 shoots. Pile: W. /2\. Knot: T, a) v. 7, h. 6, 42/sq inch; b) v. 9, h. 7, 63/sq inch. Sides: double selvage over 3 warps. Ends: plain weave bands; loose ends knotted together on (b). Colors: a) (9) red field, dark blue, deep red, light green, yellow, white, black, medium blue, apricot. b) (11) brick red, bright red, medium and light blue, white, black, gold, light green, olive green, mauve, deep pink. Both samplers are from villages east of the city of Konia. (a) is in a style suggestive of Karapinar (although probably not from that village), while (b) is likely from Ṭashpinar. Rugs from both towns appear frequently in the big bazaars, but they are seldom found in the United States.

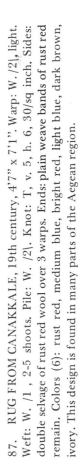

88. CANAKKALE RUG, 20th century, 6'4" x 4'1". Warp: W. /3\, light wool. Weft: W. /1 , 2-4 shoots, dyed red. Pile: W. /2\. Knot: T, v. 6, h. 6, 36/sq inch. Sides: double selvage of red wool over 3 warps. Ends: plain weave bands of red wool over 3 warps. Colors (7): red field, medium blue, ivory, yellow, orange, light green, dark brown. Earlier forms of this design are found in rugs portrayed in European paintings dating back more than three hundred years.

87. RUG FROM CANAKKALE, 19th century, 4'7" x 7'1". Warp: W. /2\, light. Weft: W. /1 , 2-5 shoots. Pile: W. /2\. Knot: T, v. 5, h. 6, 30/sq inch. Sides: double selvage of rust red wool over 3 warps. Ends: plain weave bands of rust red wool over 3 warps. Colors (6): rust red, medium blue, bright red, light blue, dark brown, remain. ivory. This design is found in many parts of the Aegean region.

Several villages in the vicinity of Melas still weave the old prayer designs in colors that basically resemble older specimens, although they are achieved mostly with synthetic dyes. Prototypes of the design may be traced back through rugs at least two hundred years old; however, there has been a gradual evolution from a more naturalistic rendition of the floral elements to lines that are now stiff and angular.

In construction the Melas resembles other small Anatolian rugs woven on an all-wool foundation. The wefts are usually dyed a rust red, and these also provide color to the woven bands at both ends. The sides are finished with a double selvage wound around three or four thickened warp strands. The knotting is of medium density, but some of the older specimens are more tightly woven.

MAKRI

In several of the older books the Makri rug is described as having been made on the Island of Rhodes, and Hawley[3] eloquently notes the blending of a more vigorous Grecian and a subtle oriental art in the designs of these rugs:

> Here was the inspiration of the sea, cloudless skies, luxuriant vegetation. Here was felt the deep influence of the Mohammedan and Christian religions, as well as early pagan mythology; and there is little doubt that the cathedral walls and picturesque church of the valiant knights of St. John made an impression on the weavers.

Despite such rhapsodic prose, there is no evidence that rugs of the Makri type were ever made on Rhodes, and current production from the island consists of very coarse fabrics in bold, simple de-

89. MELAS PRAYER RUG, 19th century, 4'7" x 6'2". Warp: W. /2\, undyed, light. Weft: W. /1, dyed red, 2-4 shoots loose. Pile: W. /2\. Knot: T, v. 8, h. 7, 56/sq inch. Sides: double selvage of pale red wool over 4 warps. Ends: upper—plain weave band of pale red, selvage, and loose warp ends. Lower—plain weave band and loose ends. Colors (6): rust red, brick red, faded yellow, mauve, dark brown, ivory. The classic Melas features a mihrab with bilateral indentations just before the top. In this example the field elements and borders are all typical.

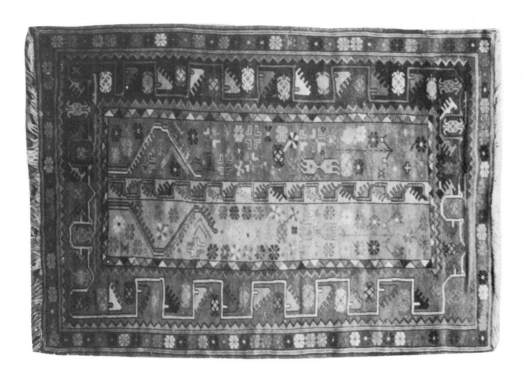

90. MAKRI RUG, 19th century, 4'1" x 6'8". Warp: W. /2\, undyed, light. Weft: W. /1, dyed pale red, 2-3 shoots. Pile: W. /2\. Knot: T, v. 6, h. 6, 36/sq inch. Sides: double selvage of light blue wool over 3 warps. Ends: upper—light blue plain weave band, selvage, loose ends. Lower—plain weave band and loose ends. Colors (6): dark and light blue, rust red, yellow, dark brown, ivory. The Makri may have 1, 2, or 3 longitudinal panels.

91. MELAS PRAYER RUG, mid-19th century, 3'8" x 5'2". Warp: W. /2\, undyed, light. Weft: W. /1, dyed red, 2-3 shoots. Pile: W. /2\. Knot: T, v. 8, h. 8, 64/sq inch. Sides: double selvage over 4 warps. Ends: narrow red plain weave bands remain. Cclors (6): rust red, light green, yellow, light blue, dark brown, ivory. The so-called "stripe Melas" is woven around the town of Karaova. Despite differences in design, these are structurally identical to the type depicted in Fig. 89.

signs. Makri rugs actually originated from the sea-coast villages of southwestern Asia Minor. The name of the principal town has since been changed from Makri (or Megris) to Fethiye, and although the population is under twenty thousand, it still functions as the largest port in the area. Wool is abundant, and large numbers of rugs were woven there through the early twentieth century. Even now the inland villages produce a small number of rugs in the old designs.

In construction Makri rugs are similar to those of Melas, although they are heavier, the knotting is less fine, and the pile is longer. The ends may have a wide woven band, frequently of light blue, and the sides are double-selvaged. In color tonality these rugs are subdued, with earth shades similar to the Melas, but a more prominent use of light and dark blue. Almost all are in scatter sizes, with designs of one, two, and three panels.

ANTALYA

Antalya is the most important seaport on Turkey's southern coast, and it serves as a collecting point for rugs made in the surrounding villages. These pieces have not established a clear identity in the West, and the relatively few that reach Europe are more likely to be known under the name of Dosmealti, a nearby town. One can examine large piles of Antalya rugs and find that perhaps eighty percent have designs that we can describe as "Lotto" variants, after the earlier rugs that we have traditionally attributed to Oushak. Probably for this reason, nineteenth-century Antalya rugs are often attributed to Bergama, where these designs are also known.

In construction Antalya rugs also resemble the Bergama, with red wefts and a color scheme built around red and blue; but here there is a much heavier use of green and yellow. There is a long woven band at both ends, often with stripes and small, woven, eye-like figures. Most examples are in scatter sizes, with surprisingly few prayer rugs.

ESKIŞEHIR

This relatively large city of west-central Anatolia has been a center of commercial rug weaving since the late nineteenth century. During the 1920s large quantities in carpet sizes were made there in designs adapted from a variety of sources, including Persia and even China. The rugs were formerly characterized by their lifeless colors, particularly dull reds and greens, but this improved after World War II. They are woven on a cotton foundation, and many of the larger, recent rugs are Persian knotted, with lusterless wool.

ISBARTA

The areas around Isbarta (formerly Sparta) and Burdur probably produce more carpets than any other part of Turkey, although these are almost exclusively commercial pieces of little interest to rug collectors. The designs are based on the same variety of sources as those of Eskişehir rugs, with no distinct local type. Most recent rugs from this area are Persian knotted on a cotton foundation, with alternate warps deeply depressed. The colors are often dull and muddy, although the wool itself may be of good quality.

IZMIR

Hand-woven carpets are not currently made in Izmir (formerly Smyrna), but there is a long tradition of such manufacture here, and the last pieces were apparently made during the 1930s. The earlier rugs were all wool, mostly in carpet sizes, and resembled the Oushak with large floral figures. There was considerable use of rust red and golden-yellow shades. Twentieth century examples tended to become stiff and lifeless. Currently Izmir is an important market center for many types of rugs from the inland, and there is a factory producing machine-made copies from older patterns.

HEREKE

The town of Hereke is located on the Sea of Marmora forty miles from Istanbul. There is some possibility that rugs were made there during the eighteenth century from silk grown in the vicinity; in 1844 the Turkish Sultan established a court manufactory there to produce rugs for the palace and for gifts to foreign potentates — no expense being spared to make them the finest available. Along with the weaving facilities, there was established a school of design which borrowed heavily from the best carpets of previous ages. Allegedly weavers were imported from Persia to supervise the copying of Persian rugs.

The finest Hereke pieces are Persian knotted, at times exceeding 800 knots to the square inch. The warp, weft, pile, and finishings were often all of silk, although rugs of fine wool were also woven.

Aside from copies of Persian masterpieces, a good many rugs were made from old Ghiordes prayer designs. In some respects these may be as fine as the originals, as the dyes, workmanship, and designs were of the highest order. The Turkish government still operates a large factory at Hereke, but the rugs are now standard commercial products, usually in carpet sizes and of no special distinction. Many rugs known to have been made in Hereke have an identifying inscription woven into the upper left-hand corner.

ISTANBUL

No doubt rugs have been made in and around Istanbul for centuries; an important group of such rugs, now mostly in museum collections, is thought to have been made in or for the Top Kapu Palace during the eighteenth century. By the late nineteenth century, however, weaving apparently took place only in workshops, some of which were operated in orphanages. There were also several commercial establishments in which copies of earlier Ottoman court pieces were woven, probably from pictures in books.

Technically these rugs present a mixed picture, with both Persian and Turkish knots, and the materials often include a heavy use of silk. They were sold under a variety of names, such as *Kum Kapu* and *Daruliçise*. Many copies of Ghiordes rugs were made, as well as large rugs in Persian designs. The turn of the century saw a brisk business in fakes around Istanbul, and likely some of these fakes are still in major museums.

PANDERMA

In Panderma (now Bandirma), on the Sea of Marmora, during the late nineteenth and early twentieth centuries, a number of wool and silk prayer rugs were woven in several workshops, usually in designs adapted from old Ghiordes and Ottoman court rugs. They closely resemble similar copies from Kayseri; there is some confusion between the two types, as the best grade of Kayseri rug is still called "Panderma." Often the Panderma rug was artificially aged and then treated to extensive repair. There are likely a number of them in museum collections today.

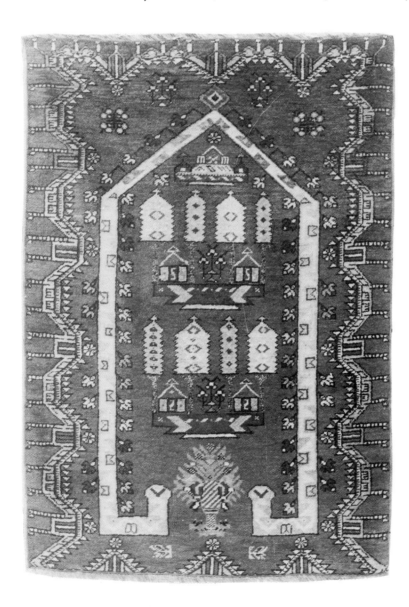

92. KIRSEHIR PRAYER RUG, late 19th century, 3'4" x 4'. Warp: W. /2\, light. Weft: W. /2\, dyed red, 2 shoots. Pile: W. /2\. Knot: T, 30°, v. 7, h. 6, 42/sq inch. Sides: .... Ends: .... Colors (7): red field, yellow, light and medium blue, aqua, red brown, brown. This rug combines features of the "Mejedieh" with the landscape figures most commonly found in Kulahs.

Courtesy of the Oriental Rug Co., Berkeley, California.

KIRŞEHIR

Kirşehir is a town of somewhat over twenty thousand inhabitants, and it serves as a market for large quantities of wool grown in the area. During the nineteenth century, and possibly before, fine prayer rugs were woven there in a remarkable variety of colors, with light blues and several shades of green. The stripe border is common, and the prayer niche often resembles the Ghiordes in configuration, at times even with similar cross panels.

The modern product of this name is typically a rug with bright synthetic dyes and some adaptation of an earlier Turkish prayer design, often from Ghiordes or Ladik. Unlike similar copies from Kayseri, these are still all of wool, and they are usually smaller than their prototypes. The wefts are red, and the sides are finished in a double selvage, often of a light green wool. Occasionally one will find runners from Kirşehir.

MUDJAR

The town of Mudjar (or Mucur) is about twenty miles southeast of Kirşehir. The area has a long tradition of weaving, particularly prayer rugs. The main border in these specimens is classically composed of diamond shapes enclosing eight-pointed floral forms, while the prayer arch is long and sharply pointed, with a cross panel generally above the mihrab. The older rugs featured subdued earth shades of beige, rust, light blue, and apricot.

In construction there is nothing to distinguish the Mudjar from a dozen other varieties of Anatolian prayer rug. They are still made in small numbers, often with extremely bright, synthetic colors.

TUZLA

The attribution of "Tuzla" is used for rugs alleged to come from the vicinity of Lake Tuz (Tuz Golu), a large, shallow expanse within a drainageless basin north of Konia. Wool is certainly plentiful in that area (inhabited for centuries by seminomadic tribes), but the rugs are usually not distinguishable from many that we label as Konias. The type most commonly called a Tuzla has a wide cross panel above the mihrab, enclosing a large octagon with simple floral figures. Some of these rugs are made of Angora wool.

KAYSERI

Kayseri (the ancient Caesarea) is one of the largest cities of the Anatolian plateau, with a population of nearly 70,000. It is still a market center

93. MUDJAR PRAYER RUG, mid-19th century, 4'1" x 5'4". Warp: W. /2\, light. Weft: W. /1, dyed pale red, 2 shoots. Pile: W. /2\. Knot: T, v. 8, h. 8, 64/sq inch. Sides: .... Ends: 2" red plain weave bands remain at both ends. Lower end still has loops. Colors (9): brick red, light and medium blue, green, yellow, mauve, light rose, dark brown, ivory. The borders, mihrab, and cross panels are all classic on this specimen, which shows clear, vibrant colors. By the late 19th century the Mudjar had been infected with particularly pernicious synthetic dyes. Dr. G. Dumas—H. Black Collection.

and collecting point for a variety of rugs made in the surrounding villages, with the nearby town of Bunyan producing the greatest number of rugs in all sizes up to the largest carpets. Few antique rugs are associated with Kayseri, nor are the rugs characterized by any specific designs. Since the late nineteenth century rugs of the area have, for the most part, been copies of Ghiordes and other popular Turkish designs.

The Kayseri rug is almost always woven on a cotton foundation, often with relatively thick wefts which may cross two, three, or more times between each row of knots. Even the sides are usually selvaged in cotton, while the pile may be wool, mercerized cotton, rayon (usually imported from Italy), a silk-cotton blend, or, more rarely, all silk. Among

94. KAYSERI RUG, late 19th century, 3'5" x 5'1".
Warp: C. /3\, white. Weft: C. /2\, undyed, 2 shoots.
Pile: W. /2\. Knot: T, v. 10, h. 10, 100/sq inch. Sides:
double selvage of white cotton over 2 warps. Ends:
loose warp ends. Colors (5): red field, dark brown border, light blue, yellow, ivory. Most Kayseri designs are
adapted from earlier Turkish rugs, frequently the Ghiordes. This design, still occasionally encountered, is an
adaptation from an Oushak original.

the more curious Kayseri types are round rugs, usually only about three feet in diameter, that are still
made in limited numbers as table covers. There are
also many saphs, usually in a material resembling
silk; often they are sold under the euphemism "Turkish silk."

SIVAS

Sivas is one of the larger cities of east-central
Anatolia. It has been a center of rug weaving at least
since the nineteenth century. Most Sivas rugs, woven in workshops or the jail, have been commercial
adaptations of Persian designs, usually woven in carpet sizes. These have a cotton foundation and rather
subdued colors.

In the villages around Sivas there is still a large
production of smaller rugs in prayer and hearth designs. Like Kayseri rugs, they may be adaptations
from older Anatolian types, but there is also a
type with intricate, complex designs of highly stylized floral forms. The foundation is usually wool,
with cotton coming into wider use. A large number
of nomad rugs are also marketed in Sivas.

YAHYALI

The town of Yahyali lies about 50 miles south
of Kayseri, but the rugs from this area resemble
more the village products from the vicinity of Sivas.
The double mihrab layout is common here, often
with crude columns. Colors are unusually somber,
although yellow is used frequently. Materials are
variable (until recently a wool foundation was standard), and the rugs tend to be among the larger scatter sizes.

THE YÜRÜK

There are approximately two million nomads
still living within Anatolia. Undoubtedly these wandering tribes have produced rugs for centuries, but,
for several reasons, the weaves are not as easily traced to local origins as are those of Persia, where the
tribes claim a wider variety of ethnic backgrounds.
(The Qashgai and Afshars are of Turkic origin, but
their arrival times in Persia are separated by at least
four centuries, while other groups of Baluchis, Bahktiaris, and Lurs are descended from Indo-European
migrants or from the Arab invaders of the eighth
century.) In Anatolia the nomads are more homo-
geneous, descended mostly from an indigenous Kurdish population and to a lesser extent from Turkic
migrants who arrived after the ninth century. Whereas groups such as the Bahktiari have been great
forces in Persia, the nomads of Anatolia have been
relatively impotent against the might of the Ottoman state. They lived within the shadow of a great
power and never coalesced into large ethnic or political organizations. We thus have a diffusion of
wandering, pastoral peoples, known collectively as
the Yürük, a word meaning simply *nomad*. They are
found predominantly in eastern Anatolia, although
elements occur as far west as Izmir.

As the Yürük live primarily from their herds,
and wool is perhaps their most important product,
the obvious result is a carpet entirely of this material. Not surprisingly, as many Yürük are of Kurdish
racial stock, their rugs resemble in some respects
those of northwestern Persia. The knotting is usual-

ly coarse, and the thick pile is of a rather harsh, dry wool. Usually the wefts are undyed, and they may be of dark goat hair. (The proportion of dark wool can be seen to increase as one travels east across Anatolia.) The ends are often braided together in long strands, while the sides are finished in a double overcast of alternating colors.

Yürük rug colors are less bright than most Caucasian pieces, with a characteristic use of green, dark blue, and a vivid crimson. More recent rugs favor a prominent use of bright orange, which has replaced the delicate apricot shades of older specimens. The designs rely heavily upon such simple motifs as latch hooks and lozenge-shaped medallions. The so-called tarantula figures and simple, stylized floral forms are also used.

New Yürük rugs are marketed in Adana, Diyarbakir, and Malatya. The shapes are often grossly irregular, with prominent wrinkling.

THE RUGS OF EASTERN ANATOLIA

Not surprisingly, in those portions of the Lesser Caucasus included within Turkey rugs are woven that closely resemble those from the Russian side of the border. These rugs, which are still made in small numbers, are called "Turkish Kazaks" by Istanbul dealers; they are collected from small villages and nomadic groups in several centers, most important of which are Kars and Erzerum.

The construction of these pieces is indistinguishable from other southern Caucasian rugs; the foundation is all wool, with wefts (often dyed pink) that may cross two, three, or more times between each row of knots. The designs are strictly Caucasian, although the colors may give some distinction. Rugs from around Kars are particularly likely to show a prominent use of brown, beige, and rust red, while there is generally an absence of the brighter shades. Many of these rugs occur in runner sizes.

KILIMS

No doubt many kilims were woven during the period that produced the village and nomad rugs now sought by collectors. For obvious reasons these relatively perishable fabrics have been less well preserved, and most of them found on the market date from later decades. The larger kilims are usually woven in two narrow strips (between 18 inches and about 30 inches in width) and then sewn together. Bold, large-scale designs are arranged horizontally across the field, and these are so similar throughout Anatolia that finding a geographic point of origin is virtually impossible. Similarly, the prayer kilims

95. YURUK PRAYER RUG, 20th century, 2'5" x 4'9". Warp: W. /2\, undyed, dark and light wool twisted together. Weft: dark goat hair, /1, 2-3 shoots: Pile: W. /2\. Knot: T, v. 6, h. 6, 36/sq inch. Sides: double overcast of multicolored wool over 6 warps. Ends: narrow plain weave bands, and loose warps braided together. Colors (6): deep red, light green, apricot, yellow, dark brown, ivory. This type of rug is woven by nomadic tribes in eastern Anatolia.
(The term Yürük may not be technically correct, although they are known by that name in the United States and Europe. Istanbul rug dealers refer to them as Kurds, reserving the former term for a particular type of nomad rug.)

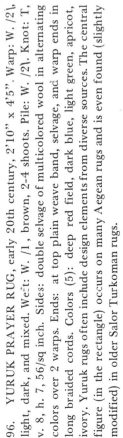

97. NOMAD RUG from eastern Anatolia, 3'6" x 11'. Warp: W. /2\, light. Weft: W. /1, light brown, 2 shoots, both loose. Pile: W. /2\. Knot: T, v. 7, h. 6, 42/sq inch. Sides: heavy double overcast with multicolored wool. Ends: narrow band of plain weave and loose ends braided together. Colors (6): brick red, dark blue, dark brown, light green, ivory, apricot. The medallions are clearly adapted from the same source as that for one of the Ezine rugs in Fig. 86. Thick, fleecy runners of this type are woven by nomadic groups in eastern Anatolia.

96. YURUK PRAYER RUG, early 20th century, 2'10" x 4'5". Warp: W. /2\, light, dark, and mixed. Weft: W. /1, brown, 2-4 shoots. Pile: W. /2\. Knot: T, v. 8, h. 7, 56/sq inch. Sides: double selvage of multicolored wool in alternating colors over 2 warps. Ends: at top plain weave band, selvage, and warp ends in long braided cords. Colors (5): deep red field, dark blue, light green, apricot, ivory. Yuruk rugs often include design elements from diverse sources. The central figure (in the rectangle) occurs on many Aegean rugs and is even found (slightly modified) in older Salor Turkoman rugs.

seldom show a clear relationship to the knotted rugs of any given locality, and, as the technique of weaving is so similar over a wide area, they are seldom specifically localized.

One feature of Turkish kilims that may help in distinguishing them from the weaves of Persian Kurdistan, Fars, and the Caucasus is the presence of loose threads at the back which connect patches of the same color. Some also have portions of the design outlined with embroidery or brocading.

Many Turkish flat-stitch fabrics are also woven exclusively with Soumak brocading and other forms of weft-float brocade. One relatively common type, woven in the latter technique, is often labeled as a "Verneh" by American dealers and collectors. For some time these pieces have been attributed erroneously to the Caucasus, but they are made throughout Anatolia. Those with a dark wool

98. TURKISH "YASTIKS," 20th century: a) 1'8" x 3'6", b) 1'9" x 3'5", c) 1'10" x 3'10". Warp: all have W. /2\, light. In (b) some warps have dark and light twisted together. Weft: all have W. /1, 2-3 shoots. Dark wool in (b), with narrow bands of yellow and red wefts. Light in (c). Pile: W. /2\. Knot: T; a) v. 10, h. 8, 80/sq inch; b) v. 9, h. 7, 63/sq inch; c) v. 8, h. 7, 56/sq inch. Sides: all are double selvaged with wool over 2 warps. Ends: all have plain weave band in colored wool. The "Yastik," or pillow cover, is found in countless designs throughout Anatolia. Often they are virtually impossible to identify as to village or even region of origin. All three of these are most likely from villages in the Konia Province.

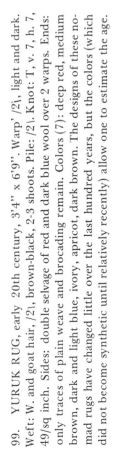

100. "TURKISH KAZAK" PRAYER RUG, early 20th century, 2'5" x 3'10". Warp: W. /2\, medium brown and ivory twisted together. Weft: W. /2\, medium brown, 3-5 shoots. Pile: W. /2\. Knot: T, v. 6, h. 6, 36/sq inch. Sides: double selvage over 2 warps in checkerboard pattern, red wool alternating with white or yellow. Ends: narrow plain weave bands of brown wool with loose warp ends. Colors (7): red field, ivory, dark blue, medium brown, yellow, yellow orange, light rust red. Rugs from the vicinity of Kars resemble Kazaks made across the border in Russia, although the colors are not so adventuresome in the former.

99. YURUK RUG, early 20th century, 3'4" x 6'9". Warp' /2\, light and dark. Weft: W. and goat hair, /2\, brown-black, 2-3 shoots. Pile: /2\. Knot: T, v. 7, h. 7, 49/sq inch. Sides: double selvage of red and dark blue wool over 2 warps. Ends: only traces of plain weave and brocading remain. Colors (7): deep red, medium brown, dark and light blue, ivory, apricot, dark brown. The designs of these nomad rugs have changed little over the last hundred years, but the colors (which did not become synthetic until relatively recently) allow one to estimate the age.

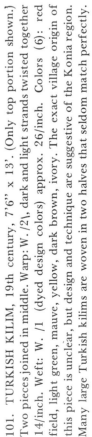

102. TURKISH PRAYER KILIM, late 19th century, 3'9'' x 5'4''. Warp: W. /2\, light brown, 16/inch. Weft: W. /2\ (dyed in design colors), approx. 28/sq inch. Colors (6): dark brown field, light green, rust red, yellow, tan, ivory. This piece was woven in the vicinity of Konia.

101. TURKISH KILIM, 19th century, 7'6'' x 13'. (Only top portion shown.) Two pieces joined in middle. Warp: W. /2\, dark and light strands twisted together 14/inch. Weft: W. /1 (dyed design colors) approx. 26/inch. Colors (6): red field, light green, mauve, yellow, dark brown, ivory. The exact village origin of this piece is unclear, but design and technique are suggestive of the Konia region. Many large Turkish kilims are woven in two halves that seldom match perfectly.

foundation are likely the products of eastern Anatolian nomads, while a similar design with a light wool foundation may occur as far west as the Bergama area.

THE "ANATOLIAN" RUG

In other portions of the book we have objected to the use of vague, nondescriptive terms to label rugs of obvious diverse backgrounds. The name "Anatolian" is surely as uninformative as Bokhara, Cabistan, Khiva, and a list of other labels appropriated by dealers to cover their ignorance. Nevertheless, in some cases we have little else. There are hundreds of obscure villages in Anatolia where rugs have been woven, and many of these, for one reason or another, have never established a distinct identity. At least the term "Anatolian" is not misleading.

TURKISH RUGS SINCE WORLD WAR I

The first world war and its succeeding social revolution in Turkey wrought a drastic change in the economy and daily life of the people. The weaving industry has never resumed its former stature, despite a sharp increase in the market.

Several factors contributed to the decline. Previously much of the weaving had been done by Greek and Armenian minorities living among the Turks; under the Sultanate they formed isolated enclaves with a well-defined (although inferior) place in the social structure. With the fall of the Empire and the violent pograms attendant upon its final years, these groups were severely persecuted. Both Greeks and Armenians left Turkey by the hundreds of thousands, and they took with them much of the carpet weaving art.

The influx of Western demand was another factor that contributed to the eventual decline in Turkey. Istanbul, the great nineteenth century trading center in oriental rugs, and other Turkish ports were thrown into close contact with Western businessmen and Western tastes. Even rugs woven in Persia, for the most part, were taken overland by camel or shipped from Trebizond to Istanbul for marketing, and rugs produced as far away as Eastern Turkestan often found their European outlet in this manner. When the demand from Europe and the United States reached enormous proportions in the early 1920s, relatively few rugs were produced in Turkey except patent commercial items to be sold in the West, thus their artistic level did not approach the freshness of the Anatolian rugs of preceding centuries.

Turkey was now firmly established as a commercial rather than an artistic center, and its products of the next decade, until the great depression reduced the demand, were among the least desirable hand-knotted rugs produced under any circumstances. In almost every respect the new rugs were inferior; they sold by the thousands only because of an enormous demand and their low prices. The dyes included some of the most objectionable anilines; the designs were no more appealing, as they were often borrowed from Persian sources and during the transformation had lost much of their original vitality. Indeed, the products of American power looms and these hand-made rugs had many similarities.

The labels under which these carpets were marketed seldom gave precise information about where they were made. Most of them were named after either Sparta (from the Anatolian city of Isbarta) or Smyrna, regions where many of them undoubtedly were woven. Another large portion came from Greek and Armenian refugees from Turkey who had settled around Athens and Thessalonika.

Weaving has steadily increased since World War II, although it has never reached its former level. One still encounters a small number of village and nomad rugs woven with the traditional designs and materials. Among commercial rugs, the larger carpets usually originate from the government-operated factory at Hereke (formerly the Sultan's manufactory) or prison workshops in Isbarta, Kayseri, Kirşehir, Konia, Sivas, Imrali, and Bursa. In many other centers, where smaller rugs are woven in homes, a government agency provides training, looms, and materials.

Recent commercial rugs are all on cotton foundations, usually a thick machine-spun thread, and the pile is often quite long. The knotting may be either Persian (which speeds production) or Turkish, while the designs are a composite from the entire Middle East.

NOTES

1. Hawley, W., *Oriental Rugs*, Dodd, Mead, and Co., New York, 1922, p. 174.
2. Lewis, G., *Practical Book of Oriental Rugs*, Lippincott, Philadelphia, 1911, p. 238.
3. Hawley, W., *op. cit.*, p. 179.

VII TURKOMAN RUGS

Among the four major categories of carpets, Turkoman rugs would seem to be the easiest to identify and classify, as their designs have changed little from their first appearance in the West to the present time. The actual situation is not so simple, however, as there is much confusion even over the names for these rugs. One often finds in the literature conflicting and misleading assertions, with the rugs assuming names that have nothing to do with place or tribe of origin. Toward the goal of clarification we will explore those elements that would allow a rug to be most meaningfully categorized.

Among the rug-making Turkoman tribes are Tekkes, Salors, Saryks, Chaudors, Yomuds (and various subdivisions such as the Ogourdjali), Ersaris, and related tribes of Beshiri, Kizil Ajak, Chubbash, and others. As many of these groups were to a greater or lesser degree nomadic until the last fifty years, their rugs cannot be accurately placed as to geographic point of origin. One system of classification, however, depends upon place names — usually the town or city where the rugs were marketed. We thus have rugs named after Bokhara and Khiva (the only two population centers of Turkestan) and several of the larger oasis areas, such as Merv and Pende. These designations might be acceptable if they bore any degree of accuracy, but their selection was so arbitrary as to be misleading. There is little evidence that a sizable carpet industry ever existed in either Bokhara or Khiva; indeed, those rugs attributed to Khiva were made hundreds of miles to the south in Afghanistan. The rugs known as Bokharas were usually made by Tekkes, who neither lived near the city nor marketed their rugs there. The oases, moreover, were inhabited by different tribes at different times, and there is nothing consistent about the designs associated with them. During the nineteenth century Merv was occupied by Tekkes, Salors, and Saryks; yet the rugs of these tribes are of markedly different design. Other important market centers have been ignored in the naming process, such as Kerki, Ashkabad, and Mazar-i-Sharif. In general such names tell us nothing about a rug.

Even more misleading are the trade names assigned by American and European rug dealers, most of whom have only the remotest conception of Middle Eastern geography and ethnography. We are given fanciful titles in the local rug shops by dealers who seek to lend an air of majesty and mystery to products that need no such apology. "Royal Bokhara" is the most common designation, usually to label products of the Tekkes. The name, however, apparently refers only to the carpets with guls, as the door rugs and prayer rugs in the so-called Katchli (or Hatchlou) design are called "Princess Bokhara," whether they are produced by Tekkes or any other tribe. Dealers speak with an air of authority in such terms, and, indeed, in the trade they are correct insofar as other merchants repeat the same misinformation.

There is little excuse for the current ignorance of authentic origins, as we have one excellent early reference with enough firsthand information to provide a foundation for our studies. This is the two-volume work of A. A. Bogolubov,[1] published in St. Petersburg by the Czarist Government in 1908. The first volume contains a text in both Russian and French; it provides a wealth of information about the history and ethnography of the area, in addition to a superb description of individual rugs. The second volume includes forty-three plates. The author was Russian Military Governor of the Transcaspian Provinces, and he had at his disposal the data of a vast bureaucracy. With each of his illustrations Bogolubov provides some data as to where the rug was made or purchased, at times listing even the exact village. In such cases we simply must take the author's word as authoritative, as we have no other primary sources of information. Using this foundation, supplemented by the work of a few anthropologists who have worked among the Turkomans, we can reconstruct a fairly reliable picture. Slowly the gaps in our knowledge are being filled.

TURKESTAN AND THE TURKOMAN PEOPLE

The area inhabited by the Turkoman peoples is over eight hundred miles wide and four hundred miles from north to south, extending eastward from the Caspian Sea over the deserts of Kara Kum and Kizil Kum, and ending in the foothills of the great mountain ranges of Central Asia: the Hindu Kush, the Pamirs, and the Tien Shen. Along the southern boundaries is a chain of mountains rising eastward from the Elburz in Persia along the Russian frontier into Afghanistan; northward, above the Sea of Aral, the central Russian steppes begin. The deserts on either side of the Oxus are for the most part flat and barren, and the climate is dry and extreme, with temperatures ranging from 120 degrees in the summer to subzero in the winter. Vegetation is scanty, except in the forests of the Oxus delta, and water is very scarce; clearly this land could support only a small population.[2] Since the technological level is low here, the only feasible way of life is a nomadic existence dependent on grazing animals. While the more desirable land near the rivers and trading centers has been frequently contested by a succession of conquerors, the deserts have been left for centuries to the Turkomans, who have inhabited mainly the foothills of the bordering mountains and the oases.

The origin of these nomads is not clearly defined, although legends among the people outline a long and glorious past. Apparently Turkic tribes arrived in Turkestan sometime around the sixth century A.D., probably from the Gobi and Tarim Basin, where they are mentioned much earlier by Chinese sources.[3] By the tenth century these nomads had absorbed the indigenous local populations and occupied the banks of the Oxus. At times, under vigorous leaders, they made forays into the settled areas of the West; during the eleventh century the most successful of these invading groups, the Seljuks, established an empire extending well into Anatolia. The Mongol invasion of the thirteenth century at first broke the Turkic dominance of the area, but as the Mongols gradually were absorbed, the actual administration of the empire fell to peoples of Turkish derivation. Other Turkic empires and dynasties were established across northern Persia and Afghanistan, while the Ottoman Turks, an offshoot of the Seljuks, ruled an empire that survived into the twentieth century.

In the midst of an incredibly complex succession of dynastic and tribal alliances, certain Turkic elements remained in the lands along the Oxus and the steppeland stretching east from the Caspian. These people gradually became separate from their more settled relatives, the Uzbegs of Khiva and Bokhara, who were also of Turkic derivation. By the sixteenth century the division was well established, with Turkomans fairly circumscribed by neighboring powers, none of whom could long dominate these nomads. Turkoman history for the next three hundred years thus became dependent upon conditions in the Khanates of Khiva and Bokhara, and

the growing Russian Empire to the north and west. Some Turkoman groups allied themselves with one power; others were employed by a rival. When Persia reached an apex of strength under Nadir Shah, all Turkestan knew his rule, but soon after his death in 1747, the Turkomans again returned to their traditional ways. Part of their prosperity depended upon raiding settled territory, a practice which the neighboring states could not completely eliminate. Finally, however, the Russians inexorably advanced into Turkoman territory, crushing the last major Tekke resistance at Geok Tepe in 1881. From that time there has been little Turkoman marauding, and the people have turned increasingly to a sedentary way of life. They constitute the major ethnic group of the Turkmen Autonomous Republic of the Soviet Union.

There is no information other than verbal tradition to explain the division of the Turkomans into tribes. Apparently a separation occurred as early as the tenth century into Yomuds, Tekkes, and Saryks, from the main Salor stock. The Yomuds for the most part settled around the Caspian and in the Khanate of Khiva, some near the delta of the Oxus. By the eighteenth century they were composed of many subtribes, the most important of which were the Ogourdjalis, who lived a sedentary life along the Caspian coast. The Ersaris, who became separated at an undefined time, settled primarily along the banks of the Oxus and around the city of Bokhara. This brought them into contact with the Uzbegs and Persians of that city, and rugs of these people show the greatest non-Turkoman influences. Other Ersari elements inhabit portions of northern Afghanistan, along with the related Kizil Ajak and Beshiri tribes.

ORIGIN OF CARPET WEAVING AMONG THE TURKOMANS

There is much speculation regarding the beginning of weaving among the Turkomans, but, as we have concluded about other historical matters, there is little concrete information from which to construct a chronology. On the one hand we have the suppositions of Bogolubov and others that these rugs had their origin in the mists of antiquity, and surely, as the rugs are of utilitarian value in the Turkoman kibitkas, some fabric must have served a similar function since the beginning of this way of life.

Nevertheless, we have no examples that could be dated with any certainty before 1800, although this may be explained by the rough wear given to Turkoman carpets. During the nineteenth century,

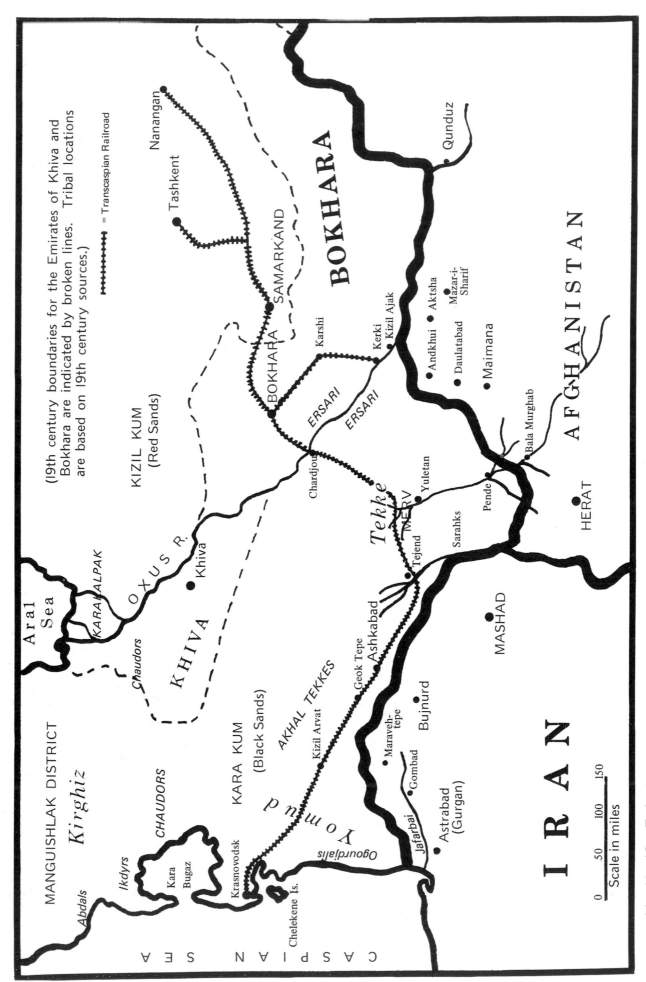

Map No. 10. Turkestan

however, we have several accounts from travelers, describing a well-developed carpet industry that probably dated back many centuries. The earliest account (1825) is from James Fraser,[4] who noted that "the manufactures of the Turkomans consist chiefly in carpets, which they weave of very beautiful fabric, and which are highly prized, fetching very large prices. They are chiefly of the twilled sort, but they also make them of a fabric resembling the best Turkey carpets, and of very brilliant patterns."

Vambery[5] in 1863 also mentioned Turkoman carpets, giving us a clear picture of how the designs were communicated:

> An important manufacture of central Asia, which reaches us in Europe by way of Persia and Constantinople, is that of carpets, which is, however, the exclusive product of the industry and skill of the Turkoman women. Besides the beautifully pure coloring and the solidity of texture, what most surprises us is how these simple nomad women preserve so well the symmetry of outline of the figures.... One carpet gives work always for a number of girls and young women. An old woman places herself at their head as directress. She first traces, with points, the pattern of the figures in the sand. Glancing at this, she gives out the number of the different threads required to produce the desired figures.

Several years later in 1881, Edmond O'Donovan[6] gave more details:

> When a Turkoman is blessed with a large number of daughters, he contrives to realize a considerable sum per annum by the felt and other carpets which they make. In this case an _ev_ is set apart as a workshop, and three or four of the girls are usually occupied upon each carpet, sometimes for a couple of months.
>
> Each girl generally manufactures two extra fine carpets, to form part of her dowry when she marries. When this has been done, she devotes herself to producing goods for the markets at Meshed and Bokhara, where the Turkoman carpets fetch a much higher price than those manufactured in Khurassan or beyond the Oxus. Sometimes these carpets are made partly of silk, brought from Bokhara. They are generally twice the size of ordinary ones, which are made from sheep's wool and camel hair mingled with a little cotton, and are almost entirely of silk.

Apparently once the Central Asian Railroad was opened, trade in Turkoman carpets expanded rapidly. By 1911, when we are given an account by W. E. Curtis,[7] the business in Bokhara had been organized along commercial lines.

> Both rugs and embroideries, however, can be bought to better advantage in London, Constantinople, Smyrna...because the best examples are picked up by agents of the big jobbers...and never appear on the local market. These jobbers have men traveling through the country and picking up bargains....The women of Turkestan do not work in the fields...so they stay at home and weave rugs, mothers and daughters taking turns at the looms.... Formerly they spun their own yarns, but they can buy it so much more cheaply now that they sell the wool from their sheep and get it ready dyed, or have it advanced to them by the commission men, or agents of the big rug houses in Bokhara, Constantinople ... or Merv.

CONSTRUCTION OF TURKOMAN CARPETS

The majority of Turkoman rugs are woven with the Persian knot, although among the Yomuds Turkish knotting is most common. In many rugs the body of the weaving is done in Persian knots, and for some reason the last few rows on each side are finished in the Turkish knot. In any event this cannot be used as a definite means of identification, as examples of Turkish knotting are found from all tribal groups. Most of the finer pieces, of course, are accomplished with the Persian knot, which allows a finer weave. This can exceed 400 knots to the square inch, while the coarsest Ersaris may have as few as 40 to 60 knots to the inch.

At the ends of a rug there is often a wide woven band in some simple stripe design. Usually this is merely a plain weave, but we have examples with a kilim stitch and an occasional use of weft-float brocade. The wide bands of many old Tekkes and Ersaris have three sets of three stripes each, colored blue or green. There is great variability. The loose ends of the warp are often left very long, and adjacent strands are sometimes knotted.

The pile may be either of sheep's wool or the soft camel fleece found beneath the coarse, outer hair. It is ordinarily twisted from two strands and varies in thickness according to the tightness of weave. In the heaviest Ersaris, it is long and loose, while in more finely knotted Tekkes and Salors, the strands are thin and closely clipped. The degree of erectness of the pile depends upon how tightly each row of knots is packed down upon the last, and varies between the Ersaris, with a loose weave and recumbent pile, and the Tekke-Salor group, in which the pile is more erect.

Occasionally silk is mixed with the wool of the pile or added in portions of the design. This is most frequent around Merv, where the material is grown, and is found in the finest rugs. Silk often dyes to a more violet shade than wool, which varies between vivid blood reds and browns.

An unusual feature of many Turkoman rugs is that they may be wider than they are long. (The warp is shorter than the weft, and the loose ends are on the long sides.) This is a characteristic of the many smaller pieces used as bag faces, which have an elaborate set of terms that describe approximately their size and function. There are three common types of bags, each with a different name:[8]

1) *Torba*—a long, narrow tent bag for small, house-items. Usual size between 14 x 36 inches and 20 x 44 inches.
2) *Joval* or *Doshaq*—a larger bag for bedding and other items, used when the tribe moves to a new location. Usual size is between 30 x 42 inches and 48 x 68 inches.
3) *Khordjin*—horse or donkey saddlebag, between 16 x 20 inches and 24 x 28 inches.

All three of these types may be either flat or pile woven, usually with the warps continuous onto the plain weave back. Among the flat stitch techniques, Soumak or weft-float brocading is most common. In addition there are a number of special pieces woven for use as animal trappings and as tent decorations. These are almost always pile woven, and many are decorated with tassels.

1) *Djollar*—a long, narrow camel hanging, often with an added fringe or tassels. Usual size between 12 x 44 inches and 20 x 64 inches.
2) The *Djollar pardar* is a related type used to hang over the inside of a doorway. The width is the same, but there are panels hanging down from the side giving it a horseshoe shape. This may also be decorated with strings of beads.
3) The *tang* is a band 6 to 14 inches wide and up to 50 feet long which extends along the entire outer circumference of the Kibitka. This may be decorated with various flat stitch techniques or may be pile woven, usually with the knots on every other warp so that the design does not show on the back.
4) *Osmulduk*—a 5-sided rug, usually, but not invariably, of Yomud weave, with tassels from the sides and base, allegedly used to decorate the lead camel in a Turkoman bridal procession. Usual size is 20 x 30 inches to 34 x 48 inches. New examples of these are still found.

Carpets come in a variety of sizes to meet different functions. There has been considerable confusion around the so-called *Katchli* (from a word meaning *cross*), which is often described as either a prayer rug or a door covering. Other forms of prayer rug are not known among the Tekkes, Salors, and Saryks, and in these cases the rugs may have had a dual function. This is less likely among the Yomud and particularly the Ersari, where the same tribe may produce a katchli to use as a door covering (known either as *pardah* or *engsi* and measuring about 48 x 60 inches to 60 x 84 inches) and smaller prayer rugs (*Namazlyk* or *Dja-namaz*, about 28 x 40 inches). The engsi, as it fastens to the tent, does not have a fringe at the top, but plain weave hemmed under; some specimens are found with a woven cord still attached.

The larger carpets also have specific terms depending upon their intended function. The house carpet (usually no larger than 7 x 11 feet) is called a *Ghali* or *Nim-ghali*, while there are other smaller types used as hearth or threshold carpets and rare rugs in a runner format, used next to larger pieces so that the entire floor would be covered.

As Turkoman rug production became more oriented toward Western markets, more of the larger sizes were produced, and eventually the standard 9 x 12 carpet was also made here.

DESIGN AND COLORS

Turkoman design motifs were long thought to have evolved from floral forms, but this supposition has been challenged by Moshkova,[9] who insists that highly stylized bird figures are the basis of much Turkoman design. Similar controversy exists around the meaning of the designs themselves, or rather the basic "gul" that forms the field pattern of most Turkoman rugs. These figures, usually octagonal, originally had a tribal significance, although with the recent commercialization of the Turkoman rug much of this has been lost. The degree to which the guls are specific to each tribe, however, is probably not as clear as we would like it to be. Even the word itself presents some controversy, as it has traditionally been taken to mean "flower." In Turkish the word means, literally, "rose flower," while there is a similar word in Persian. Moshkova distinguishes between gül and göl, which, she indicates, is a separate word referring to a tribal emblem or insignia. In this context she speaks of "dead" and "living" göls, depending upon whether a given göl is still used by its original tribe as an identifying mark on its woven products.

Such speculation is by no means conclusive. By and large we can proceed with the idea that one can identify a rug by the design of its gul, but we must be aware that there was frequent borrowing, at least by the late nineteenth century. The Salor "Mar" gul (from Merv) was used at times by both Saryks and Tekkes, while we see much borrowing by the Ersari and even Baluchi tribes.

The borders present more difficulty in terms of specific identification, as a given motif may be used by a number of tribes. Often there are many small border stripes, with one main stripe, generally showing the same ground color as the remainder of the rug. Many Salor rugs, however, do not seem to have a main border. One may also note similarities to the borders of many Baluchi rugs, particularly among the Yomud; at times there are even Caucasian-like elements.

The predominant color of most Turkoman rugs is a rich, vibrant red, varying from a pink-rose to warm, deep magenta. This was typically produced from madder, although in some places cochineal was also used. In an 1873 ethnography for the Khanate of Bokhara, John M. Trotter[10] also mentioned other dyes. He described a purple dye, resembling cochineal, from the root of a jungle shrub called *Ashik-busa*. A pink color was also noted to be obtained from a plant called *gulimachsas*, and a dark red from the branches of a shrub named *ruzan*. (*Ashik-busa* could, indeed, be madder under another name, although Trotter separately mentions this latter substance.) The enormous variety of Turkoman reds certainly suggests that dyes other than madder and cochineal were used.

The other colors are less important, and there is seldom anything approaching the brightness of a Caucasian rug. The blues, from indigo, are usually dark, and the same is true of green (a combination of indigo and a yellow dye), which is not common. Black is used for outlining the design elements, but this was usually a natural dark brown or black wool; the corrosive black iron-based dye is seldom found. Yellows are made from a variety of leaves, berries, and plant stems. The origin of a particularly bright yellow in some Ersari rugs is not clear (some sources have suggested saffron), but apparently the yellow dye called *Ispraik* (the common vine weld), was frequently used, as in other weaving areas. We also have references to yellow dyes known under the names of *Naipur* and *Rojan*, but the source of these is obscure.[11] Tumeric, henna, and gall nuts provided shades from mauve to orange.

There is a tradition that Turkoman rugs were preserved from anilines longer than other Middle Eastern products, but this does not seem to have been the case. By the 1880s, considerable quantities of synthetic dyes were finding their way into Turkestan. Many of the carpets dyed with various aniline reds show considerable running, although this in itself is no proof that a synthetic was used. In many parts of Turkestan water is so scarce that the wool may not have been properly rinsed after dyeing.

TURKOMAN TRIBAL RUG-MAKERS

On the basis of their ethnography, plus the structure and design of their rugs, Turkoman rug-weavers can conveniently be divided into three major groups. The first one includes the Salors, Saryks, and Tekkes, who inhabited roughly the same area and produced finely woven rugs of a similar structure that are often difficult to distinguish, as various design elements have become common property among them. A second group can then be made of the Yomuds, their subgroups, such as the sedentary Ogourdjalis, and the related Chaudors. The last group, inhabiting parts of northern Afghanistan and areas along the banks of the Oxus, weave a heavier, coarser rug, with more variability of design. The Ersaris are the largest of these peoples, with small numbers of Beshiris, Kizil-Ajaks, and Chub-Bash making a similar type of rug. While it is not always possible to identify a Turkoman rug as to exact tribal origin, placement into one of these three categories is relatively straightforward.

A number of other Turkoman tribes were also important during the period in which rugs have been exported from Turkestan. Among these the most numerous is the Goklan, who still occupy a portion of northeastern Iran near the border with the U.S.S.R. Vambery[12] gave their number as 10,000 tents, and he also listed smaller groups of Alielis and Karas. No doubt these tribes also wove rugs, although we are unable specifically to identify any of their older work. The Goklans now make rugs in Tekke designs, with the guls slightly smaller and more ovoid. This is likely a recent development.

SALORS

Although the Salors are traditionally regarded as the oldest and most distinguished Turkoman tribe, they have not rivaled the more numerous Tekkes for at least 150 years. From the late eighteenth century they occupied the rich oasis lands around Merv, from which they and the Saryk tribes were driven by the Tekkes in 1856. The Salors then dispersed in several directions. Some settled around Sarakhs, on land controlled by the Persian Shah, while others moved farther up the Murghab and

103. SALOR BAG FACE, mid-19th century, 2.8 x 4.4 feet. Warp: W. /2\, undyed, medium brown. Weft: W. /2\, medium brown, 1 shoot. Pile: W. /2\, with silk for portions of carmine pile. Knot: P, v. 26, h. 12, 312/sq inch. Sides: .... Ends: .... Colors (7): rust red, brick red, carmine, medium brown, light blue, dark blue, ivory. Earlier Salor rugs are likely to have more squarish and widely spaced guls. In later pieces they are flattened and closer together.

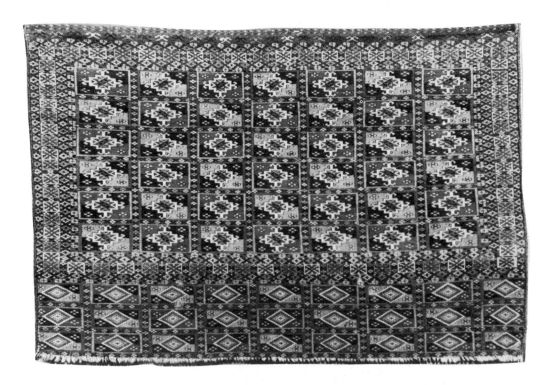

104. SALOR-TEKKE BAG FACE, 19th century, 2.6 x 3.8 feet. Warp: Goat hair, /2\, undyed. Weft: W. /2\, undyed, 2 shoots, both loose. Pile: W. /2\. Knot: P, v. 24, h. 12, 288 /sq inch. Sides: blue double overcast (not original). Ends: upper—plain weave band folded under. Lower: not original. Colors (7): red, carmine, salmon, dark blue, medium brown, ivory, yellow. Bags and rugs of this design are usually labeled as Tekkes (or, less frequently, Yomuds), but this piece, in structure and color, is certainly more Salorish. The main border is identical with that in Fig. 103.

settled among the Saryks of Pende and Yuletan. O'Donovan,[13] in 1882, notes that 150 families of Salors lived in the Merv area along a branch of the Alasha Canal. Another few hundred families lived around the villages of Mjaour, east of the river. Vambery in 1863[14] estimated the total number of Salors at 8,000 tents. A small group of Salors still live in northern Afghanistan around the town of Marutshak.

Salor rugs of several types are known, with the so-called *Mar* (or Merv) gul most characteristic. These are octagons with serrations, or small turret-like projections, which were also copied later by the Tekkes and Saryks. The earliest Salor rugs often have patches of magenta silk, and the overall color is dark and somber, with deep reddish browns. Later the colors became a brighter red, with a blood-red field; the interior of the guls, always a lighter shade, is often a bright cherry. The guls tend to be more rounded in earlier pieces.

Two other designs are also found on Salor jovals, one of which was depicted twice by Bogolubov (Plates 6 and 10). Schurmann[15] identifies these as products of the northern Salors, along the banks of the Amu Darya, but Bogolubov[16] clearly indicates a Pende origin. Another design, of rectangles, has long been associated with the Tekkes (or even the Yomuds), but at least some examples appear more likely to be Salor.

Salor rugs are Persian knotted, with occasionally a few rows of Turkish knots along the edges. The warp is light-colored wool or goat hair, while there are one or two wefts of a similar light color. The warps are usually all on the same level, while the sides are bound with a simple double overcast. A long plain-weave strip, as we often find on older Tekke rugs, does not seem prevalent among the Salors. Rugs over ten feet long are rare. No Salor Katchli design can be identified with any certainty.

a

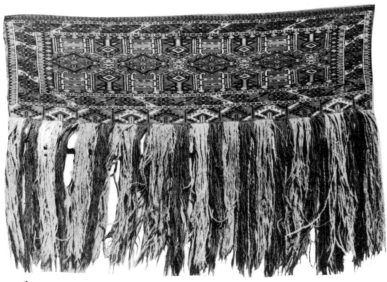

b

105. SALOR BAGS, 19th century. a) 1'3" x 3'9". b) 10" x 2'11". Warp: W. /2\, light wool. Weft: W. /2\, light wool, 2 shoots. Pile: W. /2\ (small amount of silk in a). Knot: P. In (a) left warps depressed 45°. a) v. 21, h. 14, 294/sq inch. b) v. 30, h. 12, 360/sq inch. Sides: a) ..., b) double selvage of red wool over 4 warps. Ends: plain weave bands of ivory wool. On (b) there is added embroidery in blue wool at the top. Colors: a) (6) deep red, carmine, dark blue, dark brown, ivory, yellow. b) (7) deep brick red, 2 shades of rust red, dark blue, yellow, ivory, dark brown. There is often considerable question regarding the label of small Salor pieces, particularly those without the typical gul. These examples both have Salor guard stripes, while all the border stripes on (a) are usually associated with Salor rugs. The design of (b) is also found on rugs that are obviously of Saryk origin, and another version (much more coarsely knotted) occurs among the Ersaris.

106. SALOR GULS. The configuration of (a) is usually found on older pieces, although there is considerable variation in the central figure; (b) is similarly found on old Salor rugs, but it also occurs, often in a more flattened form, on Tekke bags. Other modifications are used for recent rugs by the Saryk and Kizil Ajak in northern Afghanistan, but (c) is an adaption by the Jafarbai Yomud subtribe in northern Iran. The minor guls (d) and (e) show much variation, particularly (e), which also is used frequently by the Saryk. Both also occur on bags of Tekke manufacture; (f) has long provided controversy. It is found on recent rugs (probably Kizil Ajak) from Afghanistan. When it occurs on older pieces, the weave is usually suggestive of a Salor origin. Nevertheless, some pieces have the depressed alternate warps, Turkish knots, and darker colors of the Saryk. Often the elements of (f) are used individually, outside of any gul arrangement (as in Fig. 105b).

SARYKS

The Saryks are said to be an offshoot of the Salors, and they lived in close proximity to this group, at least during the eighteenth and nineteenth centuries. With the Tekke invasion of Merv in 1856, they too were forced to the south where they settled along the Murghab around Pende and Yuletan; some groups migrated as far as Maimana and Qaissar in Afghanistan. Vambery[17] gives their number as around 10,000 tents.

Saryk rugs are probably the most somberly colored of all the Turkomans, and many of the older pieces have a brownish-purple tonality. There are several forms of Saryk major gul, all of which are quartered and have some sort of cross-like figure in the center. The minor guls resemble those used by the Tekkes and Salors, while the border stripes show similar features.

The so-called Pende katchli has long provoked controversy as to its tribal origin. Various sources identify it as Saryk, Salor, and even Kizil Ajak. Reasons for believing it to be Saryk, however, appear most convincing. Firstly Bogolubov's[18] plate of this type clearly identifies it as from a Saryk village in the Pende area. Secondly the colors are similarly dark and somber. Thirdly, both the Katchli and Saryk rugs with guls often employ cotton for patches of white pile, while this is much less common among other Turkoman weaves. Both types may be either Persian or Turkish knotted, and both use occasional patches of magenta silk. Both are double wefted fabrics with the alternate warps depressed; the wool foundation is somewhat darker than that usually found in Tekke and Salor rugs. The design of these katchlis is distinguished by a row of arches along the top of the rug. The general layout has been compared to that of a mosque, a

107. SARYK RUG, 19th century, 4' x 6'4". Warp: W. /2\, light. Weft: W. /2\, undyed, 2 shoots. Pile: W. /2\. Knot: T, terminal 2 rows on each side; P-L, 30° for remainder of the rug, v. 16, h. 10, 160/sq inch. Sides: double overcast of dark blue wool. Ends: 1½ inch ivory plain weave band at both ends, with narrow red stripe. Colors (8): rust red field, brick red, pink, dark blue, dark green, medium brown, yellow, white. Comparison of this rug, featuring a classic Saryk gul, to the "Pende" katchli in Color Plate XVII reveals a great similarity in weave and colors. Almost certainly they are from the same tribal source.

A

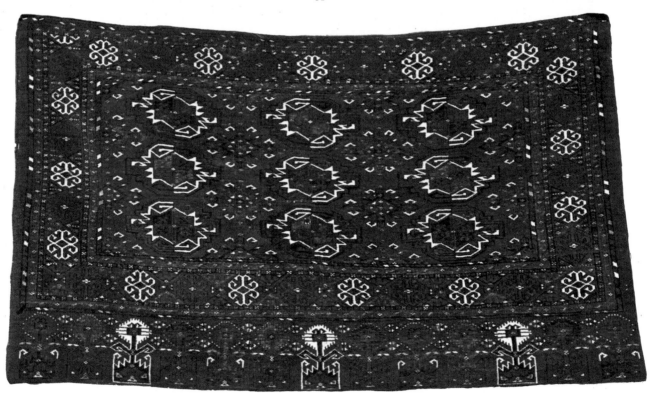

B

Color Plate XVIII. TURKOMAN BAG FACES, 19th century; a) 2'7" x 4'1"; b) 3'1" x 5'. Warp: W. /2\, medium brown. Weft: W. /2\, undyed, light brown, 2 shoots. Pile: W. /2\. Knot: P; a) v. 12, h. 7, 84/sq inch; b) v. 13, h. 7, 91/sq inch. Sides: .... Ends: .... Colors: a) (6) dark brown field, chestnut brown, mauve, deep yellow, dark blue, white. b) (6) brick red, rust red, light blue, dark blue, dark brown, ivory. The first example is a typical Chaudor, and the same design elements and colors may be found on large rugs. The second piece was purchased by the owner in northern Afghanistan from the Ersaris who made the rug. Often this type of bag is erroneously labeled as Yomud work.

Collection of Emmett Eiland, Berkeley, California.

Color Plate XIX. TURKOMAN RUG, 19th century, 6'9" x 10'3". Warp: W. /2\, medium brown. Weft: C. /2\, white, 2 shoots. Pile: W. /2\. Knot: P, v. 12, h. 8, 96/sq inch. Sides: double selvage of brown goat hair over 4 warps. Ends: plain weave remains. Colors (6): dull mauve field, pale red, dark and light blue, ivory, yellow. Despite the lack of typical "ertmen" figures in the field, we have labeled this rug as a Chaudor because of its resemblance to this latter type in color and texture. The Persian knot and cotton wefts are other features pointing away from a Yomudish origin. Courtesy of the **Oriental** Rug Co. of Berkeley, California.

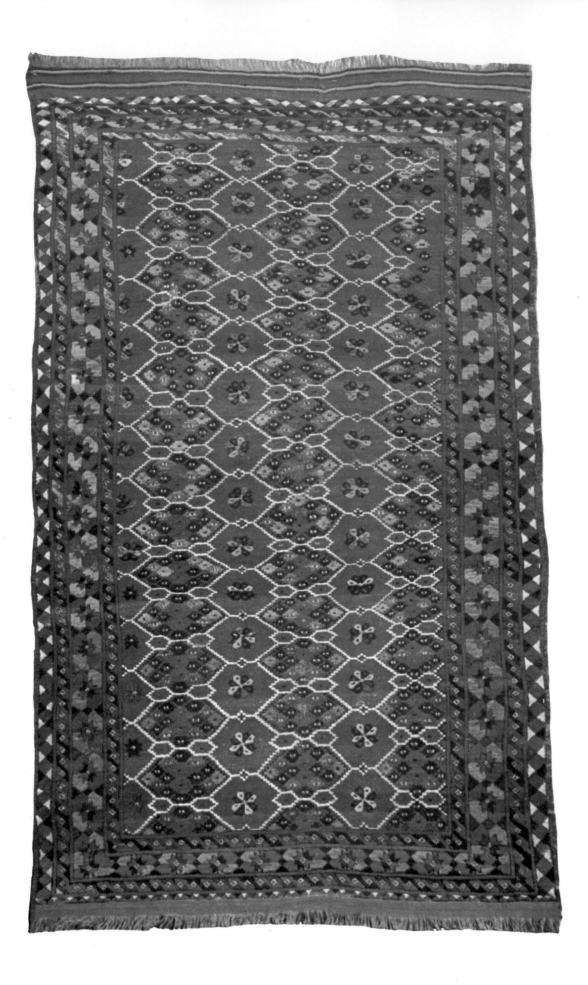

Color Plate XX. ERSARI RUG, 19th century, 4'5" x 8'1". Warp: W. /2\, undyed. Weft: W. /2\, undyed, medium brown, 2 shoots. Pile: W. /2\; Knot: P, v. 9, h. 6, 54/sq inch. Sides: double selvage of brown goat hair over 4 warps. Ends: plain weave in red, with blue and yellow stripes. Colors (6): red field, light and dark blue, yellow, dark brown, ivory. This type of rug is probably a product of the Beshiri, an Ersari-related group. It is not so heavy as the large-gulled "Afghan" type, and the colors are generally brighter.

109. SARYK BAG FACE, 19th century, 40 x 57 inches. Warp: Goat hair, /3\, undyed, light. Weft: W. /2\, undyed, 2 shoots. Pile: W. /2\ and silk for magenta. Knot: P. left warps slightly depressed, v. 14, h. 10, 140/sq inch. Sides: double selvage in red wool over 2 thickened warps. Ends: .... Colors (9): rust red, magenta silk and wool, burnt orange, yellow, light blue, dark blue, light green, dark brown, ivory. Although the colors are uncharacteristically light, this major gul is usually associated with the Saryk. Similar bags, however, are still made by Ersaris.

TEKKES

During the last several centuries, the Tekkes have certainly been the dominant Turkoman tribe; Vambery[24] estimates their number at 60,000 tents. By the late nineteenth century they probably numbered nearly 200,000, and were situated in two major enclaves. The western Akhal Tekkes, with Ashkabad as their center, lived along the northern slopes of the Kopet Dagh in the strip of grassland between the mountains and the desolate Kara Kum desert. The eastern branch underwent several migrations during the nineteenth century. When the Persian power over Turkestan waned, after Nadir Shah's death, these Tekkes had occupied the swamplands where the Tedjend River disappears; but about 1834, finding this land unsuitable, they moved to the area around Sarakhs. In 1856 they were defeated and forced to flee this region by the Persians.

Subsequently they dispossessed the Salors and Saryks of their holdings around Merv and established themselves in this relatively rich land. Even today Tekke remnants live here, as well as in an area north of Herat.

There seems to be no way in which the rugs of the Akhal and Merv Tekkes can be separated. The classic Tekke gul varies amazingly little from one rug to the next over a period of many decades. The octagon is quartered, usually by dark lines joining with the center. There are several types of minor gul, all of which resemble those found in Saryk or some Yomud rugs. The main border stripe may be a repetition of the same radiating rosette figure, or, particularly on older rugs, it may contain a great variety of diverse elements. The finishing of the ends is another indicator of age, as only the earliest specimens seem to have a long, plain-woven strip, always of the same color as the field of the rug. On the old-

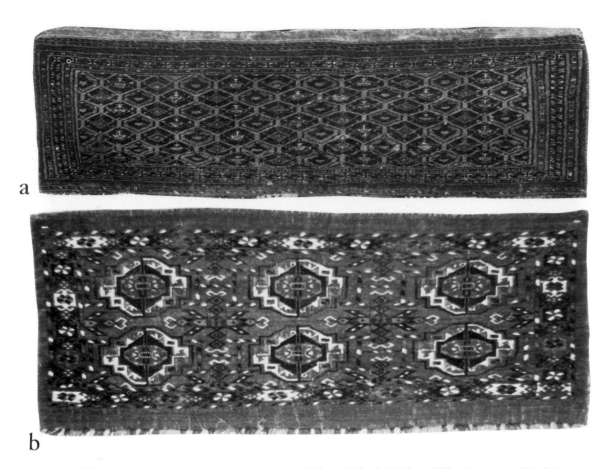

110. TURKOMAN BAGS, 19th century. a) 1'1" x 3'5". b) 1'6" x 3'8". Warp: W. /2\, light. Weft: W. /2\, light; a) 2 shoots; b) 1 shoot. Pile: W. /2\. Knot: a) T-L, 45°; b) P. a) v. 18, h. 8, 144/sq inch. b) v. 28, h. 14, 392/sq inch. Sides: .... Ends: plain weave of ivory wool. Colors: a) (5) carmine, red brown, vermillion, dark blue, ivory. b) (6) deep red brown field, deep red, apricot, dark blue, dark brown, ivory. This size bag is often described by the term "torba," and is found from all Turkoman tribes. (a) is certainly of Saryk origin, while (b) is the Tekke type which is consistently among the very finest of Turkoman weaves.

est rugs this often has three groups of three stripes each, usually in blue or green. Later rugs have only a small ivory band of plain weave, possibly with figures in weft float brocade. Even this is missing in the latest rugs.

The sides are usually finished with a simple dark blue double overcast, while the warp and weft are of light colored wool or wool mixed with goat hair. The knotting is usually Persian, although terminal rows of Turkish knots are common. Most of the rugs are double wefted, with the very finest showing only one weft between each row of knots.

There are a number of other woven products attributed to the Tekkes, although around the jovals and torbas there is some confusion. Among the Tekkes it was originally a custom for the tribal gul to appear only on larger, ceremonial pieces, while the woven products in daily, household use employed another gul.[25] This explains why one never finds the classic Tekke gul on a bag face (at least among older rugs), as another gul, often associated with the Yomud, was used for this. We thus find many Persi-

an knotted bag faces with a simple, Yomud-like gul, but a Tekke weave. Particularly when a Tekke minor gul is used, one must be cautious in attributing these pieces to either tribe.

The Tekke katchli is easily identified and is among the more common rugs of this type. There is only one arch at the top. Tekke tent bands are also found.

Tekke rugs were probably the first to be exported in large quantity, and when the Russian Central Asian Railroad was completed in 1888, great numbers of these were shipped. The increased trade also allowed for the early introduction of aniline dyes. As demand for Tekke carpets increased, the earnings of the weavers rose greatly within a few years.

Rugs with a Tekke design are still produced in large numbers. Many of these originate from Tekke, Yomud, and Goklan Turkomans living in Iran and smaller enclaves in Afghanistan. The classic Tekke gul is also frequently copied in commercial Pakistani rugs.

111. TEKKE GULS. (a) is the classic form and has varied little in rugs over a wide area for at least 150 years. Older guls are more rounded, and the central figures are slightly more complex. (b) is typical of recent modifications woven by Yomuds in northern Iran and numerous groups in Afghanistan. The configuration and central area are simpler. The ovoid shape of (c) is more typical of Goklan rugs. "Minor gul" is not exactly the appropriate term for a figure like (d), and perhaps we should find a word referring to figures between guls. Many variations of (d) are found on Tekke rugs, with similar figures also common on Yomud, Saryk, and even some Ersari rugs. (e) also occurs in many variations, and is most common on Akhal Tekke rugs and those from northern Iran.

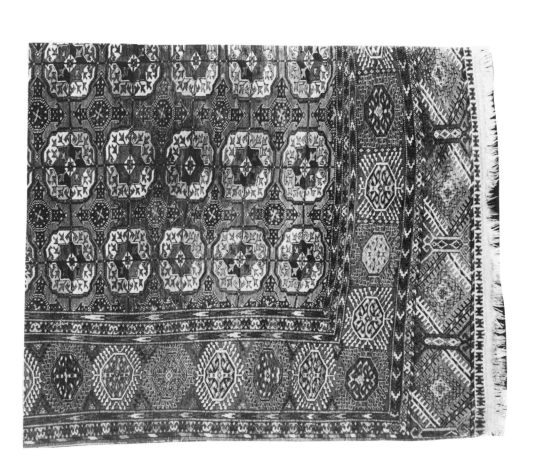

112. TEKKE RUG (portion), late 19th century, 8.2 x 11.8 feet. Warp: W. /2\, undyed, light. Weft: Goat hair, /2\, undyed, medium brown, 2 shoots. Pile: W. /2\. Knot: P-L, 15°, v. 15, h. 9, 135/sq inch. Sides: double overcast in dark blue wool. Ends: narrow band of ivo:y plain weave with weft float brocade and loose warp ends. Colors (6): brick red, carmine, dark blue, dark brown, yellow, ivory. Large Tekke rugs of several distinct types are identifiable, but as yet nobody has suggested a convincing way of dividing them up into Merv and Akhal varieties. Generally the redder rugs are more likely to have the warps on one level and a more complex border. The brownish rugs more often have moderately depressed alternate warps and simpler borders. There are two common types of minor gul.

113. TEKKE RUG, 19th century, 2'2" x 3'7". Warp: W. /2\, light. Weft: W. /2\, light, 2 shoots. Pile: W. /2\. Knot: P, v. 9, h. 12, 108/sq inch. Sides: double overcast of dark blue wool. Ends: long plain weave band of ivory wool with loose warp ends. Ornaments in weft float brocade at both ends. Colors (5): deep red field, dark blue, light blue, pale yellow, ivory. Occasional Tekke rugs are found without the usual Tekke gul. This design more often occurs on pieces of weft float brocade, and it is similar to a common Yomud type.

115. YOMUD KATCHLI, 19th century, 4'2" x 5'8". Warp: W. /2\, undyed. Weft: W. /2\, undyed, 2 shoots. Pile: W. /2\. Knot: T, v. 14, h. 9, 126/sq inch. Sides: double overcast with dark blue wool. Ends: only loose warp ends remain. Colors (6): deep purple-brown, red, dark blue, light blue, dark brown, ivory. The Yomud Katchli may or may not have a small arch at the top. Like the Tekke, they are all superficially similar, but show widely varying design elements.

114. TEKKE KATCHLI, 19th century, 3'8" x 4'6". Warp: W. /2\, undyed, light. Weft: W. /2\, undyed medium brown, 2 shoots. Pile: W. /2\. Knot: P-L, 15°, v. 18, h. 10, 180/sq inch. Sides: double overcast in red wool (not original) Ends: narrow plain weave bands and loose warp ends remain. Colors (6): brick red, bright red, dark blue, medium brown, dark brown, ivory. The Tekke katchli shows considerable variability, as comparison of a dozen specimens would demonstrate. Quite possibly some rugs of this general layout are of Salor origin.

YOMUDS

The Yomuds are a large, widely scattered tribe, and during the nineteenth century they became separated into two contingents. One segment inhabited a portion of the Khanate of Khiva, along the banks of the Oxus, where they lived under the protection of the Emir in return for their help in controlling the maraudings of other Turkomans. The other group, by far the most populous, lived along the eastern shores of the Caspian, as far east as the Akhal Tekkes and south into the lands of the Persian Shah. Vambery[26] lists their number at 40,000 tents, and notes that they occupied villages along the Gurgan and Atrek rivers. Much of the tribe devoted itself to agricultural pursuits, while relatively small portions remained nomadic with their flocks. One portion, the Ogourdjali, were completely sedentary, living in houses rather than kibitkas, and they occupied themselves as traders. Vambery indicates that they refused to recognize themselves as a Yomud tribe.

There is considerably more variation among Yomud rugs than in the three preceding groups, and this may well have resulted from the wide dispersion of a large number of smaller subtribes. In any event we can recognize at least five distinct types of guls, and the number of designs increases greatly if we also consider the numerous flat-woven Yomud pieces. In structure and basic layout, however, they show

116. YOMUD RUG (portion), 19th century, 6'4" x 10'5" Warp: goat hair, /2\, undyed, light. Weft: goat hair, /2\, medium brown, 2 shoots. Pile: W. /2\. Knot: T, v. 15, h. 8, 120/sq inch. Sides: double overcast in medium blue and brick red, alternating. Ends: ivory plain weave band with loose warp ends knotted. The last 2 inches at each corner extend 3 inches beyond other warp ends, and the plain weave has additional brocading. Colors (8): deep reddish brown, dark blue, light blue, yellow, red, deep green, dark brown, ivory. The so-called "Kepse" gul occurs on Yomud rugs from a wide area. Earlier examples are almost always in a larger format, but more recently small bag faces with the Kepse have been woven. The later pieces are also more likely to have guls all of the same colors, rather than the variation seen in this piece from one diagonal to the next.

117. YOMUD RUG (portion), 19th century, 7'1" x 11'3". Warp: W. /2\, undyed. Weft: W. /2\, undyed, medium brown, 2 shoots. Pile: W. /2\. Knot: T, v. 13, h. 8, 104/sq inch. Sides: not original. Ends: narrow band of light brown plain weave with loose warp ends. Colors (7): light brown, chestnut, dark blue, yellow, apricot, dark brown, ivory. Unlike the "Kepse," the so-called "Dyrnak" gul in this specimen may also be found in Chaudor, Chub-Bash, and Ersari weaves. Often it occurs in two forms on the same rug, and it is also found, less often, on smaller pieces.

certain similarities. The Turkish knot is much more common than the Persian among Yomud products, and seldom do we encounter a piece so fine as the best Tekkes and Salors. The warp is usually white, composed of goat hair or a wool-goat hair mixture. Alternate warps are slightly depressed, and the weft crosses twice between each row of knots. The edges are usually double overcast or selvaged, while the ends often have long woven skirts and less commonly show a long plain weave strip. There may be a great variety of ornaments in the skirt.

For the most part design motifs of the larger rugs are not the same as those used on smaller pieces and bag faces. On the latter one most often finds a quartered gul similar to that used by Tekkes and Ersaris, but, unlike the major Tekke gul, it may be drawn in a variety of ways. The borders on these pieces are usually very simple, with repetitions of small, geometric figures.

The guls of larger Yomud rugs may be colored in a way providing a diagonal orientation. The so-called dyrnak gul is the most common and may appear in two different forms on the same carpet. Bogolubov[27] attributes a piece in this design to the Ogourdjalis on the Island of Tchelekene, but we are

certain that other subtribes also used the same gul.

The so-called tauk-noshka, as discussed above under Saryk rugs, occurs in Yomud weaves frequently, usually with the typical Yomud "meandering vine" or "curled leaf" border. The "Kepse" gul is less common, while there are several others that are very rare. The colors of these and other Yomuds are still based around a dominant red or reddish brown, but in kepse rugs one is more likely to find significant use of light blue, green, salmon, yellow, and orange.

Yomud katchlis are not so common as those of the Tekkes, but they show more variation. Most older examples have no arch, the field being divided into four quadrants with the larger two uppermost. When a prayer arch occurs it is most frequently central and near the top, as in the Tekke, although one may also find a row of these same figures forming a panel across the bottom of some rugs.

The Yomuds make a variety of flat stitch fabrics of Soumak or weft-float brocading, rather than the slit-tapestry technique. Yomud tent bands are relatively common in at least two designs, and apparently all of the bands are done in a flat weave.

a

b

c

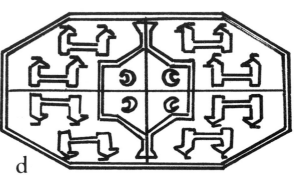

d

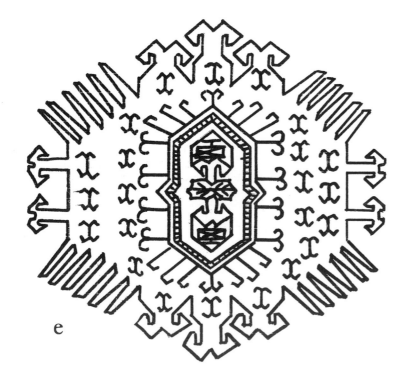

e

f

118. YOMUD GULS. The two major forms of dyrnak gul (a) and (b) are almost exclusively Yomud, except for occasional Ersari adaptations. These, along with the Kepse (c) are still used in the Soviet Union and Iran. Yomud tauk noshka rugs are less common (d), while (e), (f) and (g) were never used extensively and appear to be almost extinct now. Yomud bag faces employ numerous guls, including (h) and (i), while (j) is a common minor gul. The Yomuds of northern Iran employ a number of small guls on their rugs, including (k), which is woven by both Jafarbai and Atabai.

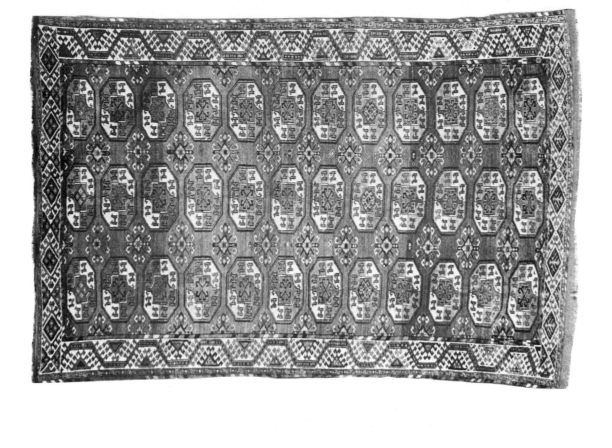

120. YOMUD RUG, 19th century, 5'8" x 9'4". Warp: goat hair /2\, undyed. Weft: W. /2\, undyed, 2 shoots. Pile: W. /2\. Knot: T, v. 16 h. 10, 160/sq inch. Sides: not original. Ends: narrow red-brown plain weave bands with loose warp ends remain. Colors (6): deep reddish-brown, bright red, light blue, dark blue, dark brown, ivory. The "tauk noshka" gul may also be found on Chaudor and Ersari rugs, but here the weave is classically Yomud.

119. YOMUD BAGS, late 19th century, a) 1'2" x 2'7"; b) 2'6" x 3'8". Warp: W. /2\, light brown. Weft: W. /2\, light brown, 2 shoots. Pile W. /2\. Knot: T, a) v. 16, h. 8½, 136/sq inch; b) v. 15, h. 9, 135/sq inch. Sides: a) .... b) double selvage of red-brown wool over 4 warps. Ends: .... Colors: a) (7) red brown field, red, apricot, light and dark blue, ivory, dark brown. b) same. Yomud bag faces vary considerably in size and design. The guls on (b) are most common, while those on (a) are relatively rare. (b) Courtesy of Oriental Rug Co. of Berkeley.

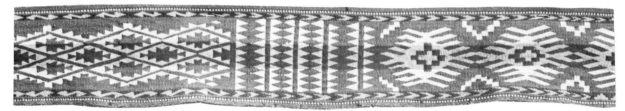

121. TURKOMAN TENT (KIBITKA) BANDS (portions).

a) Yomud tent band, l'l" x 51'. Design mostly in weft float brocade on plain weave ground. (Deep red, brown-black, ivory, yellow, dark blue.) These are found in several distinct designs and are still used by the Turkomans in northern Iran.

b) Yomud tent band, 1'9" x 52'. Plain weave ground with color provided by deep red warps; borders in weft-float brocade. Ornamentation of field (red, dark and light blue, yellow, ivory) probably embroidered with needle. This type of band is found in widths from 6 inches to about 2 feet. At times the entire field is covered by weft-float brocade, usually in just red and blue.

c) Ersari tent band, 1'6" x 54'. Ghiordes knotting (W. /2\, in deep red, rust, green, yellow, and white cotton) on cotton plain weave. The knots are probably put in by needle and run parallel to the long axis. These are made near Maimana and may be all recent; we know of no old pieces of this type. Possibly they are late adaptations of Tekke tent bands.

d) Gilza'i band, 6" x 42', weft-float brocade in rust red, ivory, yellow dark brown, light blue. These are not used the same as Turkoman tent bands (the Gilza'i live in black tents), and they are probably purely decorative. Large kilims are made by sewing these strips together.

(c) and (d) Courtesy of the Oriental Rug Co. of Berkeley.

122. YOMUD OSMULDUK, early 20th century, 27" x 43". Warp: W. /2\, undyed. Weft: W. /2\, undyed, medium brown, 2 shoots. Pile: W. /2\. Knot: T, v. 13, h. 9 117/sq inch. Sides: double overcast in brown wool, with added band of braided yarn. in bright red, brick red, green, and white. Ends: plain weave folded under, with ends of tassels looped through plain weave. Colors (7): dark brown, dark blue, green, apricot, bright red, brick red, white. These pieces are used as camel decoration on ceremonial occasions such as bridal processions.

123. YOMUD BAG, 20th century. 2'4" x 3'8". Warp: W. /2\, light, 16 strands/inch. Weft: W. ground weave dyed red, /2\, 20-24 shoots/inch. Colors (7): red, dark and light blue, white (cotton), dark brown, green, yellow-orange. These pieces seem to be made in great numbers now, and we have never encountered an example with significant age. There are a combination of flat stitch techniques used, including weft-float brocading, Soumak brocade, and slit-tapestry kilim.

a

b

124. YOMUD DOOR HANGING and SADDLE PIECE

a) 1'6" x 3'8". Warp: W. /2\, light brown. Weft: W. /2\, light brown. Pile: W. /2\. Knot: T, v. 14, h. 10, 140/sq inch. Sides: double selvage of light blue wool over 2 warps. Ends: plain weave folded under. Additional overcast at top. Colors (6): red field, light and dark blue, green, red brown, ivory.

b) 3'2" x 3'11" at widest point. 6½" strips sewn together. Design in weft-float brocade of ivory, orange, medium brown, dark brown, on red-brown field. The Yomud make a wide variety of small animal and tent decorations.

CHAUDORS

The Chaudors were described by Bogolubov[28] as being a subtribe of the Yomud, but the two have been separate at least since the sixteenth century, and now neither group recognizes a relationship. During the nineteenth century the tribe lived in an area between the Aral and Caspian seas, with two subtribes, the Abdals and Ikdyrs, inhabiting Caspian coastal areas above Krasnovodsk. Other groups lived in an arc along the northern edge of the Kara Kum, into the territory around Khiva; a southern group settled around Pende. Vambery[29] estimated their number at 12,000 tents.

Chaudor rugs are characterized by a slightly more somber color scheme than the Yomud, with a frequent use of chestnut brown and a light brown-violet. They are usually all wool, with the weft sometimes dark, but we also find some Chaudors with cotton wefts. The knotting is more likely to be Persian, particularly in the larger pieces, but Turkish knotted rugs are also found.

In design the typical Chaudor is characterized by a stepped polygonal gul known by the term *ertmen*, which appears on all sizes and types of rugs. There are usually no minor guls, but only a lattice-work of jagged lines interrupted by floral figures. Usually these, as well as the floral elements inside the guls, are drawn more naturalistically than on most Turkoman rugs. Other Chaudor rugs may appear with *Tauk noshka* or *Dyrnak* guls and are distinguished from Yomuds by their colors.

Several forms of Chaudor prayer rug are known, including one in a katchli format. On bag faces the ertmen may be so arranged that they appear only in halves.

125. CHAUDOR ERTMEN GULS. Some variation of (a) is most common on large Chaudor rugs. There are more differences among ertmen found on bag faces, the origin of which is at times obscure. (e), (f), and (g) are particularly likely to be found on long, narrow strips from northern Afghanistan, probably woven by Chub-Bash elements. (b) is usually found on more finely woven pieces that originate from the Merv area.

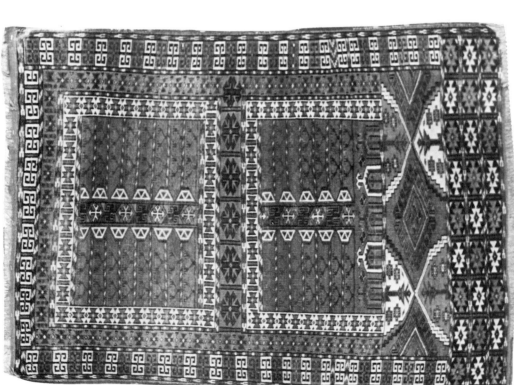

127. ERSARI KATCHLI, mid-, or early, 19th century, 3'10" x 4'8". Warp: W. /2|, undyed, dark. Weft: W. and goat hair, /2|, undyed, darker than warp, 2 shoots. Pile: W. /2|. Knot: P, v. 9, h. 7, 63/sq inch. Sides: double selvage of brown goat hair over 3 warps. Ends: ... Colors (8): brick red, apricot, blue-green, light and dark blue, yellow, ivory, dark brown. Ersari katchlis show the greatest variability of all, and this example is unusual in its clearly delineated mihrabs. On many pieces the field is quartered and there is no arch.

126. CHAUDOR KATCHLI, 19th century, 4'3" x 5'6". Warp: W. /2|, undyed. Weft: W. /2|, undyed, dark, 2 shoots. Pile: W. /2|. Knot: P, v. 12, h. 8, 96/sq inch. Sides: double selvage of dark brown goat hair with loose warp ends remaining. Ends: plain weave band of faded magenta with loose warp ends remaining. Colors (5): chestnut, magenta brown, dark blue, dark brown, ivory. The strip of "ertmen" figures and the chestnut and magenta-brown colors identify this as to tribal origin, although there are other types of prayer rugs associated with the Chaudors.

ERSARI

Ersari rugs are the subject of considerable confusion, as they have been arbitrarily divided by the rug trade into several categories, none of which involve an accurate description of the people making these rugs. For years most small Ersaris were known as *Beshires*, while the larger pieces with guls were called *Afghans*. (The name *Khiva* for these rugs is even more misleading.) Neither of these terms conveyed information as to who made the rug. While there is a town on the Oxus named Beshire, it is inhabited by Ersaris. To add to the confusion, however, there is a tribal group in Afghanistan known as the Beshiri, who make rugs we would identify as Ersaris. Elements of this tribe live around Aktsha, Andkhui, Shur-tepe, and Qunduz. They are clearly related to the Ersari, but also may be classified as a separate tribe.

The term Afghan is even less explicit, as it does not even mean that the rug was made in Afghanistan, and, contrary to what one finds in several of the older rug books,[30] there is no Turkoman tribe known under that name. The border between Russian Turkestan and Afghanistan is artificial, drawn during the nineteenth century as a result of political intrigue among European powers. In discussing Turkoman rugs, we may safely ignore it, assuming that Ersaris on one side of the border make the same rugs as Ersaris on the other.

Seemingly this would leave us with only the Ersari to consider, along with the related Beshiri, but there are several other groups that also make rugs. The Kizil-Ajak, who live in small enclaves around Herat, Aktsha, Shibergan, Andkhui, and Mazar-i-Sharif, weave a rug technically identical to the Ersari. They seem to be a more recently formed tribe and may have Yomudish elements. The Chub Bash, with groups around Shibergan and Shur-tepe, also may be of relatively recent origin, only here there are likely Chaudor elements. Chub-Bash and Chaudor rugs share certain design similarities, including use of the ertmen and the tauk noshka.

The Ersari themselves probably migrated from the Manguishlak district during the seventeenth century, with some remaining in the Khanate of Bokhara and others settling further south among the Uzbegs and Pashtuns of northern Afghanistan. They are divided into well over twenty major subtribes, inhabiting areas along the Amu Darya from Chardjou southward; in Afghanistan there are large groups around Aktsha, Shibergan, Shur-tepe, Andkhui, and Mazar-i-Sharif, with scattered enclaves as far west as Herat. Ersari groups live side by side with Beshiris,

Kizil Ajaks, Chub-Bash, and even Baluchi tribesmen. As the rugs of all but the last of these groups are virtually indistinguishable structurally, we have a difficult task in making specific identification. Some observers have approached the problem by devising a series of ambiguous names, in which some rugs are labeled as *Ersari-Beshire, Afghan of the Ersari,* or even *Afghan Ersari-Beshire.* In order to avoid such obfuscation, our solution has been to consider rugs of all these people together under the term "Ersari group," making distinctions only when our information is sufficient to justify specific labels. The rugs, indeed, share many features in common.

In color rugs of the Ersari group are generally lighter and more lively than those of other Turkoman tribes. The reds are likely to be paler, and there is more use of white, light blue, green, and particularly yellow, which may be a vivid saffron. The designs are immensely variable, but allow several basic classifications. For convenience we can identify four types:

1) The gul forms are easiest to classify, and there are numerous local variations from one subtribe to the next. The *guli–gul,* with floral elements, is most common, although the tauk noshka is frequently encountered. There are also a number of guls in which the two types seem to be combined. As was the practice among the Tekkes, until recent times the tribal guls were not employed on pieces used in everyday, household activities (bags and smaller pieces). We thus find tribal guls primarily on the larger carpets, usually of a size about 7½ by 9 feet.

2) Bags and smaller carpets commonly display some form of latticework, with jagged lines dividing the field into large, diamond shaped, gul-like areas. These pieces show great variety, with floral figures that may be highly stylized or surprisingly realistic.

3) Another category of design is often found in the older rug books, although production of these rugs seems to have ceased at least fifty years ago. These were characterized by Persian-derived patterns such as the Herati, in a characteristic crudely drawn form, often in a large, elongated format.

4) Several types of prayer rug have been made by the Ersaris, including a narrow type with a long mihrab and simple, stylized floral figures, which has become much sought after by collectors. An Ersari version of the katchli bears a resemblance to the Yomud design, although the former is larger and heavier.

A distinct type of prayer rug is found among

129. ERSARI RUG (portion), 19th century, so-called "Afghan". Warp: W. /2\. undyed, medium dark. Weft: W. and goat hair, /2\, undyed, dark brown, 2 shoots. Pile: W. /2\. Knot: P, v. 6, h. 6, 36/sq inch. Sides: double selvage of dark brown goat hair over 4 warps. Ends: long plain weave strips of red with blue stripes. Colors (7): rust red, light and dark blue, yellow, light green, dark brown, ivory. Both the "guli" gul and the minor guls occur in many forms in these rugs, and they were probably highly specific to certain tribal groups during the 19th century. These rugs typically have heavy, thick pile.

128. ERSARI RUG (portion), 19th century, 7'1" x 15'. Warp: W. and goat hair, /2\, undyed, dark. Weft: goat hair, /2\, undyed, dark, 2 shoots. Pile: W. /2\. Knot: P, v. 12, h. 7, 84/sq inch. Sides: double selvage of brown goat hair over 4 thickened warps. Ends: long plain weave band of red, with blue stripes. Colors (6): pale red, dark and light blue, yellow, white, dark brown. In portions of this rug the "tauk noshka" appears as a simple "H," and in one gul (lower left corner) we find the more typical Ersari "guli" gul.

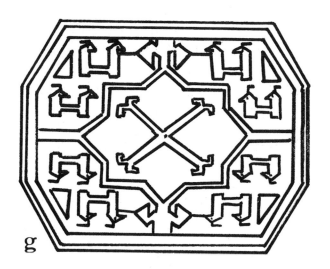

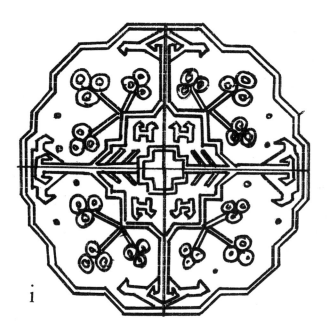

130. ERSARI GULS. Among Ersari subtribes there are literally dozens of guls and variants. Whatever tribal significance they once may have had has now virtually disappeared, as a few guls have become popular in many weaving areas, while others are virtually extinct. (a) and variants of (b) are employed over a wide area, although the former was originally more associated with the Soleimani subtribe. (c) has been traditionally used by the Dali subtribe, with (d) allegedly employed mostly around the city of Daulatabad; now it also has a wide distribution. (e) and (f) are seldom seen now and are associated with the Ghazan and Temirdshin subtribes. Of the numerous forms of tauk noshka, (g) is probably most common; both the Kizil Ajak and Chub-Bash weave rugs with similar guls. (h) is of obscure origin and rare now, as is (i), which occurs on a group of finely knotted rugs that likely date from the mid-19th century or even before.

the Kizil Ajak and several other Ersari groups, with variants among such Baluchis as the Dohktar-i-Ghazi around Herat. These rugs show designs apparently based on mosque architecture, with columns, hanging lamps, and arches.

In structure Ersari rugs are generally heavier and more loosely woven than western Turkoman rugs. Most are Persian knotted, although the Turkish knot may still be found in terminal rows on each side. Alternate warps are slightly depressed, and, as we would expect, the foundation is all wool, with the weft crossing twice between each row of knots. The wool warp tends to be darker than in other Turkoman rugs, and particularly in older specimens, there is often an admixture of goat hair. The ends may show a long band of plain weave, with blue or green stripes. Larger Ersari rugs ordinarily do not have a decorated, woven skirt, as we find on the Yomuds. The sides may have any of several types of finish. Most common, especially for larger pieces, is the double selvage of dark goat hair, similar to that found on Baluchi rugs. The bag faces, however, may have merely a double overcast of wool, usually the same color as the field. Occasionally one sees an elaborately woven selvage with a checkered pattern of two different colors (like that found on such Yomud pieces as the Osmolduks).

Among Ersaris one also sees a number of rugs with guls obviously borrowed from other tribes, particularly the Saryk and Salor. Some sources suggest that these rugs were actually made by those tribes after part of their number migrated to Afghanistan, but there is no reason to believe that they would adapt an Ersari mode of weaving merely because they changed locality. The Kizil Ajak often use a variant of the Salor gul, while the Saryk gul is found on many Ersari bags.

131. ERSARI DOOR HANGING, 3'8" x 2'1". Warp: W. /2\, gray-brown strands mixed with light. Weft: W. /2\, light wool, 2 shoots. Pile: W. /2\. Knot: P, v. 8, h. 7, 56/sq inch. Sides: double overcast of deep red wool. Ends: plain weave bands of natural wool turned under at top and bottom, with colored wool braids and tassels added. Colors (6): deep brick red, rust red, ivory, dark brown. yellow, salmon. Although all Turkoman tribes must have some form of door hanging, those of the Ersari probably show the widest variation in design. This particular design (so-called "Ashik") is also found among the Saryks and Salors.

132. ERSARI BAG FACES, 19th century. a) 1'6" x 5'3". b) 1'6" x 4'9". Warp: W. /2\, undyed, medium brown. Weft: W. and goat hair, /2\, undyed, dark brown, 2 shoots. Pile: W. /2\. Knot: P, a) v. 11, h. 7, 77/sq inch. b) v. 11, h. 10, 110/sq inch. Sides: a) double selvage of light blue wool over 2 warps. b) .... Ends: only plain weave of red wool remains. Colors: a) (6) rust red, apricot, dark blue, light blue, dark brown, ivory. b) same, except yellow instead of light blue. Long narrow bag faces of this sort are common only among the Ersari; (b) appears to be the older of the two and is most likely a product of the Kizil Ajak. The tauk noshka figures are particularly well drawn; in each one the ends are dissimilar — an unusual feature in later rugs.

133. ERSARI BAG FACE, 19th century, 3'8" x 5'9". Warp: W. /2\, medium brown. Weft: W. /2\, 2 shoots. Pile: W. /2\. Knot: P, v. 10, h. 7, 70/sq inch. Sides: double overcast of red wool. Ends: plain weave folded under. Colors (6): brick red field, dark and medium blue, ivory, yellow, dark brown. This latticework design has been woven for at least a hundred years. New specimens are almost knot for knot replicas of antique pieces, although only among the older examples is one likely to find larger rugs of this type.

134. ERSARI RUG, 19th century, 4'2" x 6'. Warp: W. /2\, undyed, medium brown, 2 shoots. Pile: W. /2\. Knot: P, w. 6, h. 6, 36/sq inch. Sides: double selvage of brown goat hair over 4 warps. Ends: plain weave bands of light brown wool. Colors (7): rust, dark and light blue, light green, dark brown, yellow, ivory. If nothing else, the Ersari are the most eclectic of Turkoman weavers, and sources for this design are not difficult to trace in rugs of other tribes.

135. ERSARI RUG (portion), 19th century, 4'5" x 10'5". Warp: W. and goat hair, /2\, light. Weft: W. /2\, undyed medium brown, 2 shoots. Pile: W. /2\. Knot: P, v. 13, h. 7, 91/sq inch. Sides: double selvage of light blue wool over 3 warps. Ends: plain weave bands of red wool. Colors (7): deep red, rust red, dark and light blue, ivory, medium brown, light yellow. It is not clear whether one should refer to the diamond-shaped design figures in this rug as guls. Likely they developed from lattice patterns. They do not seem characteristic of any particular Ersari subgroup.

136. BAG FACES from Afghanistan, 19th century. a) 1'2" x 3'4"; b) 10" x 4'4". Warp: W. /2\, medium brown. Weft: W. /2\, undyed, 2 shoots. Pile: W. /2\(traces of yellow silk in (a)). Knot: P. Ends: plain weave bands folded under. At lower end of (b) long threads are looped through plain weave. Colors: a) (6) brick red field, dark blue, yellow, ivory, dark brown, magenta. b) (6) red, apricot, dark and light blue, dark brown, ivory. These bags both have design elements derived from the Yomud dyrnak, while (a), with halved Ertmen guls, would suggest an origin from Chaudor remnants, possibly the Chub-Bash.

137. ERSARI BAG FACE, 19th century, 3'1" x 5'7". Warp: W. /2\, undyed. Weft: W. /2\, undyed, medium dark, 2 shoots. Pile: W. /2\. Knot: P, v. 12, h. 8, 96/sq inch. Sides: .... Ends: .... Colors (4): rust red field, dark blue, dark brown, ivory. Stripe designs are woven by a number of Turkoman tribes, but in this example the weave is clearly Ersari.

138. KIZIL AJAK PRAYER RUG, early 20th century, 2'11" x 5'1". Warp: W. /2\, undyed, medium gray-brown. Weft: W. /2\, undyed, 2 shoots. Pile: W. /2\. Knot: P-L, 25°, v. 12, h. 6, 72/sq inch. Sides: double selvage of red wool over 2 warps. Ends: narrow red plain weave bands and loose warp ends. Colors (6): bright red, deep red, dark blue, dark brown, ivory, light brown. The design is clearly inspired by the architectural details of a mosque, and some more recent pieces are even more realistic.

CURRENT PRODUCTION OF TURKOMAN RUGS

The great majority of the Turkoman people are now included in the Soviet Union, with whom trade has been limited by political considerations; yet we find dealers in both the United States and Europe with large supplies of rugs in the ever-popular Turkoman patterns. While there is still significant rug production in Turkestan under the Soviet regime, most of the currently available materials originate in Persia, Afghanistan, and, more recently, Pakistan. The old tribal designs have been expropriated rather indiscriminately, and one may find curious combinations with borders of one origin and guls of another.

New Turkoman rugs from the Soviet Union do not reach the United States in large quantity, as they are expensive relative to the products of other areas, and customs duties are assessed at a much higher rate. The Free Port of London, however, has a large stock of these rugs, and examination of hundreds of new pieces leaves one with the feeling that craftsmanship is maintained at a high level. While the dyes are no doubt synthetic (but of good quality), and the bright red is usually subjected to some form of "London wash," the designs and actual weaving can be favorably compared to the standards prevailing early in the century. Most of the rugs have Tekke designs, with the guls drawn faultlessly, and even the borders (unlike those on Persian "Tekkes") show considerable variation. Yomud "Dyrnak" and "Kepse" rugs are available, as well as a smaller number with Chaudor "Ertmen" guls. There is no reason why these rugs should not mellow into fine antiques.

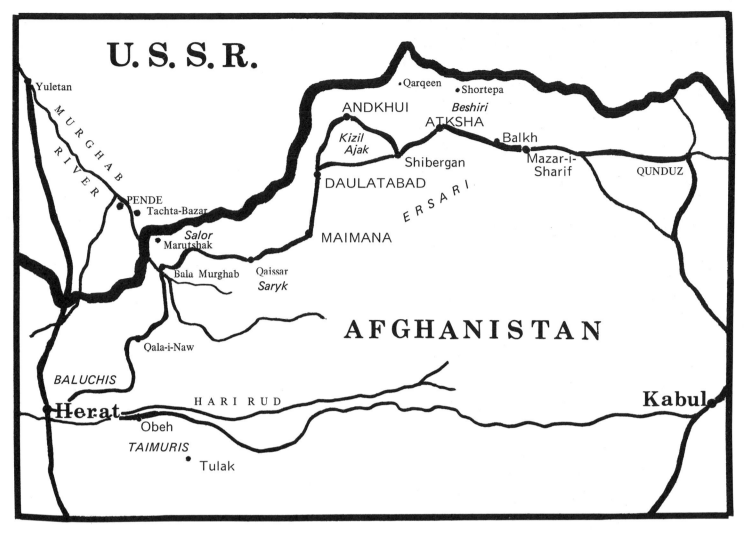

Map No. 11.   Rug-Weaving Areas of Northern Afghanistan

IRAN

The case is somewhat different in Iran, where the drawing is often defective, and most modern products will never attain character with age. Here much of the weaving comes from two Yomud sub-tribes, the Jafarbai and Atabai, and some Tekkes who migrated southward during the 1930s. The Tekkes settled just below the Soviet border around Marvehtepe and other villages north of Gombad. Their rugs are woven much as before, with the traditional gul and rather unstable bright red dyes.

The Yomuds weave in both traditional and Tekke designs. The Jafarbai, for the most part, produce two distinct types (usually small) in a medium grade weave of about 100 knots to the square inch. One design involves a repeated gul-like rhomboid figure that resembles that found on brocaded pieces; the other common motif superficially resembles the Salor gul, with similar serrations, but it is relatively flattened and arranged diagonally across the field with no minor guls.

The Atabai weave larger rugs in the traditional Dyrnak and Kepse designs. Although most of them are brightly colored, a small number are found with the old brown field. The Atabai also weave bags and large rugs in Tekke-like designs. The gul is usually somewhat simplified, with the configuration more rigid and rectangular. (These are to be distinguished from the similar Goklan rugs with Tekke guls, in which the configuration becomes more ovoid, with the corners rounded.) These rugs have unimaginative borders, with little variation from one section to another. They are still made on a wool foundation, however, and the craftsmanship may be surprisingly good. Meshed and Tehran serve as market centers for these rugs, and the same merchandise seems to be available in both places.

AFGHANISTAN

The material available in Afghanistan differs dramatically from what one encounters in Iran. At least for the last fifty years the Ersaris and related tribal groups have been fairly sedentary, and nomads found in the Turkoman areas are primarily of Pashtun or Baluchi origin. Ersari subtribes are thus increasingly mixed, among themselves and their Uzbeg neighbors, and this leads to a considerable diffusion of old tribal designs. In addition a number of important rug merchants have set up workshops in some of the larger towns, and they supply dyed yarn and even designs to weavers who work in their own homes. The situation is becoming one in which we may more accurately refer to a rug by local rather than tribal origin. The Kabul dealers thus describe a rug as from Aktsha or Daulatabad, rather than in terms of the Ersari subtribes who live there.

The best of the Afghan carpets are the so-called *Mauri* (named after Merv), and are made in a number of centers throughout northern Afghanistan. Marutshak (still inhabited by Salorish remnants) and the Herat Province are important weaving areas, and even the city of Herat has a number of workshops, including an orphanage where boys do the weaving. (The carpets made there have moderately depressed alternate warps, and the Persian knots are tied with a hook.) The Tekke gul is far the most common design (some of the weavers are Tekke), while production is increasing in the so-called *Zaher Shahi* design, based on an old Akhal Tekke motif and named after the current King of Afghanistan. This is usually found on a white background.

Mauri carpets of the best quality are distinguished from lesser grades by being knotted with single rather than double plied yarn, thus allowing the weave to be tighter. The colors bear a good resemblance to those found in older carpets, but a visit to the dyers of Herat reveals the same rows of boxes from Bayer and Hoescht that one finds elsewhere in the Middle East.

Also included with Mauri carpets are the so-called *Sarooq* types (the traditional spelling in rug books has been *Saryk*, but the word is actually pronounced to rhyme with *book* or *look*). These are a little coarser, have slightly more depressed alternate warps, and occur mostly with a Salor major gul and no minor guls. Until fairly recently a number of them displayed considerable use of silk, but this has apparently stopped. Saryk katchlis are apparently no longer woven. (I have made a careful and fruitless search for them.)

The second best quality of carpet, and the finest of the traditional Afghans, is the Daulatabad, woven around that town and Maimana. A number of old Ersari guls are used, along with Tekke-like guls (more widely spaced); the border stripes are relatively narrow, and the fabric somewhat stiff. Colors in Daulatabad rugs range from bright red to reddish brown.

Similar in design are the carpets made around Andkhui, which are somewhat heavier and are more likely to be found in adaptations of old Ersaris patterns. In many of these carpets Karakul wool is used for the white, natural gray, and black. The best carpets from this region are known by the village name of Altibolak.

A medium grade of carpet is also produced in Aktsha and surrounding villages, and here much of the production is controlled by Kabuli merchants. Consequently the colors and designs are more responsive to market conditions in Europe. An example is the so-called "Golden Afghan," which was originally the result of a London bleach job that changed bright red to a sickly yellow. Now carpets are woven in Aktsha that are yellow to begin with, as well as pink, beige, and dull brown. These pieces do not require a bleach. The designs feature traditional Ersari large guls, as in Daulatabad, although there are usually a greater number of border stripes.

The lower grades of Afghan carpets now come from Qarqeen and Shibergan. These resemble Andkhui carpets in design, but while the weave is just as fine, they are more pliable and lighter. This results from the use of thinner yarn, spun from Karakul wool, which gives a coarser feel.

Despite the loss of specific tribal identification among Ersaris, several groups still weave characteristic designs. Recently the most prominent of these has been the Djengal-Arjuq, who live around Aktsha and make rugs with fairly naturalistic floral designs. Many bear a superficial resemblance to early Turkish prayer rugs, with columns, hanging lamps, and elements of mosque architecture, but the borders and cross panels may be relatively curvilinear. The rugs have probably been produced only during the last several decades, and I have found no old pieces. They seem to be popular export items.

PAKISTAN

In Pakistan the carpet industry has expanded greatly within the last twenty years, prospering primarily from patterns borrowed from the Turkomans. Indeed, market conditions alone determine the type of rug woven; yet the finished product has some desirable features. The cotton foundation allows for a straight fabric that lies better on the floor than a rug with a wool warp. The knotting in the better grades is quite dense and may exceed even the earlier Turkoman pieces. Cashmere wool of a lustrous softness is used for the so-called *Mori* rug (another variant of Merv). The dyes are all synthetic, but of good quality.

Nevertheless, the colors in these new rugs are probably their most objectionable feature, as they are often acceptable in other respects. One may find rugs with gray or green fields with patches of bright orange or gold. To one schooled upon the subtleties of the old Tekkes or Yomuds, these innovations seem gaudy and contrary to the original spirit. This probably represents the low point in the use of Turkoman designs.

OTHER RUGS FROM TURKESTAN

Turkomans are not the only weavers in Turkestan. There are products woven by the Kirghiz, Karakalpaks, Uzbegs, Tadjiks, Gilza'i, and Hazaras, as well as a number of other groups such as the Teimuri, Djamshidi, and Bahluri, who are considered under the section on Baluchi rugs. Relatively few fabrics from these peoples reach markets outside of their immediate area, and those that do are usually not properly identified. Certainly few of us are able to recognize woven products of the Uzbegs and Tadjiks, although the brilliantly colored Hazara kilims (woven with a warp sharing technique) are readily distinguished. The Gilza'i, cattle-raising Pashtun nomads, make a characteristic fabric of narrow strips sewn together, with the design in weft-float brocade.

Other migrating Pashtun groups, including also some Gilza'i, are known simply as *Kuchis*, a term applying to many peoples of diverse origin among the country's two million nomads. In the bazaars from Kabul to Kandahar and Herat to Mazar-i-Sharif, the same types of small bags and tent pieces are found. They are attributed simply to Kuchis, and dealers are unable to give precise origins. As these people are notoriously shy of strangers, and they have not been systematically studied, we cannot make precise attributions, but often their products are very appealing, woven in designs imaginatively adapted from Turkoman work. The colors, however, are brighter, and often the sides and ends are finished elaborately with tassels and braids. (I have never seen these for sale outside of Afghanistan.)

The Waziris are another Pashtun group weaving a distinctive rug not well known outside the country. These rugs are usually small and relatively narrow, and the field design consists of medallion-like, asymmetric, stylized floral figures arranged longitud-

inally. Many of these rugs are subtly colored and pleasing, but production is quite low. At any given time there are probably no more than a dozen for sale in the Kabul shops.

Both the Karakalpak and the Kirghiz weave pile carpets; yet we have considerable difficulty in making clear identifications. A recent Soviet publication[31] deals with the latter group in some detail. The rugs are all wool, Persian knotted, and resemble Baluchis in coloring. We are told that both the Karakalpaks and Kirghiz learned weaving from the Turkomans, but there is every likelihood that they have carried on the art for many centuries.

THE RUGS OF EASTERN TURKESTAN

Rugs from Eastern Turkestan are seldom found in the United States, and they have never been available in quantities allowing wide distribution; yet there are several reasons for including them in our discussion, despite our intention of avoiding Chinese rugs in general. Firstly we should correct one clear error of attribution — the rugs are known in the trade as Samarkands, which is an inaccuracy probably stemming from their being marketed frequently, but not invariably, in that city. There is no tradition to support a claim to any significant carpet industry in Samarkand, and the rugs can be demonstrated as originating in the eastern Turkestan cities of Yarkand, Kashgar, and most importantly, Khotan. This area is the westernmost portion of China and was part of the Sinkiang Province until 1955 when it was divided into semiautonomous areas of different tribal groups.

Our second reason for considering Eastern Turkestan rugs involves another mistake, but one more difficult to prove. It has long been assumed that these rugs, because of similar construction and apparently related design motifs, were derivative from the rugs of China and somehow became distinct only through closer proximity to rug weaving centers of the West. In the literature we see repeated references to Chinese influence from Grote-Hasenbalg to Rosa Belle Holt, who describes the rugs as showing ". . .distinctly Chinese characteristics. . . . As in all rugs of this description, the Chinese element is plainly seen, both in design and color, showing what proximity of location will affect."[32]

The opposite case is more likely, and for information bearing on this we are indebted to Hans Bidder's[33] extensive monograph devoted to these rugs. After a thorough historical review Bidder con-

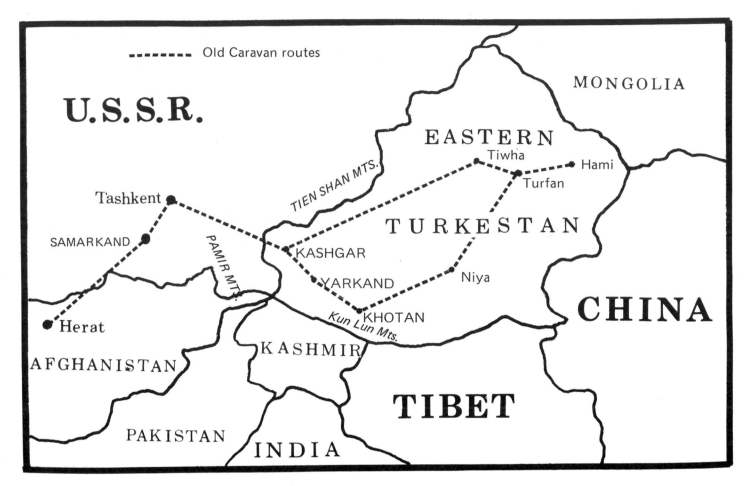

Map No. 12.   Eastern Turkestan

cludes that China's accomplishments in carpet manufacture are almost exclusively derivative from the West, particularly Turkestan. Furthermore, this has occurred in relatively recent times, as we have no documentation of early Chinese rug weaving or surviving examples that could be dated before the 18th century. Bidder identifies the oasis of Khotan as the center of rug production in eastern Turkestan, with the oases of Kashgar and Yarkand as somewhat less important. He presents a well-documented theory that carpets have been produced continually in this area for 2000 years. While not completely convincing, the possibility is certainly established.

If, indeed, there has been an unbroken chain of development in these towns, one reason would be various geographic features of the surrounding area. In the great central portion of Eastern Turkestan lies the Takla Makan desert, extending 1500 miles from east to west, 250 miles from north to south, which is not only unexplored but virtually unhabitable. Surrounding this are formidable mountain ranges with the Pamirs to the west (in places rising over 25,000 feet), the Tien Shan on the north,

and the Kun Lun range to the south, extending eastward in a northerly direction and cutting off free access to central China. A drainageless basin is thus created, with the water run-off from the mountains winding through the wastes of the Takla Makan and disappearing in salt marshes. As the annual rainfall is in most places less than fifteen inches per year, this makes possible the habitation only of oasis towns fed by the rivers, and along both northern and southern edges of the desert lie a string of small inhabited areas.

From these data we may make several observations: 1) the area is accessible from the outside only with great difficulty, 2) the land is not of a richness to invite settlement or colonization from outside, but can support only a small population, and 3) it lies in the only natural corridor for trade between China and the West, including India. We thus have an area of fairly static population exposed to influences from both East and West, with towns along the trade routes dating back at least to the first several centuries B.C. when the area was controlled by the Han dynasty of China, although the settled inhabitants of the oases were likely of an Indo-European stock.

The region passed under many powers during the next two thousand years. The Chinese control, from the second century B.C. to the fourth century A.D. and from the seventh to tenth centuries, was primarily a matter of maintaining garrisons to secure the silk routes to the West, and no attempts at colonization were made; this was true even after the Manchus reconquered the western province in 1757. In the interim, under various Turkish and Mongol overlords, the cultural orientation was westward, particularly after the Turkish ninth-century migrations through the basin, which imposed a Turkish language and the Mohammedan religion. Nevertheless, the resident population of the oases remained almost unchanged, and even today they show distinct Indo-European facial characteristics and coloring.

Our first direct evidence of carpetmaking in Khotan is contained in the finds of Sir Aurel Stein,[34] who traveled widely in the area from the 1920s until his death in 1953. In several burial sites around Niya, east of Khotan, and near Lake Lop Nor, he found knotted carpet fragments that have been dated anywhere from the third to the sixth century A.D., which places them as the second oldest finds of knotted pile rugs. There is still some question as to just where these carpets were produced, but the writings of Chinese travelers suggest that at least during the seventh century pile carpets were made in Khotan and Kashgar, although Marco Polo, who traversed the same territory, fails to mention such an industry. Information is sparse as to whether carpets were made during the period of Western orientation from the tenth through mid-eighteenth centuries, but quite possibly production continued. With the return of Chinese ascendancy we have many descriptions of carpets from travelers.

Still there are several unanswered questions. We know that Stein's findings were of an entirely different construction from more recent carpets of Khotan. The older rugs are distinguished by the Turkish knot (about 8 x 4 to the square inch), a wool warp, and four loosely twisted wool wefts between each row of knots. This, of course, differs markedly from the modern Khotan carpets, even those that are dated to the eighteenth century. The later rugs are nearly all Persian knotted, as are the rugs of China, and such a change in the type of knot would not likely have evolved gradually. It could be taken as evidence that the Stein finds and the later carpets from the area represent two entirely separate traditions.

In any event we have no evidence of a carpet industry in China predating the known eastern Turestan carpets, and there are no Chinese carpets that we could date with any certainty as being before the eighteenth century. The Chinese have not demonstrated a great fondness for woolen fabrics, and only with the demand for carpets from the West did manufacture begin on a large scale. Surveys of Chinese industry in the early nineteenth century make no mention of carpets, and likely few were made before the 1890s. While this leaves us without a clear answer, we may tentatively view the Khotan rugs as having a longer lineage than those from central China, and we can accept them as distinct in themselves rather than derivative.

Recent carpets from Eastern Turkestan are notable for their soft wool, grown mostly by Kirghiz tribesmen inhabitating the foothills of the Kun Lun range. The dyes are similar to those found in other oriental carpets before the influx of analines after 1870. Cochineal and indigo were long imported from India, and there was a particularly bright, rich red in many of the old carpets (called Tibetan red) which allegedly came from the saffron flower. Dark colors, browns and black, were usually natural shades of wool, and thus do not show increased wear as in many Persian carpets. Basically the palette was somewhat limited, with primary use of only light and dark blue, bright and wine red, light and dark yellow, and various natural shades. With the advent of synthetic dyes, we have a wider range, particularly with magenta and orange.

The designs are generally of three varieties: 1) one or more medallions, 2) variations of the vase and pomegranate motif, or 3) gul designs reminiscent of western Turkoman patterns, but usually surrounded by a geometrical coffering. There are also occasional rugs with overall patterns obviously based on the Herati or other classic Persian designs, but these can usually be distinguished at a glance from their western counterparts. By far the commonest design is the medallion, with one, two, or three nearly circular medallions arranged longitudinally on a rectangular field. If there are more medallions, the arrangements differ; with five we find one in each corner and one in the center, and with an even number, they may be arranged side by side. The three-medallion carpet is most frequent.

Whatever the field design, the same limited range of border designs is found, with one main border and from 3 to 9 smaller stripes. These are often derived from the swastika, in various connected forms. The cloudhead motif is also common, along with simple Greek or Chinese key motifs.

139. EASTERN TURKESTAN RUG, probably from Khotan, 19th century, 4'4" x 9'. Warp: C. /6\, undyed, white. Weft: W. /2\, undyed, medium dark, 2-5 shoots, some straight and some loose. Pile: W: /3\, untwisted. Knot: P, v. 8, h. 7, 56/sq inch. Sides: .... Ends: loose warp ends. Colors (5): red-magenta field (considerable abrash), blue gray, dark brown, faded yellow, ivory. The feel of these rugs is loose, and considerable weft is visible from the back.

In size Eastern Turkestan rugs are more uniform than those from most areas; the classic examples usually measure twice as long as they are wide; the commonest dimensions are about 3.6 x 7 feet and 7 x 14 feet. Those specimens we consider the earliest are more likely to be nearly square; and by the early twentieth century we find another group of rugs in dimensions more suitable to Western tastes; among these one may encounter some 9 x 12 foot carpets.

Structurally these rugs show little variability, and this adds to the problem of specifically assigning them to any one oasis center or another. Virtually without exception they have thick cotton wefts, of four to six strands plied together, and they appear to be essentially all Persian knotted. (The rare pieces with Turkish knotting usually have additional questionable features that make their origin doubtful.) In some pieces of apparently early manufacture, alternate warps are significantly depressed, and the knotting is relatively fine. Recent rugs show wefts more or less on the same level, with a knot count usually between 30 and 80 to the square inch. Usually one will find three wefts of dark wool between each row of knots, although there may occasionally be four or more. One group of rugs, however, shows undyed or blue cotton wefts, often only two strands, and another group has two or three strands of light wool. Schürmann[35] has attempted to localize these techniques to Yarkand and Kashgar, respectively, but the evidence is meager. Particularly when dealing with rugs alleged to be over one hundred years old, we are on dangerous ground when we attempt to make too specific a localization.

Silk rugs are occasionally found, probably from all three oases, and may have a foundation of cotton or, rarely, of silk. Some specimens show portions embroidered with metal thread.

The dating of these rugs presents a problem, as we have little information on which to base our conclusions. A sixteenth-century origin has been claimed for some, and others have been assigned to the seventeenth and eighteenth centuries. As with rugs from western Turkestan, however, this seems tenuous, and we cannot be certain about anything before 1800. We do know that early in the nineteenth century the rugs had entered into commercial channels and were directed toward at least three markets. Eastward the outlet was through the Kansu province of China, and the rugs were known by that name in the Chinese trade. A number of carpets also made their way by camel caravan through the mountains to the south and west into British India, and from there to English markets. Probably more were taken west through Samarkand, which, fairly soon after the Russian occupation in 1868, had railroad connections with the larger trading centers. There was also probably a large market for these carpets within Central Asia itself, and many travelers have noted their extensive use within Samarkand.

In recent years the markets have seen little of Eastern Turkestan rugs. There was some exporting up to World War II, but we have no way of knowing what changes have occurred under the Communist regime. Within the last year I have seen a few new pieces for sale in Kabul.

Eastern Turkestan rugs have never been popular in the United States. Their loose construction would seem ill-suited to many American homes. They are much more common in Europe, particularly on the London market.

NOTES

1. Bogolubov, A. A., *Tapisseries de L'Asie Centrale*, St. Petersburg, 1908, 2 vols.
2. Gregory, J. S., and Shave, D. W., *The U.S.S.R.*, Harrap and Co., London, 1944.
3. Barthold, V. V., *Turkestan down to the Mongol Invasion*, Luzac, London, 1958.
4. Fraser, J. B., *Narrative of a Journey into Khorassan*, London, 1825, p. 281.
5. Vambery, A., *Travels in Central Asia*, Harper and Brothers, New York, 1865, pp. 473-74.
6. O'Donovan, E., *The Merv Oasis*, London, 1882, vol. II, p. 352.
7. Curtis, W. E., *Turkestan, the Heart of Asia*, New York, 1911, pp. 167-168, 320-321.
8. Wegner, D., "Nomaden und Bauern-Teppich in Afghanistan," *Baessler-Archiv*, Neue Folge, Band XII, pp. 151-152.
9. Moshkova, W. G. "Gols auf turkmenischen Teppichen," *Archiv für Völkerkunde*, vol. III, Vienna, 1948, pp. 39-42.
10. Trotter, J. M., *Topography, Ethnography, Resources, and History of the Khanate of Bokhara*, Calcutta, 1873, pp. 50, 55.
11. *Ibid.*, p. 55.
12. Vambery, *op. cit.*, p. 352.
13. O'Donovan, *op. cit.*, vol. II. Data given on fold-out map.
14. Vambery, *op. cit.*, p. 350.
15. Schürmann, Ulrich, *Central Asian Rugs*, Verlag Osterrieth, Frankfurt, 1969, pp. 82-83.
16. Bogolubov, *op. cit.*, p. 10.
17. Vambery, *op. cit.*, p. 351.
18. Bogolubov, *op. cit.*, p. 10.
19. Gogel, F. W., *Teppiche*, Moscow, 1950.
20. Clark, H., *Bokhara, Turkoman, and Afghan Rugs*, John Lane and Bodley Head Ltd., London, 1922, pp. 89-90.
21. Thacher, A. B., *Turkoman Rugs*, E. Weyhe, New York, 1940, Plate 39.
22. Schürmann, *op. cit.*, p. 103.
23. Bogolubov, *op. cit.*, p. 11.
24. Vambery, *op. cit.*, p. 351.
25. Moshkova, *op. cit.*, pp. 33-34.
26. Vambery, *op. cit.*, p. 355.
27. Bogolubov, *op. cit.*, p. 11.
28. *Ibid.*, p. 12.
29. Vambery, *op. cit.*, p. 349.
30. Thacher, *op. cit.*, p. 25.
31. Umetalieva, Dzhamal, *Kirghiz Carpets*, U.S.S.R., 1966.
32. Holt, R.B., *Rugs, Oriental and Occidental*, Garden City Publishing Co., Garden City, New York, 1937, p. 102.
33. Bidder, Hans, *The Rugs of Eastern Turkestan*, Universe Books, New York, 1953.
34. Stein, Aurel, *On Ancient Central Asian Tracks*, Pantheon, New York, 1964.
35. Schürmann, *op. cit.*, p. 45.

VIII RUGS OF THE CAUCASUS

There have probably been more errors and misleading statements about rugs from the Caucasus than any other major group. Anyone consulting more than one source is inviting a potent dose of inconsistency and fantasy. The misinformation begins at a basic level—the names themselves are suspect. Most Caucasian rugs marketed in the West have been sold under the labels of Kazak and Cabistan; the remainder have been called by such terms as Karabagh, Shirvan, Daghestan, Kuba, and Baku. Rug dealers seem confident when they use these labels, and, if one were not to look closely, there would seem to be a clear means for distinguishing the origin of these rugs. Beneath the veneer, however, lies a chaos, as no one seems to know precisely what any of these terms means.

Cabistan (also spelled Kabistan, Capristan, and Cabristan) would appear from its construction to be a place designation. It even occurs on several maps in rug books; yet there is no such geographical location, and writers present a wild array of explanations for its use. Mumford[1] insists that misplacement of one letter was responsible for the error, as he attributes these rugs to the city of Kuba and its vicinity. Kubistan thus becomes Cabistan. Jacoby[2] notes, however, that the rugs were from Shirvan, and the name represents a contraction of Kiaba-Shirvan. (*Kiaba* is a term describing the size of most Shirvans.) In their introduction to the Metropolitan Museum of Art's *Ballard Collection of Oriental Rugs*, Breck and Morris[3] note that "Some Daghestan rugs are called Kabistan; Kouba gives its name to another group." Jacobsen[4] sticks to the dealer's terminology, noting that most of the rugs are undoubtedly Daghestans, but he explains an arbitrary classification in which only a certain type of prayer rug is called a Daghestan, while those rugs showing Persian influence (flowers and angular designs) are called Kabistans. One last curious suggestion from several other sources[5] is that the word is derived from Cabristan (land of graves), and refers to some funereal use of a certain size or type of carpet.

After reading such conflicting assertions, one could be excused for showing some confusion as to just what is meant. Clearly the word does not have a precise meaning, and it can easily be discarded from our classification. Most dealers now use it to describe any finely woven Caucasian rug that they cannot identify more specifically.

A question also exists about the other common term, *Kazak*, as here we are describing the carpets of a people who apparently do not exist in any context outside of rug books. Many writers assure us that the word is a corruption of Cossack and that the rugs are products of either a tribe closely related to Russians[6] of that name, or people who are in fact those Russians who dwell along the banks of the Don.[7] Mr. Hawley[8] notes that rugs were produced by the Tcherkess, or Circassians, who lived along the eastern coast of the Black Sea and, after their conquest by the Russians, migrated into the southern Caucasus.

Actually Kazak rugs were made (and modern versions are still woven) in that portion of the southern Caucasus between Tiflis and Erivan, bordering the Gendje area on the northeast and the Karabagh area on the southeast. Ethnographic studies of the Caucasus show that the area is inhabited primarily by Armenians and Azerbaijani (Azeri) Turks,[9,10,11,12] with a smaller population of Georgians and Kurds. In the anthropological literature there is nowhere described a group in this area by the name of Kazak, nor do we find Circassians within several hundred miles—they are located well north of the Caucasus. This does not imply that the data are incomplete, as official Russian census figures are available from 1886 and 1897 that categorize the inhabitants of each area specifically into tribal groups. We can thus say with some certainty that the people living in the villages that make Kazak rugs are Azeri Turks and Armenians, often living side by side. Still, there may be sufficient reason to retain the term, as the rugs are known by no other name, and their exact village origins are so obscure as to make designation on this basis impossible.

One might speculate as to why such conflicting information abounds about Caucasian rugs. The most likely explanation is that the region is so geographically isolated that travel until recent times has been difficult. Few Westerners in the rug business have traveled there, and most writers reveal that their research is faulty. Actually, although the rugs themselves have been imperfectly studied, we have an immense compilation of information about the Caucasus, and there is no reason to regard it as

Color Plate XXI. ERSARI BAG FACE, 19th century, 3'7" x 5'8". Warp: W. /2\, undyed, dark gray-brown. Weft: W. /2\, undyed, dark, 2 shoots. Pile: W. /2\, silk. Knot: P, v. 12, h. 7, 84/sq inch. Sides: double selvage of brown goat hair over 4 thickened warps. Ends: upper—plain weave band folded under. Lower—loose warp ends. Colors (9): light and dark blue, yellow, white, red, pink, light green, dark brown, ivory. In the upper half of the field, the centers of the repeating figures are in silk (light green, light blue, pink, and yellow).

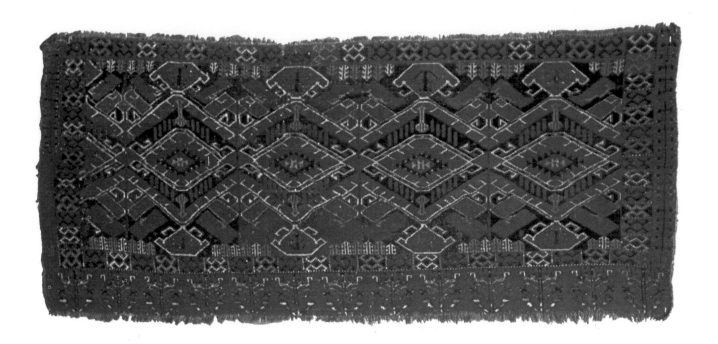

Color Plate XXII. BAG FACES from Afghanistan. a) 2'2" x 4'10''; b) 3'5" x 6'2" (with fringe). Warp: W. /2\, medium brown. Weft: W. /2\, 2 shoots. Pile: W. /2\. Knot: P; a) v. 11, h. 8, 88/sq inch. b) v. 8, h. 7, 56/sq inch. Sides: a) double selvage of red wool over 2 warps; b) fringe sewn along 3 sides; 1'' strip of weft float brocade with webbing and tassels added. Ends: .... Colors: a) (8) brick red field, dark blue, medium blue, medium brown, ivory, apricot, deep green, yellow. b) (6) rust red field, yellow, green, dark blue, dark brown, ivory. Interesting bags are woven by many of the smaller ethnic groups in Afghanistan. (a) is a product of the Ersari-related Beshiri. (b), although obviously influenced by Ersari designs, is not Turkoman work. Kabul rug dealers label these as "Kuchi" bags, which means simply nomad. Probably this was made by the Kara-Kirghiz.

Color Plate XXIII. RUG FROM SOUTHERN CAUCASUS, 18th century, 5'1" x 6'2". Warp: W. /2\, light brown. Weft: W. /2\, dyed pale red, 2 shoots. Pile: W. /2\. Knot: T-L, 20°, v. 9, h. 7, 63/sq inch. Sides: double selvage of pale red wool over 3 warps. Ends: selvaged at both ends. Colors (8): pale red field, dark blue, light blue, deep green, yellow, mauve, dark brown, ivory. This rug is clearly descended from a group dating back at least to the 17th century and possibly before. The origin of these pieces is obscure, and may be either in the southern Caucasus or north-western Persia.

Color Plate XXIV. KAZAK RUG, 18th or early 19th century. 4'3" x 6'11". Warp: W. /3\, light. Weft: W. /2\, undyed, 2-6 shoots. Pile: W. /2\. Knot: T, v. 6, h. 6, 36/sq inch. Sides: double selvage of red, blue, and yellow-brown wool over 6 warps in zig-zag pattern. Ends: .... Colors (5): red field, medium blue, yellow, medium brown, ivory. This piece is probably from the Bordjalou area, and the bold design suggests an origin possibly as early as the 18th century. The rug is particularly heavy, and the back appears irregular because of the variable number and thickness of the wefts.

Color Plate XXV. KAZAK RUG, 19th century, 6'1" x 9'3". Warp: W. /3\, light brown. Weft: W. /2\, dyed red, 2-4 strands, all loose. Pile: W. /2\. Knot: T, v. 6, h. 6, 36/sq inch. Sides: double selvage of red wool over 3 warps. Ends: upper—narrow plain weave band and selvage. Lower—loops. Colors (7): blue field (light and dark), brick red, pink, apricot, dark brown, ivory. Rugs of this type were made near Erivan, and some specimens over twelve feet long can be found.

Color Plate XXVI. KAZAK, 19th century, 4'4" x 7'10". Warp: W. /3\. Weft: W. /2\, dyed
red, 3-4 shoots. Pile: W. /2\. Knot: T, v. 7, h. 7, 49/sq inch. Sides: double selvage of red wool over
three warps. Ends: red plain weave and selvage remain at the top. Colors (7): rust red, blue green,
light and dark blue, white, yellow, dark brown. Kazak rugs in this design were apparently made in
several areas, as they show considerable differences in construction, colors, and wool.

Color Plate XXVII. PICTORIAL KARABAGH, early 20th century, 4'11" x 6'1". Warp: W. and C. /2\; medium brown wool twisted together with white cotton. Weft: W. /2\, undyed, 2 shoots. Pile: W. /2\. Knot: T-L, 45°, v. 9, h. 8, 72/sq inch. Sides: .... Ends: loops at lower end, plain weave at upper end. Colors (12): red field, pink, deep red, dark brown, medium brown, light brown, black, yellow, gray, gray-green, light green, ivory. From the beginning of the Russian occupation of the Caucasus, there was a production of pictorial and floral rugs from the Karabagh area, primarily from the vicinity of Schusha. They are characterized by curvilinear designs, often from European sources, and a wide range of colors.

Color Plate XXVIII. SHIRVAN PRAYER RUG, 19th century, 4'5" x 5'4". Warp: W. /2 , light. Weft: W. /2 , undyed, 2 shoots. Pile: W. /2 . Knot: T, v. 9, h. 8, 72/sq inch. Sides: .... Ends: .... Colors (6): pale red field, light blue, dark brown, pale yellow, red brown, ivory. While this wildly imaginative rug would seem to be unique, there is an almost identical piece, with different colors, depicted by Schurmann.

Courtesy of S. W. Shear, Berkeley.

a mysterious and uncharted wasteland. There are about nine million people in the Transcaucasian Republics of Armenia, Azerbaijan, and Georgia, and some of their natural resources, such as the oil around Baku, have become important for the Soviet economy. Both geographic and ethnographic studies are plentiful, and we may draw from a number of sources.

There is also a wealth of historical data beginning in Greek and Roman times, and parts of the southern Caucasus were Byzantine colonies. From the eighth to the twelfth century there was a succession of powerful Georgian kings, but, particularly after the Mongol conquest, more and more people used the Caucasus for refuge as they were driven from their homelands. Finally, with the gradual Russian subjugation of the Tartars, the Czarist regime advanced into the mountains. After a series of wars with Persia and Turkey, the present boundaries were settled. As late as 1946 there was still a dispute between the Soviet Union and Iran as to the control of Persian Azerbaijan.

GEOGRAPHY OF THE CAUCASUS

The Caucasus could be said roughly to include the land between the Black and Caspian seas, and essentially to comprise a border between Europe and Asia. The mountains themselves are easily divided into two groups, the Greater and Lesser Caucasus, with the first consisting of a steep, narrow chain running diagonally across the isthmus between the northeastern shore of the Black Sea to the Apsheron Peninsula on the Caspian. The elevation across this area, between 9,000 and 18,000 feet, presents a great natural barrier 60 to 100 miles wide. The northern slopes are more abrupt than the southern, and they merge with the vast steppe area extending into central Russia. To the south is a broad valley through which the Rioni River drains westward and the Kura empties to the east into the Caspian. This is the Transcaucasian area and comprises a fertile plateau of varying elevation. Further to the south, beyond the river valleys, the Lesser Caucasus rise, blending imperceptibly with the highlands of the Anatolian Plateau and the mountain chains of northern Iran.

Because of great differences in altitude the climate varies considerably. In the Rioni Valley and the Caspian coastal areas there is heavy rainfall and dense vegetation, with mild winters and cool summers. In the Greater Caucasus, the Armenian highlands, and the Kura Valley the climate is one of extremes: little rainfall, hot summers, and subzero winters. On the higher mountains are perpetual snows.

ETHNIC GROUPS

The Caucasus has been inhabited continually from Paleolithic times; there are archeological sites from numerous peoples and civilizations. The area has been used both as a corridor for migrations and as a refuge for nations driven out of more desirable territory. For thousands of years it served as a passage between Asia and Europe, and portions have been invaded and occupied by so many peoples that a classification has until recently been all but impossible. Only after advances in Caucasian linguistics have we been able to categorize the various racial and national groups, which are usually divided into Caucasian and non-Caucasian types. The first group includes all peoples speaking languages unrelated to any found outside the Caucasus, and the second is composed of those speaking languages from later migrations: the Indo-European, Turco-Tartar, and Semitic stocks. The true Caucasians are further divided into three branches; the northwestern, northeastern, and the southern.

In the northwestern Caucasus are the Abkhaz and the Circassians (or Tcherkess), about whom so much has been written in the rug books. Mumford[13] narrates their migration in 1864-66, half a million strong, from ancestral homelands through the Caucasus to Anatolia. He describes their rugs as very much like Kazaks. He gives a highly questionable account of their fortunes, and other writers seem to have picked it up. We often see rugs described as Tcherkess, although no one seems able to distinguish them from Kazaks. Those Circassians remaining in Russia, according to census figures, number over 200,000,[14] and Turkish data of 1945 show about 75,000 of these people residing in Anatolia.

A great number of separate tribes inhabit the northeastern Caucasus, the two largest being the Chechens in the north (who were deported by the Soviets to the central Asian steppes in 1943), and the Lesghians to the south. The area north of the Greater Caucasus is called Daghestan, and the cities of Derbend and Kuba are located there. Ethnographic maps show dozens of small enclaves of different peoples throughout Daghestan, and it is impossible to assign specific rug patterns or weaving methods to them. We can, however, present new findings. Although Mumford, Hawley, and others refer to the Chechens as makers of rugs commonly called Chi-chis (Tschichi and other spellings), these rugs originate from the Kuba district — a fact confirmed by details of construction. It is unlikely that Chi-chi rugs have anything to do with the Chechens, who

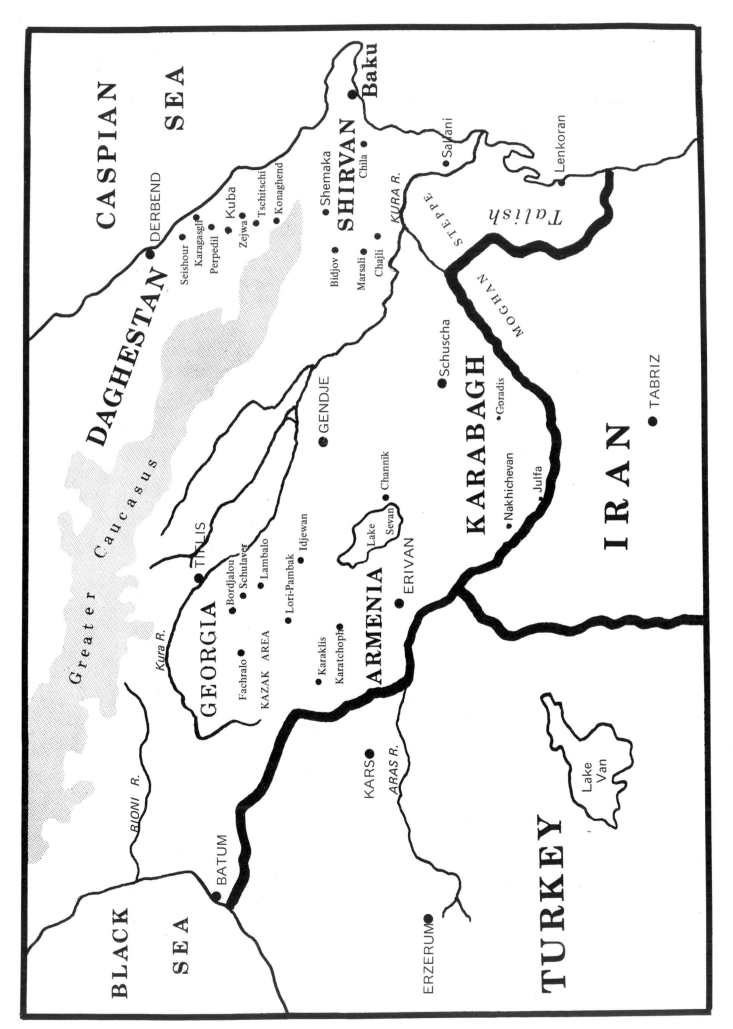

Map No. 13. The Caucasus

live several hundred miles north of where the rugs were made.

The southern Caucasus is by far the most populous area and produces the bulk of Caucasian rugs. The Georgians, numbering several million, are the largest group with a Caucasian language, although they apparently have never been great weavers. Rugs were for a time marketed in Georgia's capital of Tiflis, but these were probably the products of tribes to the south. We have an account from 1875 (von Thielmann[15]) of the bazaar in Tiflis in which it was noted that carpets were generally brought from Persia, although inferior specimens could also be obtained from Nucha and Baku.

Around the Georgians live smaller groups of Mingrelians, Svans, and Laz, none of whom are known for their carpets. More important as weavers are the Armenians, inhabiting areas of the Lesser Caucasus and the portions of the Anatolian plateau bordering Turkey. These people number about three million, and they have probably made rugs for centuries. The last important group is a mixture of Turco-Tartar origin referred to as Azerbaijani (Azeri) Turks, a term that does not imply ethnic homogeneity. They inhabit most of the Shirvan area and the city of Baku. A great many Caucasian rugs are produced by these people.

There are two remaining small groups of Indo-European origin, the Kurds and Talish. The former inhabit mountainous territory bordering Persia, while the Talish live in a small area off the Caspian coast around the city of Lenkoran. Both peoples have been heavily influenced in their carpet making by the Turkic population around them, and it is often impossible to distinguish their products.

GENERAL CHARACTERISTICS OF CAUCASIAN RUGS

Perhaps the most important point in the identification and classification of Caucasian rugs is that distinctions can very seldom be made by pattern alone, as we have often done with Turkish, Persian, and Turkoman rugs. Although one could say much about the great natural barriers presented by the mountain chains, there has been considerable communication between peoples, as few groups have economies that are truly self-sufficient. Moreover, the area producing Caucasian rugs extends at most only about three hundred miles inland from the Caspian (in most places considerably less), and, except for the Talish region, is only several hundred miles from north to south. This stricture and the economic necessity of trade have resulted in a widespread diffusion of patterns throughout the entire region. This is not to say that there are no differences among various localities, rather that we cannot point to any particular design motifs and say categorically that they are from one area and not another. A given border stripe, for example, may be found from northern Daghestan to southern Shirvan with little variation. To make a closer identification we must study more carefully the construction of a rug.

The warps are almost always of natural colored wool, twisted of two, three, or four strands, which themselves may be of different shades from white to dark brown. The strands may also be arranged to present a flat or nearly flat surface on the back (as the Kazak, Shirvan, and Gendje), or alternate warp strands may be depressed up to 75 degrees in some Daghestans. Rugs from the southern Caucasus have the warp looped over a pole or rope at one end of the loom rather than tied to it, so that when the carpet is finished and the beam is removed, the exposed warp at one end consists of loops; the other end is fringed where the strands have been cut. Often the ends are too worn for intact loops to remain, but there is some protection when they have been woven into a thick band. By teasing apart the strands it is possible to see that the warp is looped at one end. On north Caucasian pieces all the warps are cut from the loom, and the fringes are similar at both ends.

The weft is less frequently of wool than the warp, and variation is introduced by dyeing in many rugs. Again the natural colors may vary greatly, and there may be two or three strands (including one occasionally of cotton) twisted together. Often in Kazak or Gendje rugs the weft is dyed red or, rarely, blue; the Talish may dye the strands light blue, a feature that also occurs in many Persian rugs. Classically the weft is passed twice between each row of knots, and this is nearly always the case with the finer weaves. In some of the coarser Kazak and Gendje rugs we may find three or even four or more strands, and they may vary considerably in thickness.

There are also distinguishing features in the way the ends are finished, as we may find narrow bands of plain weave at one or both ends. In some rugs one end has a several-centimeter woven band turned and bound under the rug, while the other end has a woven band and a fringe. This band is seldom long on Caucasian rugs, and when a long kilim is found on an all-wool, brightly colored geometric rug, one should consider an Anatolian origin. Kuba and Daghestan rugs often have the warp ends tied in a series of knots.

Binding of the sides may be either in wool or cotton. Daghestan rugs almost always have a thin white or blue wool overcast or selvage. Kuba rugs often follow this pattern, with more variation, while in Shirvan rugs white cotton is the most common material for edging. In some Gendje and Talish rugs the yarn may differ in color along the length of the edge or rarely on some south Shirvan pieces may be so arranged as to present a checkered pattern. As with the warp ends, this edge is among the first parts of a rug to wear, and caution must be used in determining whether the binding found on a rug is original. Often it has been replaced with something entirely foreign to the rug, and other means of identification must be used.

The type of wool is also revealing, although it may have undergone changes over the years from wear or cleaning. Talish rugs are characterized by the coarseness of their wool; poorer wools are also used in Derbent, Gendje, and in some varieties of Kazak rugs. Other types of Kazaks, Kubas, Shirvans, and the most finely woven Daghestans often have a lustrous wool that imparts a velvety quality to the fabric.

Much has been written to the effect that the wild nomads making Caucasian rugs have not thus far been corrupted by Western commercial influences, but, at least so far as dyes are concerned, this again is an exaggeration. Synthetic dyes were available as early as the 1870s, although they apparently did not become so widespread as in other areas. Otherwise one finds the same dyestuffs as in other Middle Eastern rugs, with the reds either of madder or cochineal, and the blues almost always of indigo. The first synthetics were the familiar bright orange (that mellows not at all with age), mauve-magenta, and some shades of pink. Fading is extreme in many of these rugs.

140. KAZAK RUG, late 18th or early 19th century, 5'8" x 7'4". Warp: W. /3\, undyed. Weft: W. /2\, undyed, 2 shoots. Pile: W. /2\. Knot: T, v. 10, h. 9, 90/sq inch. Sides: .... Ends: .... Colors (7): ivory field, red, dark and light blue, yellow, deep green, dark brown. The narrow borders and richly embellished design suggest considerable age for this piece. Grote-Hasenbalg depicts a rug of similar layout without the latch-hooks.

TYPES OF CAUCASIAN RUGS

KAZAK RUGS

In many respects Kazak rugs are archtypical of other Caucasian weaves, with their bold, vigorous designs and vivid color schemes. Their area of manufacture, roughly between Tiflis and Erivan, includes hundreds of villages, each with its own peculiarities of design and color. Some authors distinguish between rugs of the most important villages: Lambalo, Schulaver, Bordjalou, Lori-Pombak, Karaklis, Idyawan, Fachralo, and Karatchoph. Such localization must be approached with caution, as there has been a considerable diffusion of design, and the features of construction do not allow for a precise identification.

Generally Kazak rugs have large-scaled patterns, often of several medallions, in clear, brightly contrasting colors. The warp is without exception naturally colored wool, usually twisted in three strands of slightly differing shades, while the weft is also wool. Often this weft is dyed red, but at times is natural colored and, rarely, blue. There may be as many as four or more weft strands between each row of knots, and the knotting varies from medium to extremely coarse. As previously noted, one end has a cut fringe, and the other consists of loops, while the sides may be of several types. Often one finds a double selvage formed by looping the weft strands in figure-of-eight fashion around three or four thickened warp strands and reinforced with additional yarn. The pile is among the thickest found in Caucasian rugs, with a heavy, lustrous quality in the better pieces. Some Kazaks are almost square, with the dimensions differing by only a few inches between length and width.

141. KAZAK RUG, 19th century, 6' x 8'2". Warp: W. /3\, undyed. Weft: W. /2\, undyed brown wool, 2 shoots. Pile: W. /2\. Knot: T-L, 0-15°, v. 9, h. 8, 72/sq inch. Sides: double selvage of pale red wool over 2 warps. Ends: upper—narrow brown plain weave band and selvage. Lower—loops. Colors (8): dark blue field, rust red, light blue, yellow, light tan, dark brown, ivory, deep green. Kazak rugs with a central square show great structural variability and were clearly made over a wide area. The four corner figures of this example are rather unusual.

143. KAZAK RUG, 19th century, 6' x 7'7''. Warp: W. /3\, light brown. Weft: W. /2\, undyed, 2-3 shoots. Pile: W. /2\. Knot: T, v. 6, h. 6, 36/sq inch. Sides: double selvage of red, blue-green, and brown wool (alternating about every 4 or 5 inches) over 2 warps. Ends: upper—selvage. Lower—narrow red plain weave band and loops. Colors (8): red field, dark and light blue, blue green, yellow, mauve, ivory, dark brown. Three-medallion rugs of this type are a relatively common Kazak variety. Apparently they were woven in large numbers throughout the 19th century.

142. KAZAK RUG, 19th century, 5' x 8'9''. Warp: W. /3\, light brown. Weft: W. /2\, undyed, 2-4 shoots. Pile: W. /2\. Knot: T, v. 8, h. 8, 64/sq inch. Sides: double selvage of multicolored wool over 4 thickened warps. Ends: upper—selvage. Lower—loops. Colors (6): red field, blue, light green, yellow, dark brown, ivory. These design elements are clearly descended from figures in the dragon carpets, and occur on a variety of rugs from the Kazak and Karabagh areas. Some sources identify the design with Lenkoran rugs, but this is certainly not invariably the case.

145. KAZAK RUG, mid-19th century, 5'2" x 7'1". Warp: W. /3\, light brown. Weft: W. /2\, dyed red, 2-4 shoots. Pile: W. /2\. Knot: T, v. 7, h. 7, 49/sq inch. Sides: double selvage of red wool over 2 warps. Ends: upper—plain weave band folded forward and brocaded in red and blue green. Lower—loops. Colors (7): red field, blue, light blue-green, light brown, yellow, ivory, black. The so-called cross design occurs in Kazak rugs which come from several areas and differ significantly in technical details.

Courtesy of the Oriental Rug Co. of Berkeley, California.

144. KAZAK PRAYER RUG, "Borchalu," 19th century, 5'2" x 4'. Warp: W. /2\, undyed. Weft: W. /2\, undyed medium brown, 2-4 shoots. Pile: W. /2\. Knot: T, v. 9, h. 7, 63/sq inch. Sides: .... Ends: .... Colors (5): red field, dark blue, light blue, dark brown, ivory. Prayer rugs of this basic layout cover a span of at least the last hundred years, with gradual simplification of the field motifs and borders.

A great number of wild stories have circulated about these rugs, which would seem to need no romanticizing; yet one finds such ramblings in many of the well-known references. Mumford refers to the people (Kazaks) as "an old offshoot of the great hordes whose home is in the Kirghiz steppes and whose kinsmen are scattered over the Southern districts of Russia away to the banks of the Don. 'Kazak' means virtually a rough rider. It describes the whole race of these restless, roaming, troublesome people who in a sense are born, live, and die in the saddle."[16] What a pity that none of the ethnographic studies of this region bear out such impressions, although the Armenians who make most of these rugs have had an interesting history of their own.

The natural vigor and power of Kazak rugs have made them much sought after, which is another illustration of the axiom that the merits of a rug cannot be judged by such academic criteria as the number of knots per square inch. Many of the most crudely woven rugs may be much prized for their design. The elements are the same as we find in other Caucasian pieces, with stars and stylized animal and floral forms, but the combination of colors may be most striking.

146. KARABAGH, "Sunburst," 19th century, 4'6" x 7'6". Warp: W. /2\, undyed, medium brown. Weft: W. /2\, undyed dark brown, 2-3 shoots, loose. Pile: W. /2\. Knot: T, v. 8, h. 7, 56/sq inch. Sides: double selvage of dark brown wool over 4 warps. Ends: .... Colors (7): red, light and dark blue, ivory, dark green, yellow, dark brown. Whether or not these rugs are actually from the village of "Chelaberd," as alleged in some rug books, they are clearly of Karabagh origin (despite their frequent label of "Eagle Kazak"). The design is descended from earlier "dragon" rugs.

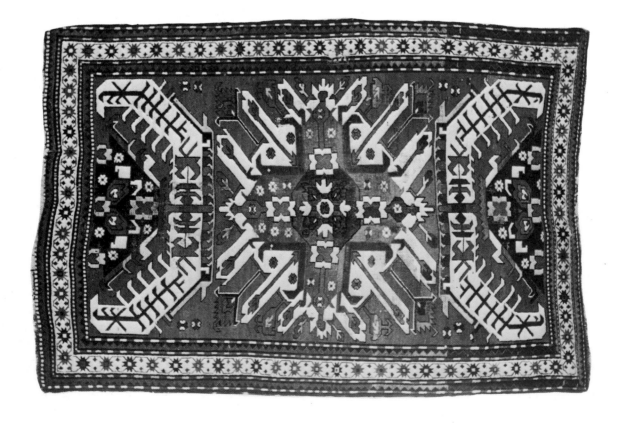

KARABAGH

The rugs of Karabagh (a term referring to an area, not a people) are made south and east of the Kazak district, although they often have great similarities to Kazak design and construction. In many works on the subject, the rugs of Azerbaijan have been divided into the categories of *Karabagh* and *Karadagh,* with the latter term referring to products from the Persian side of the border. (*Karadagh* also is used for many Kurdish rugs.) There is actually no such clear distinction, as on either side of the border one finds that the rug weavers are Azeri Turks of the same linguistic and cultural backgrounds. One could say, however, that the closer the weaving center is to Persia, the more the influences of this country are seen in the rugs, as we note in Karabaghs more curvilinear forms than in other Caucasian types. This has also been a result of market influences from the West, as the Russians were exporting carpets from Karabagh as early as the mid-nineteenth century.

The warp of these rugs is not invariably wool, as in other Caucasian products, but may be all cotton (in later rugs) or at least have a large admixture of cotton. The weft also is occasionally of cotton, although usually there are two strands of undyed wool, at times of a very dark shade. The ends, sides, knotting, and pile may be so similar to the Kazak as to provide little differentiation, and it is unclear whether some rugs should be labeled as Kazaks or Karabaghs. A case in point is the Eagle Kazaks, or "sunbursts," which have a medallion that is likely floral in derivation. These are alleged by many sources to come from the village of Tchelaberd, west of Schusha, but evidence is sparse. (Indeed, the village itself does not seem to occur on any maps outside of rug books.) Most rugs of this type have a double weft of dark brown wool, which is certainly a Karabagh feature. One may also examine earlier examples of the so-called dragon rugs and find design elements that are clearly forerunners of the sunburst medallion. As the motif has clearly undergone a long period of development over at least several centuries, localizing its appearance in modern Caucasian rugs to one small area in Karabagh seems naive.

A similar controversy exists around the so-called Cloudband or Dragon Kazak, which is often assigned to the village of Chondoresk in the Karabagh region. This type shows diverse structural characteristics, and the likelihood of a multiple origin is great.

Among other designs found in Karabagh rugs are stylized floral patterns, more naturalistically

147. KARABAGH RUG, 19th century, 3'8" x 6'7". Warp: W. /3\, light. Weft: W. /2\, undyed light brown, 2 shoots. Pile: W. /2\. Knot: T, v. 9, h. 7, 63/sq inch. Sides: double selvage of dark blue wool over 3 warps. Ends: .... Similar medallions, outlined by jagged lines, are found in many Karabagh runners and even carpets.

drawn than in the Kazak; generally the colors are also more muted. Many of the finest rugs come from the area around Schusha, where the knotting is tighter and the pile somewhat shorter.

148. KARABAGH RUG, early 19th century, 4'2" x 7'5". Warp: W. /3\, light and dark wool twisted together. Weft: W. /2\, dyed pale red, 2-4 shoots. Pile: W. /2\. Knot: T, v. 7, h. 7, 49/sq inch. Sides: .... Ends: .... Colors (7): dark blue field, light blue, pale red, light green, yellow, dark brown, ivory. Also containing elements that can be followed back to much earlier rugs, the design takes up an unusually large area of the field on this piece.

149. KARABAGH RUG, 19th century, 4'4" x 6'8". Warp: W. /3\, light. Weft: W. /2\, medium brown, 2 shoots. Pile: W. /2\. Knot: T, v. 8, h. 8, 64/sq inch. Sides: .... Ends: .... Colors (6): red field, dark blue, dark brown, light green, yellow, ivory. This design may well share a common ancestor with the more common "sunburst."

150. KARABAGH, "Cloudband," 19th century, 3'10" x 5'6". Warp: W. /2\, undyed, light brown. Weft: W. /2\, undyed, dark brown, 2-4 shoots, loose. Pile: W. /2\. Knot: T, v. 7, h. 7, 49/sq inch. Sides: double selvage of brown wool over 3 thickened warps. Ends: ... Colors (5): dark brown field, deep yellow, rust red, dark blue, ivory. The so-called "Cloudband" or "dragon Kazak" has been given a variety of attributions, including the village of Chondoresk, in the Karabagh area. Unlike the "sunburst," however, it shows great structural variability, and was likely woven over a wider area. Many examples are runners with three or four medallions.

151. KARABAGH RUNNER (portion), dated 1212 A.H. (1797), 3' x 15'1". Warp: W. /3\, light. Weft: W. /2\, lighter than warp, 2 shoots. Pile: W. /3\. Knot: T-L, 35°, v. 9, h. 9, 81/sq inch. Sides: .... Ends: .... Colors (12): cochineal red, pale green, surma, pale yellow, black, red brown, ivory, pink, buff, purple, dark maroon, yellow-green. Runners and small rugs with birds and characteristic medallion figures were made throughout the 19th century and likely well before. Many of them are dated, and they are usually known under the name "Lampa," which may refer to a village.

Courtesy of Peter Saunders, Berkeley, California.

GENDJE

The city of Gendje (known more recently as Kirovobad and Elizabethpol) is also inhabited by Armenians and Azeri Turks, and the rugs produced in this locale are thus not greatly different from Karabaghs or Kazaks. There are, however, several features that occasionally may allow them to be distinguished, particularly the binding of the sides, which often shows several colors of yarn wound as a double selvage. The warp is uncolored wool, and the weft strands are either dyed red or of light, sometimes grayish, wool. In knotting, pile, and texture, there is no discernible variation from the Kazak.

The patterns are slightly more distinctive, as Gendje rugs are not so floral as those of Karabagh, and they less frequently have large medallions. More characteristic is a smaller, geometrical repeating pattern throughout the field, often arranged in diagonal stripes. The colors are usually lighter (with more white and light blue) than in most Kazak rugs.

There is some question as to the need for distinguishing Gendje rugs from Kazaks, as the areas of manufacture are adjacent, the peoples are the same, and weaving methods are virtually indistinguishable. Also we seldom have real evidence to support the assertion that a given rug actually came from the area of Gendje, which makes this identification all the more tenuous. In some of the older books Gendje is alleged to be derived from the name of Genghis Khan (the rugs are actually called Genghis by Hawley, Lewis, and Mumford), and, of course, the weavers are alleged to be fierce nomads. Actually the town was known as Ganja as early as the sixth century.

TALISH RUGS

The Talish inhabit a mountainous area adjacent to the Caspian Sea around the city of Lenkoran. Of Indo-European origin, these people speak a language unrelated to Turkish or the Caucasian languages, although their carpets are Caucasian in feeling. Rug production has probably never been great here, and most Talish rugs are runners, with a few prayer rugs.

Older Talish rugs have a warp of natural wool, but the weft, either of wool or cotton, may be natural colored or dyed red or blue. The knotting is tighter and the pile shorter than Kazaks or Karabaghs, while the sides may have a double overcast in several colors of yarn.

152. GENDJE RUNNER, 19th century, 4'1" x 8'1". Warp: W. /3\, undyed light. Weft: W. /2\, dyed red, 2-4 strands. Pile: W. /2\. Knot: T, v. 8, h. 6, 48/sq inch. Sides: double overcast of dark wool over 3 warps. Ends: .... Colors (5): light blue, red, ivory, dark brown, yellow. Generally the Gendje is somewhat lighter in color than the Kazak, with more light blue and less red. In texture and feel, however, they are essentially identical. A significant percentage of the Gendje rugs depicted in rug books have either stripes (usually diagonally oriented) or some small figures arranged in stripe-like fashion across the field. In itself this is a poor criterion. Stripe designs are common among Shirvans, Kubas, Kazaks, and particularly Karabaghs. Multiple medallion designs, usually three lozenge-shaped figures with edges serrated in small 90° steps, are also common from the Gendje area, although they are usually mislabeled as Kazaks.

154. GENDJE RUNNER, 19th century, 3'4" x 9'2". Warp: W. /3\, light. Weft: W. C. /2\, white, 2 shoots. Pile: W. /2\. Knot: T, v. 7, h. 6, 42/sq inch. Sides: .... Ends: .... Colors (6): light blue field, pale red, dark blue, yellow, dark brown, ivory. The field elements and border stripes could occur on Caucasian rugs over a wide area, but the colors and structure of this piece suggest a Gendje origin.

153. GENDJE RUG, 19th century, 4'10" x 7'5". Warp; W. /3\, light. Weft: W. /2\, undyed, 2-5 shoots. Pile: W. /2\. Knot: T, v. 5, h. 6, 30/sq inch. Sides: double selvage over 4 warps of yellow, blue, and red wool in alternating bands. Ends: .... Colors (5): dark brown field, pale red, medium blue, yellow, ivory. The pile is exceedingly long and shaggy in this loosely woven rug.

155. TALISH RUNNER, 19th century, 3'5" x 7'8".
Warp: W. /3\, light. Weft: W. and C. mixed, /2\, undyed,
2 shoots. Pile: W. /2\. Knot: T, v. 8, h. 7, 56/sq inch.
Sides: remnants of selvage yarn at intervals penetrate 1-
2" into body of rug. Ends: .... Colors (6): light blue field,
ivory border, yellow minor borders, dark blue, dark
brown, red. This example shows the border characteristic
of Talish pieces, although other designs are also found.
The field may be completely open or covered with repeating figures.
(Talish rugs well represent a peculiar quirk of the rug
market in recent years. As soon as a Caucasian type
establishes a distinct identity [i.e., when it is published
and given a village or tribal name in rug books], it simul-
taneously acquires great value through some mysterious,
poorly understood process. One may find Talish rugs
with aniline colors, in poor condition, and of little distinction in design being offered for staggering sums. The
same is true of the so-called "Chi-chis," "Perpedils,"
"Marsalis," and others, while even good rugs without a
name attract less attention.)

There is probably no way to distinguish Lenkoran rugs from Talish rugs in terms of structure.
The Lenkoran, however, frequently occur with a particular medallion, while there is often a characteristic main border on Talish rugs. During the early
twentieth century many low-grade runners on cotton foundations were made in this area. The designs were taken from other parts of the Caucasus.

MOGHAN

Closely related to the Talish are rugs of the
Moghan Steppe just to the north. The people of
this area are descendants of Azeri Turks — a group
rather isolated for several centuries. Nineteenth-century Moghans are all wool and almost always in a
runner format, with a medium weave and either undyed or red wefts. Many twentieth-century runners
have also come from this same area, and most of
these show some cotton in either the warp or weft,
often plied together with strands of wool. The designs are more likely to involve small, repeating
figures than medallion forms.

SHIRVAN

The Shirvan district is a loosely defined area
south of the Greater Caucasus and east of Gendje.
It includes the Apsheron Peninsula, where the city
of Baku is located. (Rugs from lands immediately
adjacent to the Caspian are usually labeled by the
name of that city). The inhabitants are almost entirely Azeri Turks, with a few groups of Kurds.

Shirvan rugs are often constructed on a warp
of brown strands twisted with white. The wefts are
usually of white wool, but some of the later specimens are of cotton. One end is fringed, and the
other shows loops, often woven into a selvage,
while the sides are almost always double overcast in
white wool or cotton. The knotting is among the
finest in Caucasian fabrics, often with a short pile
in the older rugs. In design there is almost nothing
that can be used to distinguish the Shirvan, as motifs from all over the Caucasus are used. The dimensions range from small scatter sizes to some
over 5 x 10 feet, and these include runners and
prayer rugs. Many have medallions, while others
show small repeating figures, including a great number of stylized animals and even human forms. The
colors are somewhat more subdued than on the
rugs previously discussed, with more use of blue
and ivory.

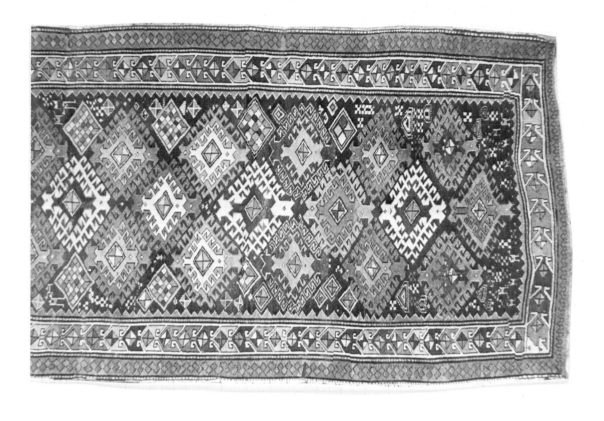

156. LENKORAN RUNNER (portion), 19th century. Warp: W. /3\, light brown. Weft: W. /2\, dyed red, 2-3 shoots. Pile: W. /2\. Knot: T, v. 7, h. 6, 42/sq inch. Sides: double selvage over 3 warps of red, light green, and brown wool in alternate bands. Ends: loops at lower end. Colors (5): red field, light green, light blue, dark brown, ivory. Lenkoran rugs might well be considered as a Karabagh variety; 20th century rugs from this area used cotton first for the weft, and by the 1920s the entire foundation was cotton.

157. MOGHAN RUNNER, 19th century, 4'4" x 10'6". Warp: W. /3\, medium brown. Weft: W. /2\, dyed red, 2 shoots. Pile: W. /2\. Knot: T, v. 9, h. 8, 72/sq inch. Sides: ... Ends: ... Colors (7): dark blue field, light blue, red, yellow, dark brown, light green, ivory. This is more finely woven than the typical southern Caucasian rug and shows an unusually dark color tonality.

One feature that distinguishes Shirvans from the finely woven north Caucasian fabrics is the arrangement of the warps so that adjacent strands lie flat across the back. In the Kuba alternate strands are somewhat depressed, and in the Daghestan they may be depressed as much as 75 degrees.

In general the older Shirvans were more floral and less rigidly geometric. The so-called Kufic border is common both in later and earlier pieces, and many books label any rug with this motif as a Shirvan. Examination of the construction, however, will quickly reveal that many are from the Kuba district.

There are several widely recognized subtypes of Shirvans from particular villages or areas. Chajli, Akstafa, Bidjov, and Marsali rugs are similar in construction, but show characteristic designs. As with the village-produced Kazak rugs, however, their labels are usually speculative.

BAKU

The city of Baku is located on the Apsheron Peninsula and is an important Caspian port. Recently the population has expanded to over 800,000 because of the great oil industry, and even in the nineteenth century Baku was a major commercial center of trade in Caucasian rugs. In most rug books the surrounding towns are classified together with Baku, including an area to the south along the Caspian coast. One will see references to Chila, Surahani, and Saliani, villages bearing the same general group characteristics, but which produce rugs that have distinctive features of design.

The warp is similar to that of Shirvan rugs, and the strands lie flat; but the weft, often of brown wool, may be mixed with some cotton, and the pile is cut short. Unlike other Caucasian products, there are often multiple shades of a single color in the same rug, and all the colors are generally subdued.

Shades of light blue and turquoise characterize Baku rugs, while the most typical design consists of a simple central medallion and matching pieces at each corner. The intervening field is then covered with large, complex, and brightly colored Boteh figures, usually on a dark blue ground. Other patterns are also found, but there is great difficulty in separating these from Shirvan rugs in general. Occasionally a Baku rug will be found with a typical Persian pattern, such as the Herati, and only an examination of the weaving technique will reveal its Caucasian origin.

158. SHIRVAN RUG, 19th century, 3'4" x 4'5". Warp: W. /2\, light. Weft: W. /2\, light, 2 shoots. Pile: W. /2\. Knot: T, v. 9, h. 8, 72/sq inch. Sides: double selvage of white wool over 2 warps. Ends: .... Colors (7): pale red field, dark blue, light blue, ivory, dark brown, yellow, medium brown. Eight-pointed star figures of this type are found throughout the Caucasus and even among Kurdish groups in Iran and Turkey. Certainly they cannot be attributed to any particular people or region, although the construction of this example indicates a Shirvan origin.

160. SHIRVAN PRAYER RUG, "Marsali," 19th century, 3'3" x 4'4". Warp: W. /3\, light. Weft: C. /2\, undyed, 2 shoots, both loose. Pile: W. /2\. Knot: T, v. 12, h. 9, 108/sq inch. Sides: .... Ends: upper—ivory plain weave band and selvage. Lower—ivory plain weave band and loops. Colors (6): dark blue field, light blue, pale red, ivory, dark brown, yellow. Prayer rugs with Boteh figures covering the field are relatively common in many parts of the Caucasus.

159. SHIRVAN RUG, 19th century, 4'4" x 5'. Warp: W. /3\, medium brown. Weft: W. /2\, undyed, 2 shoots. Pile: W. /2\. Knot: T, v. 8, h. 8, 64/sq inch. Sides: double selvage of white cotton over 2 warps. Ends: .... Colors (7): dark brown, light green, dark and light blue, red, yellow, ivory. This rug, with a compartment design, is somewhat more squarish in shape than most Shirvans, although both border and field motifs are typical.

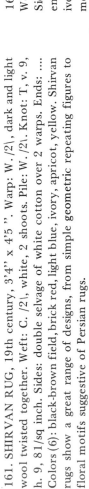

162. SHIRVAN RUG, 19th century, 3'11'' x 5'1''. Warp: W. /3\, brown wool. Weft: C. /2\, white, 2 shoots. Pile: W. /2\. Knot: T, v. 10, h. 10, 100/sq inch. Sides: double overcast of white cotton. Ends: ivory plain weave remains at both ends. Colors (7): red field, dark and light blue, yellow, light green, dark brown, ivory. The figures at the base of the field appear to represent a family and domestic animals.

161. SHIRVAN RUG, 19th century, 3'4'' x 4'5 ''. Warp: W. /2\, dark and light wool twisted together. Weft: C. /2\, white, 2 shoots. Pile: W. /2\. Knot: T, v. 9, h. 9, 81/sq inch. Sides: double selvage of white cotton over 2 warps. Ends: ..... Colors (6): black-brown field, brick red, light blue, ivory, apricot, yellow. Shirvan rugs show a great range of designs, from simple geometric repeating figures to floral motifs suggestive of Persian rugs.

163. SHIRVAN RUG, 19th century, 4'2" x 4'9". Warp: W. /3\, light and dark strands twisted together. Weft: W. /2\, undyed, 2 shoots. Pile: W. /2\. Knot: T, v. 9, h. 8, 72/sq.inch. Sides: double overcast of white cotton. Ends: .... Colors (7): buff-yellow field, brick red, light blue, ivory, dark brown, light yellow, light green. Like Fig. 160, this could also be labeled a "Marsali," although the two pieces have dissimilar colors, construction, and texture. While superficially alike, the Botehs are also of a different design.

164. SHIRVAN RUG, 19th century, 3'5" x 5'4". Warp: W. /3\, light and dark strands twisted together. Weft: W. /2\, undyed, 2 shoots. Pile: W. /2\. Knot: T, v. 9, h. 7, 63/sq inch. Sides: double overcast of white cotton. Ends: upper—remains of knotted fringe. Lower—loops. Colors (5): dark blue field, red, deep yellow, dark brown, ivory. This design can be traced to floral arabesque rugs of the 17th century, and it most likely is of non-Caucasian origin.

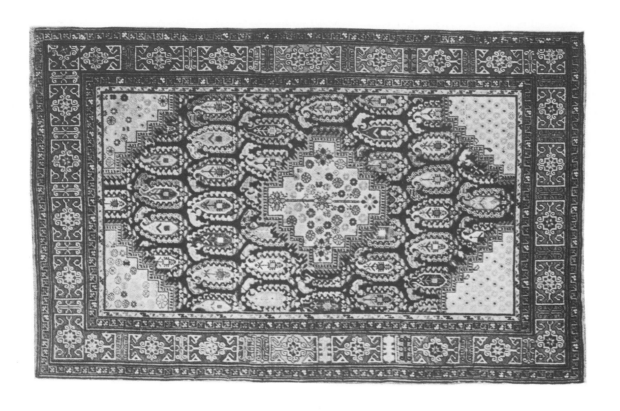

166. BAKU RUG, 19th century. Rugs of this design are often attributed to the town of Chila and are characterized by elaborate Boteh figures on a dark blue field and considerable use of light blue.

165. SHIRVAN RUG, 19th century, 3'8" x 6'2". Warp: W. /3|, 2 dark and 1 white strand. Weft: W. /2|, undyed, 2 shoots. Pile: W. /2|. Knot: T, v. 8, h. 8, 64/ sq inch. Sides: .... Ends: .... Colors (7): red field, light and dark blue, light green, yellow, ivory, dark brown. This design is most frequently found on Shirvan kilims. (Refer to Fig. 178).

Courtesy of the Oriental Rug Co. of Berkeley, California.

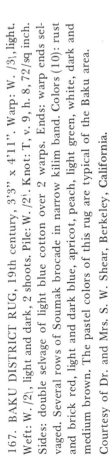

168. KUBA RUG, 19th century, "Perpedil," 4'4" x 6'2". Warp: W. /3\, 2 strands light and 1 dark brown. Weft: C. /2\, undyed, 2 shoots. Pile: W. /2\. Knot: T, v. 12, h. 12, 144/sq inch. Sides: double overcast of white cotton. Ends: only loose warp ends remain. Colors (8): ivory field, light blue, blue-green, red, light green, deep yellow, yellow brown, dark brown. This design occurs on a variety of Daghestan and Shirvan rugs, although some sources identify it particularly with the village of Perpedil in the Kuba area.

167. BAKU DISTRICT RUG, 19th century, 3'3" x 4'11". Warp: W. /3\, light. Weft: W. /2\, light and dark, 2 shoots. Pile: W. /2\. Knot: T, v. 9, h. 8, 72/sq inch. Sides: double selvage of light blue cotton over 2 warps. Ends: warp ends selvaged. Several rows of Soumak brocade in narrow kilim band. Colors (10): rust and brick red, light and dark blue, apricot, peach, light green, white, dark and medium brown. The pastel colors of this rug are typical of the Baku area. Courtesy of Dr. and Mrs. S. W. Shear, Berkeley, California.

KUBA

The city of Kuba and its surrounding villages are actually part of Daghestan, although the rugs are often classified separately; in many ways they are intermediate between weaves from farther north and those of Shirvan. In construction they bear many resemblances to their southern neighbors, and a clear distinction is often difficult. Again there are a number of local names under which these rugs are known, and the weaves of Konaghend, Perpedil, Sejshour, Zejwa, Tschitche, and Karagashli are allegedly identified by design.

The warp in most Kuba rugs is naturally colored wool, but the weft is variable. The later ones may have a cotton weft (or a cotton-wool mixture) while the older classical pieces may even be single wefted. The sides are finished with a double overcast or selvage of blue or white yarn wound over several warp strands. In older pieces this yarn is usually fine and tightly applied. Both ends are finished the same, often with the loose warps tied in a series of knots. Between this knotted band and the last rows of pile there may be a several-centimeter band in a reinforcing flat weave (often a Soumak stitch).

Several characteristic Kuba designs are often given special names, with the designation Chi-chi being the most common. As with many other designs attributed to only one village, there is great likelihood of multiple origin, as different specimens with the same pattern may vary greatly in construction.

169. KUBA RUG, 19th century, "Konaghend," 3'10" x 5'11". Warp: W. /3\, 2 light and 1 dark strands. Weft: W. /2\, undyed, 2 shoots. Pile: W. /2\. Knot: T, v. 7, h. 7, 49/sq inch. Sides: double overcast of dark blue wool. Ends: upper—selvage, with several rows of Soumak brocading after last row of knots. Lower—loose warp ends. Colors (6): pale red field, dark blue medallion, yellow, orange, dark brown, ivory. The design elements of this rug are more typical of the many large pieces of Soumak brocade that originated from the same area.

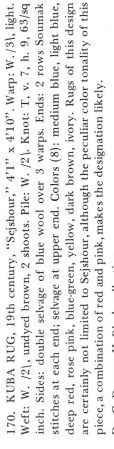

171. KUBA RUG, 19th century, "Zejwa," 3'11" x 4'10". Warp: W. /3\, light wool. Weft: C. /2\, undyed, 2 shoots. Pile: W. /2\. Knot: T-L, 25°, v. 11, h. 10, 110/sq inch. Sides: double overcast of white cotton. Ends: upper–selvage. Lower–loose warp ends. Colors (6): dark blue field, light blue, rust red, yellow, dark brown, ivory. The design is obviously related to the Karabagh "Sunburst," which is likely descended from earlier "dragon" rugs.

170. KUBA RUG, 19th century, "Sejshour," 4'1" x 4'10". Warp: W. /3\, light. Weft: W. /2\, undyed brown, 2 shoots. Pile: W. /2\. Knot: T, v. 7, h. 9, 63/sq inch. Sides: double selvage of blue wool over 3 warps. Ends: 2 rows Soumak stitches at each end; selvage at upper end. Colors (8): medium blue, light blue, deep red, rose pink, blue-green, yellow, dark brown, ivory. Rugs of this design are certainly not limited to Sejshour, although the peculiar color tonality of this piece, a combination of red and pink, makes the designation likely. Dr. G. Dumas–H. Black collection.

173. KUBA RUG, 19th century, "Chi-chi," 3'9" x 4'10". Warp: W. /3\, light and dark strands twisted together. Weft: W. /2\, undyed, 2 shoots. Pile: W. /2\. Knot: T, v. 9, h. 8, 72/sq inch. Sides: double overcast of white wool. Ends: .... Colors (5): dark blue field, faded red, yellow, dark brown, ivory. This field design is not often found with a Chi-chi border.

172. KUBA PRAYER RUG, nineteenth century, 3'11" x 4'5". Warp: W. /3\, 2 light and 1 dark strand twisted together. Weft: C. /2\, white, 2 shoots. Pile: W. /2\. Knot: T-L, 10-20⁰, v. 12, h. 8½, 102/sq inch. Sides: double overcast of white cotton. Ends: portions of plain weave (white cotton weft) and selvage remain. Colors (7): red, light blue, ivory, yellow, light green, red-brown, dark brown.

Color Plate XXIX. KUBA-DAGHESTAN, 19th century, 4'10" x 3'11". Warp: W. /3 . Weft: W. /2 , undyed white, 2 shoots. Pile: W. /2 . Knot: T-L, 80°, v. 15, h. 11, 165/sq inch. Sides: overcast of light blue cotton over 2 warps, with short sections of dark blue. Ends: plain weave of blue cotton; selvage at top. This unusual rug poses a question of attribution, as there are elements in the field characteristic of "Chi-chi" and "Perpedil" rugs, but the colors and construction are not suggestive of either. The deeply depressed alternative warps suggest a Daghestan origin.

Dr. G. Dumas — H. Black collection.

Color Plate XXX. "CHI-CHI" RUG, 19th century, 6' x 4'. Warp: W. /3\, 2 white and 1 dark. Weft: W. /2\, light, 2 shoots. Pile: W. /2\. Knot: T-L, 20°, h. 8, v. 10, 80/sq inch. Sides: double overcast of white cotton. Ends: plain weave of white wool, with adjacent strands knotted together. Colors (10): medium blue field, light blue, rust red, brick red, dark brown, ivory, light green, yellow green, yellow, red-brown. The classic Chi-Chi has an overall greenish tonality, despite the meager use of this color.

Courtesy of the Oriental Rug Co. of Berkeley, California.

Color Plate XXXI. DAGHESTAN PRAYER RUG, 19th century, 4'1'' x 4'10''. Warp: W. /3\, brown and white twisted together. Weft: W. /2\, white, 2 shoots. Pile: W. /2\. Knot: T–R, 80°, h. 12, v. 14, 168/sq inch. Sides: white cotton overcast around 4 warps for about half of rug; selvage of 2 cords on remainder. Ends: white cotton weft in ¼ inch plain weave bands, with warp ends selvaged.

D. G. Dumas—H. Black collection.

Color Plate XXXII. SOUMAK RUG, dated 1890, 7'1" x 11'. Warp: W. /3\, strands of light
and dark wool twisted together, 20 warps/inch. Weft: W. /2\, undyed, 1 shoot between each row
of brocading. Sides: .... Ends: loose ends knotted together. Colors (8): red field, dark and light
blue, yellow, apricot, dark brown, white, magenta. Many features of this piece are typical, including the four medallion format and the "running dog" outer border strips.

RUGS OF THE NORTH CAUCASUS

Three different labels are frequently attached to rugs from the northern Caucasus, although the distinctions are not at all clear. The most common label, Daghestan, refers to the entire area, while the name Derbend signifies a Caspian port that is the area's chief town. Concerning Lesghi, the third term, ethnographic maps and those in rug books are in disagreement. Schurmann's map places the Lesghians along the northern slopes of the Greater Caucasus, well to the north of Derbend. Anthropological studies of the Caucasian peoples, however, locate the Lesghians (or Kurins) as living south of Derbend, inhabiting villages around Sejshour and Perpedil, in the area north of Kuba. By superimposing maps of tribal habitation over the names of cities, we might conclude that these people wove many Kuba rugs. Still, as we have no reliable data on Lesghi rug designs, it is probably best to abandon the name as a rug classification. No one seems able to differentiate the so-called Lesghi rugs from Daghestans on a structural basis, and most writers apparently depend upon color, particularly a heavy use of yellow and green, to make an identification.

This leaves us essentially with only two varieties of north Caucasian rugs to distinguish, which involves separating the rugs of Derbend from those made in the surrounding area. Here there are some distinguishing features, as Daghestan rugs have a warp and weft all of naturally colored wool, while in the Derbend both often have admixtures of cotton, usually one strand twisted with two strands of white wool. In the Daghestans there is usually a white or blue double overcasting, while Derbend rugs are often bound with a double selvage of blue wool. Generally Daghestans are of a fine to very fine weave, but they differ from other finely woven Caucasian products in having a deeper pile. Even when the nap is short, the rug has a characteristic stiffness because of the depressed alternate warps. The Derbend is almost universally described as being of coarser weave and having thicker pile. As a good many so-called Daghestans were marketed in Derbend, the distinction is, of course, difficult and possibly unnecessary. Often the use of one name instead of the other seems quite arbitrary.

In design the north Caucasian pieces show little that does not also appear in the south. One particular prayer design is almost universally labeled as a Daghestan, with a cream field and an overall design made up of tiny compartments of small lozenges. (Many of these appear, on structural grounds, to be Shirvans.) Otherwise we have the same borders and field motifs as elsewhere, and on design alone we can make no identification.

174. DERBEND RUNNER, late 19th century, 3'2" x 11'7". Warp: W. /3\, light. Weft: W. /2\, light, 2 shoots. Pile: W. /2\. Knot: T, v. 8, h. 7, 56/sq inch. Sides: double selvage of dark blue wool over 3 warps. Ends: narrow band of Soumak brocading in dark blue, adjacent warp ends knotted together. Colors (7): medium blue field, yellow, ivory, red, mauve, medium brown, light blue. The "Kufic" border is usually associated with more tightly woven rugs of the Kuba district.

176. DAGHESTAN RUG, 19th century, 4'5" x 9'6". Warp: W. /3\, light brown. Weft: W. /2\, light brown, 2 shoots. Pile: W. /2\. Knot: T, left warps depressed 45°, v. 10, h. 10, 100/sq inch. Sides: double selvage of light brown wool over 2 warps. Ends: .... Colors (10): light and dark blue, light red, mauve, green, yellow, ivory, light and medium brown, dark brown. The borders and field elements could occur over a wide area from Derbend to south of Baku. The deep depression of alternate warps in this case, however, suggests a Daghestan origin. Courtesy of Peter Saunders, Berkeley, California.

175. DAGHESTAN PRAYER RUG, 19th century, 3'11" x 5'10". Warp: W. /3\, undyed light and dark brown. Weft: W. /2\, undyed, white, 2 strands. Pile: W. /2\. Knot: T, left warps depressed 40°, v. 10, h. 9, 90/sq inch. Sides: .... Ends: narrow bands of ivory plain weave remain. Colors (6): ivory field, bright red, light green, light blue, yellow, dark brown. In border and field design this is a classic Daghestan, at least according to tradition. There is no way of resolving the issue here, but most of these rugs seem indistinguishable from Shirvans in construction.

177. DERBEND RUG, late 19th century, 3'2" x 4'9". Warp: W. /2\, light. Weft: W. /2\, light brown, 2 shoots. Pile: W. /2\. Knot: T, v. 10, h. 9, 90/sq inch. Sides: double selvage of dark blue wool over 3 warps. Ends: narrow band of dark blue Soumak brocading; adjacent warp ends selvaged together. Colors (8): dark blue field, light blue, rust red, pink, yellow, gray-brown, ivory, medium brown. Many Derbend rugs have designs associated with other parts of the Caucasus. In slightly more complex form this design is found on many Shirvan rugs.

PILELESS RUGS

Pileless Caucasian fabrics are often more difficult than pile carpets to identify as to exact origin, as we find several clearly different types of construction. Most common are the kilim, which is much the same as the Anatolian or Persian product, and the Soumak.

Caucasian kilims are generally simple in pattern, with small geometric figures arranged in horizontal stripes. Often there is some question as to their origin, but many have warps of light and dark strands twisted together, a typical Shirvan feature.

The so-called *Soumak* (the term here refers to a particular type of Caucasian fabric rather than the Soumak technique) also involves some uncertainty, as many writers insist that the word is merely a corruption of the name Shemaka, a large market town in the Shirvan area. Allegedly Soumaks were made

in and around this city and often sold in the United States under the name of Kashmere, as the loose ends at the back somewhat resemble the weave of the shawls from northern India. (Likely dealers adopted the term in an effort to make the Soumak sound more exotic.) Actually there is no evidence that this type of carpet was made only in Shemaka. From the variety of patterns, some being quite similar to those found on pile carpets from other areas, we may conclude that many places outside of the city itself made these fabrics. The Kuba district produced many Soumaks, and they were also woven around Derbend.

Soumaks often show three large, diamond-shaped or octagonal medallions surrounded by smaller medallions at the sides and small geometric figures in between. The outermost border is often a stripe of narrow latch hooks, usually in red and black. Occasionally there are typical borders from

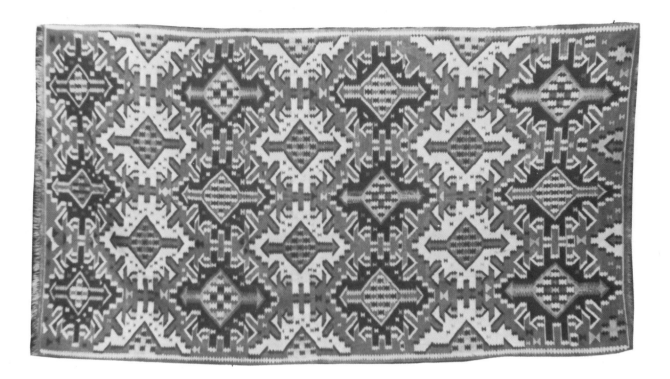

178. SHIRVAN KILIM, 19th century, 6'4" x 9'6". Warp: W. /3\, light and dark strands twisted together, 14/inch. Weft: W. /2\, 42 shoots/inch. Ends: warps knotted together. **Colors** (5): red field, dark brown, light green, yellow, ivory. This is among the relatively common designs found on Shirvan kilims.

179. SHIRVAN KILIM, 19th century. (Technical data unavailable.) Horizontal stripes make up the most common design for Caucasian kilims, most of which are labeled as Shirvans. They are almost always uniformly of wool, with /3\ warps of light and dark wool twisted together. Likely these were made over a wide area of the Caucasus, as they show considerable differences in color and texture.

pile rugs, such as the crab or wineglass patterns. Generally the borders are narrow in proportion to the field. In color these rugs are often bold and vibrant, with vivid reds and blues. Because of the stitch (requiring that the wool be tightly spun), the Soumak often feels coarse to the touch.

One particular type of Soumak depicted in many of the books is the so-called *Sileh*. Most writers include them under Shirvan carpets, although no one appears to know whether the name refers to a city, region, tribe, or design type. The usual pattern consists of a number of large stylized *S*-shaped figures in symmetrical rows, usually four by four. (There are occasionally other designs also called Sileh. The colors are vivid, and the patterns quite intricate; usually the piece consists of two smaller portions sewn together. We have no definite information as to where these were made.)

Another case in point is the so-called *Verneh* rug, generally constructed in a weft float brocade. As depicted in books, it is usually two segments sewn together, with stripes of stylized animal figures. The most common design consists of bird-like forms in alternating colors, although there are also camels and other animals. Just as with Sileh, no one appears to know whether Verneh refers to a town or a style, but most writers suggest a Karabagh origin. The colors are usually subdued, with much blue and red. Another type often known by the name Verneh, with squares and lozenges on a foundation of dark wool, is usually of Anatolian origin.

Apparently few pileless Caucasian rugs have been made since the 1920s, or at least new ones have not been imported into the United States. Although there have been revivals in production of pile carpets, these less durable fabrics have aroused less interest.

CURRENT PRODUCTION OF CAUCASIAN RUGS

Production of Caucasian rugs was probably at a maximum by the beginning of World War I, although the industry had developed slightly later than in Persia. With the decrease of the European market after 1924 and the subsequent upheavals in Russia, weaving at the old level was never resumed, as the Soviets made many changes in the Caucasus.

The area now comprises the Transcaucasian Republics, and the populace has turned largely from its former industries to new ones and to mining. However, during the twenties there were again periods when rugs were shipped to the West in large quantities, and at the same time, to raise capital, the Soviets exported many of the older pieces that had been used in Russia.

Often these later rugs are almost impossible to identify specifically, as the patterns, materials and weaving methods had become more uniform. Use of cotton warps increased (they were almost never found in the older pieces), and synthetic dyes became almost universal. During World War II exports apparently ceased altogether, and during the late 1940s there was a period of several years when no newly made Caucasian rugs appeared on the market. Still, American travelers in Russia reported seeing new rugs in Moscow department stores, and finally in about 1960 the first of the post-war pieces began to appear in the West. This may have been stimulated by the great demand rising in western Europe at that time.

These latest products have never been brought to the United States in large numbers, as they are expensive and subjected to heavy import duty. They are compactly woven, with designs assembled from all areas of the Caucasus, a heavy cotton foundation, and rather harsh colors. Currently they are manufactured in a limited number of patterns, with much less variety than among the older group. For rugs to be sold in Russia, the Caucasian weavers occupy themselves with contemporary designs ranging from realistic floral motifs to graphic scenes with a propaganda poster message.

Not to be confused with the Soviet products are rugs now woven around Ardabil and Meshkin, in northern Iran, where carpet making has developed on a large scale since about 1950. This area is just south of the Russian border, and most of its inhabitants are Azeri Turks of the same stock as those on the Soviet side of the border; so it is not surprising that their rugs may be identified more readily as Caucasian than Persian. The patterns are taken from classical Caucasian sources and combined in much the same way as in modern Soviet exports. The Meshkin tend more toward the Kazak styles, while the Ardabil rugs are suggestive of old Shirvan pieces.

In construction these rugs are solid, but coarsely knotted. The foundation is cotton and the pile of good wool, medium to short. Generally the colors are duller than Caucasian products, with many of the rugs having ivory or rust red fields.

NOTES

1. Mumford, J. K., *Oriental Rugs,* Scribners, New York, 1900, p. 108.

2. Jacoby, H., *How to Know Oriental Carpets and Rugs,* Pitman, New York, 1949.

3. Breck, J., and Morris, F., *The Ballard Collection of Oriental Rugs,* New York, 1923, Metropolitan Museum of Art, p. xxiv.

4. Jacobsen, C., *Oriental Rugs,* Tuttle, Rutland, Vermont, pp. 223-224.

5. Pushman, G. T., *Art Panels from the Handlooms of the Far Orient,* Chicago, 1911, p. 64.

6. Holt, R. B., *Rugs, Oriental and Occidental,* Garden City Publishing Co., New York, 1937, p. 107.

7. Roberts, E. H., *Oriental Rugs,* Textile Publishing Co., New York, 1928.

8. Hawley, W., *Oriental Rugs,* Tudor, New York, 1937.

9. *Narody Kavkaza,* Institut Ethnografii, Moskow, 1960, vol. I, p. 22.

10. Field, H. *Contributions to the Anthropology of the Caucasus,* Cambridge, 1953.

11. Luzbetak, L., *Marriage and the Family in Caucasus,* Vienna, 1951.

12. Geiger, B., et al., *Peoples and Languages of the Caucasus,* Moulton and Co., 'S-Gravenhage, 1959.

13. Mumford, *op. cit.,* p. 113.

14. Luzbetak, *op. cit.*

15. Thielmann, Max von, *Journey in the Caucasus, Persia, and Turkey in Asia,* London, John Murray, 1875, p. 226.

16. Mumford, *op. cit.,* p. 123.

APPENDIX A

A Note on Attribution and Documentation

Any new rug book is soon subjected to a popular game among rug collectors — confident second-guessing of the labeling of the plates. While this can be great fun, particularly with some earlier books where the errors are obvious, I am naturally less objective in imagining the same process occurring around my own attributions. Some of my labels will be questioned, and this is a healthy exercise. Some readers will wonder how I know that a particular rug was made in a given locality. While many desire most specific information, whether accurate or not (e.g., labeling an old Caucasian rug as from the tiny village of Idjewan and dating it to about 1830—clearly something no one could possibly know for certain), another group would have the author take a more cautious, less assertive approach (e.g., labeling rugs known in the trade as "Bergama" as merely "western Anatolian" rather than specifying the exact village or area).

Not having approached this work with a deliberate desire to provoke controversy, I have taken something of a middle course. Except when I know a piece to be relatively recent, datings are educated guesses, like those of everyone else. The attributions, however, are another matter, as I have tried to include here rugs about which I have some reasonable certainty. The skeptic, of course, will wonder how I came by this information, as I have not always provided documentation. (Indeed, the most interesting parts of many rug books are omitted by the author in his neglecting to tell us how he learned certain "facts.") Actually, the matter often is not simple. In certain cases I have observed the rugs in their areas of manufacture. When I purchase rugs in Ezine or Canakkale, find similar rugs in the shops and mosques, and see other examples on the loom in that area, then I feel absolutely confident. The same certainty applies when I purchase a Kizil Ajak prayer rug from a tribesman in Afghanistan purporting himself to be a member of that group, or when a Dohktar-i-Ghazi Baluchi sells me a rug with this tribe's characteristic design.

I am on less firm ground, but still relatively confident, when I purchase rugs in city bazaars, as here also one can gather much information. If several of the best informed rug dealers in Shiraz (plus an American anthropologist in residence with the tribes) tell me that a given rug is woven by the Shishbuluki subtribe of the Qashgai, then I tend to believe this is true, even though I have never been among these nomads. The same applies to other bazaars where the locals are expert, and I lack a thorough acquaintance with the village sub-types.

However, in dealing with older rugs (of a type either no longer made or not identical to the modern products), another level of doubt arises. How do I know, for example, that the Shiraz rug I identify as made by the Baharlu was not woven by another group, as this type of rug surely has not been produced for many years? Well, of course, I am not certain. All I can say is that very knowledgeable rug dealers and connoisseurs in Shiraz have informed me that they have no doubt, and at the same time have pointed out structural reasons for their opinions. I believe them, but naturally have less faith than I would from direct personal knowledge.

The final level of uncertainty comes with rugs that were made so long ago that there is not even a reliable local tradition around their manufacture. Here I have relied on the older rug books and the "accumulated wisdom" of the rug trade, recognizing the defects in both sources. I thus cannot say with certainty that the two Ladik rugs depicted in this book were actually made near a village by that name, although I am sure that most people knowledgeable about rugs would agree with the attribution. Still, it is best that one keep an open mind even about these "certainties." The rug literature is improving rapidly, and the next several decades may well witness a reevaluation of many traditional ideas.

APPENDIX B

The literature on oriental rugs involves words from many languages, and those written in Arabic script present a particular problem. The name of a Persian city, for example, could be translated into our alphabet in several ways: e.g., Senneh, Sehna, Sinne, etc., all with approximately (but not exactly) the same sound that a native of the city would use. This is complicated by the fact that authors in English, German, French, and Italian have contributed most of the works on rugs, choosing spellings most appropriate to their languages. To compound the matter further, there is often no unanimity within Iran as to how certain place names are pronounced, and a Tehrani would speak the name of his city with a decidedly different inflection from the provincial's.

Fortunately our task does not require our taking sides on any momentous issues of orthography, but at the same time we wish our readers to be spared unnecessary confusion. We have chosen, for the most part, what we believe to be the simplest and most common spellings. In a few cases, however, we have retained forms most familiar to rug fanciers rather than those in current use. The city of Senneh, for example, is now called Sanandaj by Iranians, but we have retained the old name more widely associated with rugs.

In Turkey, when the government adopted a Romanized alphabet during the 1920s, the spelling of town and city names was standardized. We thus are on relatively firm ground in using "Izmir" and "Kayseri" at times for the older "Smyrna" and "Caesarea." Still we have introduced some modifications for clarity. Certainly "Ghiordes" is better known to rug collectors than the new "Gördes." Confusion still might arise, however, when the Turkish letters have a sound different from their English equivalent. For example, the letter "c" in Turkish is pronounced as an English "j". Thus the Turks write "Demirci" and "Mucur" rather than "Demerji" and "Mudjar." We have tried to use forms that would result in the least confusion, even though this involves a certain lack of consistency.